Robert Rogers, John Bradstreet

Diary of the Siege of Detroit in the War With Pontiac

Also a Narrative of the Principal Events of the Siege by Major Robert Rogers

Robert Rogers, John Bradstreet

Diary of the Siege of Detroit in the War With Pontiac

Also a Narrative of the Principal Events of the Siege by Major Robert Rogers

ISBN/EAN: 9783337019044

Printed in Europe, USA, Canada, Australia, Japan

Cover: Foto ©ninafisch / pixelio.de

More available books at **www.hansebooks.com**

Munsell's
Historical Series.
No. IV.

DIARY

OF THE

Siege of Detroit

IN THE

WAR WITH PONTIAC.

ALSO A

Narrative of the Principal Events of the Siege, by Major ROBERT ROGERS;

A

Plan for Conducting Indian Affairs, by Colonel BRADSTREET;

AND OTHER

AUTHENTICK DOCUMENTS,

NEVER BEFORE PRINTED.

EDITED WITH NOTES
BY *FRANKLIN B. HOUGH.*

Albany, N. Y.:
J. MUNSELL, 78 STATE STREET.
M.D.CCC.LX.

TO

J. Carson Brevoort, Esq.

OF BROOKLYN, N. Y.

Sir:

HE Contemporary Records of the Hoſtilities which followed the Surrender of Canada in 1760, *muſt ever poſſeſs an unuſual Degree of Intereſt, as illuſtrating the Indian Character, and the Succeſs of the Line of Policy adopted by the French in their Northern Colonies of America, as contraſted with that of the Engliſh.*

Having early acquired an intimate Knowledge of the Interiour, by a Series of enterpriſing Explorations, the French adopted a rational Method of ſecuring the Benefits to be derived from a Monopoly of the Indian Trade, and with ſuch Succeſs that the Friendſhip they gained could not be annulled

A

nulled by Treaties, or readily assigned to a Nation whom they had been taught to hate.

Deceived by the Statements of zealous Partizans in the French Interests, the Natives fondly hoped for the Return of their ancient Allies to Power, and in the Ardour of their Enthusiasm they sought to merit returning Favours by anticipating the Arms of France in the Reconquest of the Country, and the Expulsion of the English.

The Journal and Documents here printed, from their undoubted Authenticity and great Diversity of Subject, are believed to offer a valuable Addition to our previous Knowledge of the Events attending the Indian Wars of 1763 *; and the Publisher, by inscribing these Pages to a zealous and discriminating Student of American History, has the Gratification of believing that his own Labours for the Extension of Historical Literature have met with an intelligent Approval.*

CONTENTS.

CONTENTS.

Introduction, - - - - - - - - - - - - vii
Diary of the Siege of Detroit, - - - - - 1
Journal of the Siege of Detroit, - - - - - 121
General Bradftreet's Statement upon Indian Affairs, - - - - - - - - - - - - 137
Papers relating to the Indian Wars of 1763 and 1764, and the Confpiracy of Pontiac, - - - 159
Index, - - - - - - - - - - - - - 288

INTRODUCTION.

OTWITHSTANDING the Englifh found themfelves Mafters of Canada, by the Capitulation of Montreal in September, 1760, the French retained a Place in the Memory of the Indian Tribes which could not be alienated by Treaties; and this Regard, which was gained by a long Series of kind Offices and well-timed Prefents, was ftrengthened rather than diminifhed by the Neglect and Ill-ufage which thefe Sons of Nature received at the Hands of the Englifh.

There was no longer any European Rival to contend againft; no Competition exifted for the Monopoly and Profits of the Indian Trade, and no Rifk of an Alliance with any civilized Power, to moleft the long Frontier which had through many Years been defolated with Fire, and kept in Mourning by the cruel Hand of a lurking Enemy. The Motives for cultivating the Friendfhip of the Indians, which had been dictated

by

by Policy, no longer exifted, and thofe of Humanity and common Juftice foon proved inadequate to fecure thofe Favours which the Natives had long been accuftomed to receive from the Whites, and which the Introduction of the Weapons and fome of the Arts, if not the Vices, of Civilization, had to a certain Degree rendered neceffary to their Comfort and Contentment.

It was impoffible for them to fall back upon the Ufe of the Bow and Arrow, and the Club, after having become accuftomed to Fire Arms, and the only Means of their procuring thefe Articles which had thus been made neceffary to their Exiftence, was from the Englifh, now fole Mafters of the Country, upon fuch Terms and with fuch Sacrifices as unprincipled Traders or haughty military Officers might exact or permit, and if any Grievance arofe there was no longer an Appeal to a friendly Ear, or Hope of better Times for themfelves or their Children.

It will be remembered that the French ftill retained Command of the Pofts upon the Miffiffippi; that moft of the Inhabitants of this Nation, who were fcattered around the military Pofts in the Interiour, garrifoned by Englifh Troops, were ftill living in Terms of Intimacy with the Indians, and although yielding a formal Allegiance to their new Mafters, were ftill national in Language and in Heart, and finally that French Miffionaries and Emiffaries were ftill living in the Indian Villages throughout the Country. The War between France

Introduction. ix

France and England, although fettled in North America, was ftill raging in Europe, and a Series of fuccefsful Operations in the old World, might have ftill enabled the French to claim the Relinquifhment of Canada, as one of the Conditions of Peace, as had occurred but a few Years previous in the Refurrender of Louifburgh, upon the Ifland of Cape Breton, after its Capture by New England Troops.

If in addition to thefe we remember, that the Indians had been taught by their French Allies, that the Grand Monarch of France was fcarcely lefs Omnipotent than Deity, that he loved his red Children and would ultimately protect them,—and that greatly perverted Accounts of the true Relations exifting between the two Countries were circulated among the Indians, we fhall have fufficient Reafons to account for the War which devaftated the Frontiers in the Summer of 1763, and in which Pontiac, the great Ottawa Chief, acted fo confpicuous a Part.

Sir William Johnfon, whofe Opportunities for knowing Indian Affairs were unfurpaffed, and whofe Judgment is entitled to the higheft Refpect in every thing that concerns thefe People, thus wrote to the Lords of Trade at the Period under Confideration:

"Without any Exaggeration, I look upon the North-
"ern Indians to be the moft formidable of any unci-
"vilized Body of People in the World. Hunting and
"War are their fole Occupations, and the one quali-
fies

Introduction.

"fies them for the other; they have few Wants, and
"thofe are eafily fupplied; their Properties of little
"Value, confequently Expeditions againft them, how-
"ever fucceffful, cannot diftrefs them, and they have
"Courage fufficient for their Manner of fighting, the
"Nature and Situation of their Countrys require not
"more.

"As the French well knew the Importance of the
"Indians, they wifely took Advantage of our Neglect,
"and altho' they were not able to effect a proper Re-
"conciliation with the Six Nations, took Care to cul-
"tivate a good Underftanding with the Weftern In-
"dians, which the Safety of their Colony, and their
"ambitious Views of extending their Bounds, rendered
"indifpenfably neceffary; to effect this, they were at
"an immenfe Expence in buying the Favour of the
"Indians.

"On the Reduction of Montreal, whereby the Fron-
"tiers claimed by Canada were ceded to His Majefty,
"I thought it prudent to fend Mr. Croghan, one of
"my Deputys, with the Troops, who were to take
"Poffeffion of Detroit, etc., whereby I reconciled the
"Change to the neighbouring Indians, then in Arms
"againft us, and the next Year went in Perfon to
"Detroit, where I held a Conference with the feveral
"neighbouring Nations, the Particulars of which will
"appear from my Tranfactions laft Year tranfmitted
"to your Lord^{pps}; but apprehenfive that our occupying

Introduction. xi

"ing thefe Outpofts would never be approved of,
"unlefs the Indians fhared our Favours, as they had
"been accuftomed to thofe of the French, I reprefented
"to the Commander-in-Chief, the neceffity of weaning
"them therefrom gradually, as well as the repeated
"Accounts I had conftantly tranfmitted me of the
"Uneafinefs amongft the Indians, and my Apprehen-
"fions thereon.

"The Indians of the Ottawa Confederacy (& who
"begun the prefent War) and alfo the Six Nations,
"however their Sentiments may have been mifrepre-
"fented, all along confidered the northern Parts of
"North America as their fole Property, from the Be-
"ginning; and although the Conveniency of Trade
"(with fair Speaches and Promifes) induced them to
"afford both us and the French, Settlements in their
"Country, yet they have never underftood fuch Set-
"tlement as a Dominion, efpecially as neither we, nor
"the French ever made Conqueft of them; they have
"even repeatedly faid at feveral Conferences in my
"Prefence, that 'they were amufed by both Parties with
"Stories of their upright Intentions, and that they
"made War for the Protection of the Indians' Rights,
"but that they plainly found it was carried on, to fee
"who would become Mafters of what was the Property
"of neither the one nor the other.' The French in
"order to reconcile them to thefe Encroachments,
"loaded them with Favours, and employed the moft

B intelligent

"intelligent Agents, of good Influence, as well as art-
" ful Jesuits, amongst the several western and other
" Nations, who by Degrees prevailed on them to admit
" of Forts, under the Notion of Trading Houses, in
" their Country; and knowing that these Posts could
" never be maintained contrary to the Inclinations of
" the Indians, they supplied them thereat with Ammu-
" nition and other Necessaries in abundance, as also
" called them to frequent Congresses, and dismissed
" them with handsome Presents; by which they en-
" joyed an extensive Commerce, obtained the Assist-
" ance of these Indians, and possessed their Frontiers in
" Safety; and as without these Measures, the Indians
" would never have suffered them in their Country, so
" they expect that whatever European Power possesses
" the same, they shall in some measure reap the like
" Advantages. Now, as these Advantages ceased,
" on the Posts being possessed by the English, and
" especially as it was not thought prudent to indulge
" them with Amunition, they immediately concluded
" we had Designs against their Liberties, which Opin-
" ion had been first instilled into them by the French,
" and since promoted by Traders of that Nation and
" others who retired amongst them on the Surrender of
" Canada and are still there, as well as by Belts of
" Wampum and other Exhortations, which I am con-
" fidently assured have been sent amongst them from the
" Illinois, Louisiana and even Canada, for that Purpose."

The

Introduction.

The Treatment which the Indians were accuftomed to receive from the Englifh Traders has been fpecified by Sir William Johnfon.[1]

"The Frontier Traders, fenfible they have little to
"apprehend from their Conduct, went ftill greater and
"more dangerous Lengths than their Superiours; from
"a Variety of unheard of Frauds, I fhall felect a very
"few Inftances which will tend to fhew to what Lengths
"fome of that Character will go when fubject to no
"Controul, and becaufe two of thefe Inftances were
"the Occafion of our lofing the Trade and Affections
"of fome powerful Tribes of the Ottawaes, who were
"perfuaded to come the Length of Ofwego to Trade
'with us, and the laft Inftances caufed the Defection
"of the moft powerful Tribes of the Senecas.

"Several of the Ottawaes having traded for a con-
"fiderable Time at Ofwego, where they got fome Arti-
"cles which they could not procure from the French,
"an Ottawa Chief of great Influence with his Family,
"brought his Packs to a Trader there, in order to try
"the Market; the Trader, after the ufual Practice of
"deceiving him in the Weight, hurried the Peltry into
"a private Room, telling the Indian that all Mer-
"chandize was very dear, owing to the Severity of
"Dutys (a ftale, but dangerous Artifice ftill practifed)
"defired him to choofe out what Goods he wanted;
"the Indian having made a Choice, was aftonifhed to

[1] Col. Hift. of N. Y., vii, 955.

find

"find that his Skins produced not one third of what
" he had been accuftomed to receive for the like Quan-
" tity (for the Trader had befides his Extortion on
" the Goods reckoned the Peltry at only one third of
" its real Weight) went away difcontented, but return-
" ing faid, he was afhamed to go back with fuch fmall
" Returns, and begged for a fmall Keg of Rum,
" which the Trader gave him, as he faid, as a high
" Favour, but on opening the Keg foon after his De-
" parture it proved to be Water. Another Trader for
" fome valuable Furrs, which he received from an Ottawa
" Chief of great Influence, who came likewife to try
" the Market, and defired to have his Returns in Rum
" for a general Feaft, gave the Indian 30 fmall Kegs with
" Directions not to open them by the Way, otherwife
" the Trader would be punifhed for letting them have
" fo much; but the Indian before his Return to Nia-
" gara, being defirous of fome Liquor, opened them
" and found them all Water. This has been often
" acknowledged by thefe Traders, and on its coming
" to the Knowledge of the French, they made fo good
" a Ufe of it, that thefe People and all their Friends
" were ever after our most implacable Enemies. The
" next Inftance is that of a Seneca Warriour, whofe Influ-
" ence and Abilities were fo well known, that I found it
" a very hard Tafk to bring them over, which however
" I at length effected in 1756, when he came to me
" with a large Party of Warriours, who were to fet out

on

Introduction.

" on public Service in a few Days, but having some
" Furrs to dispose of, I gave them at their Desire a
" Passport to Schenectady, wherein I recommended it
" to a Merchant and Trader there, to use them very
" kindly, and to do them the strictest Justice, notwith-
" standing which, this Enemy to the Interests of his
" Country, imposed upon them in the grossest Manner;
" it appearing from their Account, & his own Confes-
" sion since, that as they were Strangers, he had doubled
" the Prices of his Goods and allowed them but half
" the Weight of their Peltry; this was resented ac-
" cordingly, the Indians took another Route back, and
" the Chief sent me a Belt of Wampum with a Mes-
" sage informing me of the Imposition (the Particulars
" of each Article being marked on the Handle of an Axe)
" and assuring me that he should always continue to have
" a personal Regard for me, but not the least for the
" English who had served him so often, but the last
" Instance was of such a Nature, that he had accepted
" of an Invitation from the French, who knew how to
" treat them, and their Services; he made his Words
" good; in a few Days cut off a large Settlement, and
" continued our most violent Enemy ever since, par-
" ticularly at Niagara in 1759, whilst it was not in my
" Power to have the unworthy Author punished. To
" this I must subjoin an Instance in the Case of the
" Chief of all the Senecas, a Warriour, whose Influence
" and Capacity were, and are well known here, whom I
had

"had steadily preserved in the British Interest, when
"we were almost totally abandoned, this Man at the
"Eve of the late War, was thro' the Means of Liquor
"seduced by some *Agents* at *Albany* to subscribe his
"Name to an Indian Deed for a Tract within the
"Bounds of Pennsylvania, but claimed by the Con-
"necticut People, in Virtue of their obsolete Charter,
"which extended their western Limits to the South
"Seas. This being a most iniquitous Proceeding
"highly resented by the Six Nations; the few who sub-
"scribed to it became obnoxious to the rest, particu-
"larly the Chief before mentioned, so that he was
"obliged to fly to the French for Protection, who so
"far won upon him, that he with a powerful Party
"who followed his Fortunes took up Arms shortly
"after, attacked a Body of Provincials at Lake George,
"whom they totally defeated and killed 45. Since
"which he was concerned in the most important Ser-
"vices against us, cut off some of our Settlements, and
"occasioned the Deaths of more than 400 of our
"People. These, it is presumed, will suffice to shew
"the Effects of the Resentment of a few Indian Indi-
"viduals."

Such being the Causes of Disaffection, and such the Motives still remaining with the French to encourage Indian Hostilities, there was wanting only a Leader around whom to Rally and upon whom to rely for Direction

Introduction. xvii

Direction and Counfel, and fuch a Chieftain was found in the Perfon of Pontiac.

By Merit as well as by Birth he had gained the Pofition of principal Chief of the Ottawas, and his Achievements and Talents had gained him an Influence fcarcely lefs powerful over the Ojibwas, Pottawottamies, and in fact over almoft all the Races of the Algonquin Stock. The Seneca Tribe of the Six Nations were alfo brought into this Alliance, and led by this energetic, crafty and vindictive Enemy of the Englifh to unite in a Plan for the fimultaneous Deftruction of the Pofts along the whole Frontier, as the Prelude of a general War of Extermination.

Pontiac was about fifty Years of age. He was a Friend to the French, whofe Fortunes he ardently defired to retrieve in Canada, and from whom he had without doubt been promifed large Reinforcements and unlimited Supplies. The Merchandife ftored at Detroit and other Pofts in the Interiour, at the Time Hoftilities began, were alone fufficient to provoke the Cupidity of the Savages, with much fewer Grounds for Grievance than actually exifted, and at Detroit alone, the Value of Goods was eftimated at half a million Pounds Sterling.[1]

In the Code of Indian Warfare, that Meafure is honourable which is fucceffful, and Treachery, Craft and Force may be alike employed, as Circumftances favour

[1] Lanman's Hift. Michigan, p. 107.

xviii   *Introduction.*

one or another. With thefe People, a Parole of Honour or the Obfervance of a Truce, would have been faithfully kept only fo far as a Fear of Confequences compelled them, and the Incidents concerning the Detention of Col. Campbell and Lieut. McDougal, as related in the following Pages, furnifhes but one of a Multitude of Inftances which Hiftory affords in Proof of the Fact, that the Natives knew no Code of Honour where an Advantage could be gained by a Breach of Truft.

The Hatred felt by the Indians towards the Englifh, began to affume a centralized and efficient Form in 1762, in the Fall of which Year Pontiac fent Meffengers with War Belts far and wide, calling every where upon the Warriours of his Race to unite and at a concerted Moment to fall upon and deftroy the neareft Military Pofts of the Englifh, affuring them that their Father, the Grand Monarch, would fuftain them in their Effort, and that they would be able to drive thefe hated Englifh from their Land.

The Incidents which marked the Execution of this Defign are related in the following Pages, and the high Degree of military Merit which faved Detroit from the Fate of many other Frontier Pofts, will long remain a Subject of Admiration.

The Diary printed in the following Pages, we believe to be now for the firft time publifhed, and although its Author is unknown, we have Reafon to infer from

feveral

Introduction. xix

several Allusions to himself, and References to other Records kept along with it, that he was the Secretary of the Commandant, and that he was fully in his Confidence. The Manuscript is all in one Hand-writing, and is written upon about half a dozen Sizes of Paper, which were evidently in loose Sheets at the Time, and have since been bound in one Volume.

It was purchased from a Bookseller in London, and its former Owner had begun to print it; but finding, after getting through thirty-two Pages, that the Sheets had not been bound up in Chronological Order, the Enterprise was abandoned, until it came into the Hands of the Publisher of the present Series. It bears conclusive Evidence of Authenticity, and is believed to offer new and valuable Contributions to our Knowledge of the Events to which it relates.

The Tribes, one by one, were gradually won back to Peace with the English through the Address of Sir William Johnson and others, whose Sagacity led them to this Pacification by Detail, rather than to attempt a general Treaty with all the hostile Tribes, as this might lead to a Union among them that would be dangerous in its Tendencies and difficult to controul.

The Pride and Hatred of Pontiac long kept him aloof from these Negotiations, and many an ineffectual Effort he made to interrupt them; but the final and conclusive Intelligence of Peace between France and England, received from the French themselves, at length

length convinced them that the laſt Hope of Succour had vaniſhed, and that no Effort of theirs could Benefit their loved and cheriſhed Allies, or controul the Progreſs of the Engliſh.

Pontiac concluded a Peace with George Croghan, Deputy of Sir William Johnſon, at Detroit, in Auguſt, 1765, and promiſed to meet Sir William at Oſwego in the Spring following to ratify the Peace in Perſon, and from this Viſit he returned laden with Gifts to the Maumee, where he ſpent the ſucceeding Winter. In 1767, new Sources of Annoyance to the Indians were encountered by the Inſults and Aggreſſions of the Frontier Settlers, and a brief but bloody War enſued on the Borders of Virginia, in which Pontiac is not known to have been concerned. During the Summer of 1767, he went to the Illinois, and ſoon after repaired to St. Louis to viſit his Friend St. Ange, who then commanded at that Poſt. He was treated with great Kindneſs, and two or three Days after, hearing that a large Number of Indians were aſſembled at Cahokia, on the oppoſite Side of the River, for ſome ſocial Purpoſe, he reſolved to croſs over and ſee what was in Progreſs. He was adviſed to the Contrary, but relying upon his own Courage and ſeeing no Danger, he went.

The cloſing Scene of his Life we cannot ſo well relate as in the Language of Francis Parkman, Jr., of Boſton, whoſe beautifully written Hiſtory of the Conſpiracy

Introduction. xxi

ſpiracy of Pontiac, evinces a great Amount of Reſearch, and a high Degree of literary Merit.

* * "The Place was full of Illinois Indians; ſuch
"a Scene as in our own Time may often be met with
"in ſome ſqualid Settlement of the Border, where the
"vagabond Gueſts, bedizened with dirty Finery, tie
"their ſmall Horſes in Rows along the Fences, and
"ſtroll idly among the Houſes, or lounge about the
"Dram-ſhops. A Chief ſo renowned as Pontiac could
"not remain long among the friendly Creoles of Ca-
"hokia without being ſummoned to a Feaſt; and at
"ſuch primitive Entertainment the Whiſkey Bottle
"would not fail to play its Part. This was in truth
"the Caſe. Pontiac drank deeply, and, when the
"Carouſal was over, ſtrode down the Village Street to
"the adjacent Woods, where he was heard to ſing the
"Medicine Songs, in whoſe magick Power he truſted
"as the Warrant of Succeſs in all his Undertakings.

"An Engliſh Trader, named Williamſon, was then
"in the Village. He had looked on the Movements
"of Pontiac with a Jealouſy probably not diminiſhed
"by the Viſit of the Chief to the French at St. Louis;
"and he now reſolved not to loſe ſo Favourable an
"Opportunity to deſpatch him. With this View, he
"gained the Ear of a ſtrolling Indian belonging to the
"Kaſkaſkia Tribe of the Illinois, bribed him with a
"Barrel of Liquor, and promiſed him a farther Reward
"if he would kill the Chief. The Bargain was quickly
made.

"made. When Pontiac entered the Foreſt, the Aſſaſ-
"ſin ſtole upon his Track, and watching his Moment,
"glided behind him, and buried a Tomahawk in his
"Brain.

"The dead Body was ſoon diſcovered, and ſtartled
"Cries and wild Howlings announced the Event.
"The Word was caught up from Mouth to Mouth,
"and the Place reſounded with infernal Yells. The
"Warriours ſnatched their Weapons. The Illinois
"took Part with their guilty Countryman, and the few
"Followers of Pontiac, driven from the Village, fled
"to ſpread the Tidings and call the Nations to Re-
"venge. Meanwhile the murdered Chief lay on the
"Spot where he had fallen, until St. Ange, mindful of
"former Friendſhip, ſent to claim the Body, and
"buried it with warlike Honours, near his Fort of St.
"Louis.

"Thus baſely periſhed this Champion of a ruined
"Race. But could his Shade have reviſited the Scene
"of Murder, his ſavage Spirit would have exulted in
"the Vengeance which overwhelmed the Abettors of the
"Crime. Whole Tribes were rooted out to expiate it.
"Chiefs and Sachems, whoſe Veins had thrilled with
"his Eloquence, young Warriours, whoſe aſpiring
"Hearts had caught the Inſpiration of his Greatneſs,
"muſtered to revenge his Fate, and from the North
"and the Eaſt, their united Bands deſcended on the
"Villages of the Illinois. Tradition has but faintly
preſerved

Introduction. xxiii

"preferved the Event; and its only Annalifts, Men "who held the inteftine Feuds of the Savage Tribes in "no more Account than the Quarrels of Panthers or "Wild-cats, have left but a meagre Record. Yet "enough remains to tell us that over the Grave of "Pontiac more Blood was poured out in Atonement "than flowed from the Hecatombs of flaughtered "Heroes on the Corpfe of Patroclus; and the Rem- "nant of the Illinois who furvived the Carnage re· "mained for ever after funk in utter Infignificance.

"Neither Mound nor Tablet marked the Burial- "place of Pontiac. For a Maufoleum, a City has rifen "above the Foreft Hero; and the Race whom he "hated with fuch burning Rancour trample with un- "ceafing Footfteps over his forgotten Grave."

The Papers which follow the Diary in this Volume are now moftly printed for the firft Time, from original Manufcripts in the State Library at Albany, and will be found to have an interefting Relation to the Confpiracy of Pontiac and the Wars of that Period. The Alarms which thefe Events occafioned on the Frontier were fcarcely lefs Diftreffing than actual Hoftilities, and thefe were often greatly aggravated by Rumours of Invafions and Murders which proved groundlefs and abfurd. The Refources of the Country, and the Spirit of the Inhabitants were, however, tefted by this Crifis, and Hiftory is enriched with Details, which might not have been otherwife preferved.

Albany, Feb. 1, 1860. F. B. H.

DIARY

OF THE

SIEGE OF DETROIT.

DIARY

OF THE

SIEGE OF DETROIT.

Detroit, May 1, 1763.

HE 1ſt of May Pondiac, the moſt conſiderable Man in the Ottawa Nation, came here with about 50 of his Men,[1] & told the Commandant[2] that in a few Days when the reſt of his Nation came in he intended to come and make him a formal Viſit, as is the Cuſtom with all the Na-

1763.
May 1.

[1] The Pontiac MSS. quoted by Parkman and aſcribed to a French Prieſt, ſays the Party numbered *forty*. The Commandant in writing to Sir Jeffrey Amherſt, ſtates the Number as *fifty*. They came for the nominal Purpoſe of dancing the Calumet Dance and declaring their Friendſhip for the Engliſh, but in reality to aſcertain the Strength of the Garriſon, and the Nature and Extent of their Means of Defence. While moſt of them were dancing, the others were ſtrolling about the Premiſes, narrowly examining everything.—*Parkman's Pontiac*, p, 201.

[2] Major Henry Gladwyn, had but a ſhort Time previous to this Date, ſucceeded Major Campbell in the Command of this Poſt. He had accompanied Braddock in his unfortunate Expedition in 1755, was made Captain in the 80th or Gage's Light Armed Foot, Dec. 25,

tions

1763.
May.
7

tions once a Year.³ The 7th he came with all the Ottawa and Part of several other Nations, but we saw from their Behavior & from Reports that they were not well intentioned, upon which the Commandant took such Precautions that when they enter'd the Fort (tho they were by the nearest acc^{ts} about 300 hundred and arm'd with Knives, Tomahawks, & a great many with Guns cut short and hid under their Blankets) they were so much surpriz'd to see our Dispositions that they wou'd scarcely sit down to Council; however in about half an Hour after they saw that we were prepared for the worst, they sat down & made several Speeches which were answer'd as calmly as if we did not suspect them at all, and after receiving some Tobacco & Bread & some other Presents they went away to their Camp.⁴ This Morning a Party sent by him for that Purpose took Capt. Robinson & Sir Robert

1757, and commissioned Major of that Regiment, June 20, 1759. In December of the Year following, he became a Major in the regular Army.

He continued in Command at Detroit through the Seige of Pontiac, and until relieved, Aug. 31, 1764, upon the Arrival of the Army under Col. Bradstreet.

He was promoted to the Rank of Lieutenant-Colonel, Sept. 17, 1763, and to that of Major-General, Sept. 26, 1782. He died at Stubbing, near Chesterfield, County of Derby, England, June 22, 1791.

³ Referring to the Ojibwa, Pottawattamie and Wyandot Tribes, who were leagued together in this Enterprise.

⁴ Other Authorities state that but sixty Indians were permitted to enter the Fort. All the Troops and Employées about the Premises were drawn up in military Array, and as Pontiac and his Men passed on to the Council House, he found Major Gladwyn and his Officers sitting armed with Swords and Pistols. It was evident that the Purpose of the Visit was understood, and the crafty Savage was overawed. As he came to that Part of his Speech in which he was to have given the Signal for Attack, a roll of Drums and clash of Arms at the Entrance confused him, and he sat down. The Commandant has been censured for not detaining him, which he probably would have done had he suspected the Extent of the Plot.

Davers

Pontiac's Siege of Detroit.

Davers in a Barge near the Mouth of Lake Huron, which Capt. Robinson went to sound. They with Part of the Boat's Crew were put to Death,[5] the rest they took Prisoners as we were afterwards informed. The 8th Pondiac return'd with a Pipe of Peace in order to ask Commandant leave to come next Day with his whole Nation to bury all bad Reports, but the Commandant wou'd not give him leave but told him if he had any thing to say he might come with the rest of the Chiefs and he would hear them. However instead of coming the 9th in the after Noon he struck his Camp and cross'd the River within ½ a Mile of the Fort,[6] but being inform'd by the Interpreter that he would not be permitted to come in, he embark'd again & he commenc'd Hostilities by killing the King's Cattle that were on an Island about 3 Miles from the Fort,[7] with the People that took care of them, and a poor English Family that had just built a little House there,[8] as also another English Family that liv'd just behind the Fort.[9] He also cut of the Communication

1763. May.

9

---

[5] An anonymous Letter, dated at Detroit, July 9, 1763, and printed in the Pennsylvania Gazette, Nos. 1,807, 1,808, states that the Body of Sir Robert Davers was boiled and eaten. Mr. Paully (whose Escape from the Enemy is elsewhere noticed) saw the Skin of Capt. Robertson's Arm in use as a Tobacco Pouch. These Murders occurred May 9, 1763.—*Parkman's Pontiac*, p. 207.

[6] The Ottawa Camp had previously been about five Miles above on the east Side of the River.

[7] Isle au Cochon or Hog Island, is now on the American Side of the National Boundary. It is two Miles long and one wide.

[8] The Person killed here was named James Fisher, who had been a Sergeant of the Regulars. A further Account of this Murder is given in Rogers's Narrative in the subsequent Pages of this Volume. His Wife and four Soldiers are by some Accounts reported as having been murdered at the same Time.—*Thatcher, Lanman.*

[9] This Family was that of an from

Pontiac's Siege of Detroit.

1763.
May.
from the Fort to the Inhabitants on each Side so that we cou'd not get the least Thing brought into the Fort. He told the Inhabitants that the first of them that shou'd bring us any Provisions or any thing that cou'd be of any Service to us, they wou'd put that Family to Death. They also surrounded the Fort & fired a vast Number of Shots at it and the Vessels which were anchor'd so as to flank the Fort both above and below.[10] The Garrison lay upon the Arms all Night, not being above 120 Men,[11] Merchants, Sick & Officers. The

English Woman, named Turnbull, who lived outside of the Fort on a distant Part of the Common. Major Gladwyn had given her a Piece of Land for her Residence.—*Lanman's Michigan*, 106.

[10] There were two small armed Vessels lying before the Fort at this Time, named the *Beaver* and the *Gladwyn*. They rendered efficient Service in the Siege, and kept the Enemy from approaching by Water.

[11] The Garrison at the Beginning of the Siege consisted of one hundred and twenty-two Men and eight Officers, besides about forty Fur-traders and Engagées, who were more inclined to the French and were willing to be neutral. The Fort was Quadrilateral, with one Side near the water's Edge, and consisted of a single Row of Palisades twenty-five feet high, with Block-houses over the Gates and at the Angles. It contained two Six-pounders, one Three-pounder and three Mortars, badly mounted and calculated rather to inspire Terror than to do Execution among the skulking Savages

who so assiduously watched the Fort, seldom venturing in Numbers within Range of the great Guns, but ready to take off the unlucky Person who might chance to show his Head above the Pickets, or his Body before a Port hole.

This Enclosure contained about 100 small Dwellings, closely built upon narrow Streets, a Council-house, a small Church and Barracks for the Troops. A wider Street, called the *Chemin du Ronde*, led around the Buildings adjacent to the Pickets. The Buildings were of Wood and very liable to be set on Fire by burning Arrows. The Church was particularly exposed to this Casualty, as it stood near to the Palisades, but the Indians were threatened by the French Priest with the anger of the Great Spirit, if they did not desist from their Attempts to fire this Building. The Garrison by keeping constant Watch and plenty of Water in Cisterns, prevented Fires from taking. The River is here half a mile Wide.— *Discourse of Lewis Cass, before the Hist. Soc. of Michigan*, Sept. 18, 1829, p. 29.

10th

Pontiac's Siege of Detroit.

10th they surrounded it again and fired very briskly till about 11 or 12 o'Clock when they made some Proposals for an Accommodation (which was lucky for us, as it gave us Time to get Provisions in to the King's Store as we had not above three Weeks at short allowance), and Capt. Campbell and Lieut. McDougal,[12] with the principal Part of the French, who said they would be answerable for their Return, went out to hold a Council with him, but as soon as Pondiac got them in his Possession, he chang'd his Mind & would not come to Terms as he had a few Hours before promis'd the French, who seem'd to do all in their Power to make him disperse his People, but on the contrary sent Word to the Commandant that he must leave the Fort

---

[12] Major Donald Campbell had been succeeded by Gladwyn but a few Days before. M. Gouin, a friendly Canadian, finding that these Men were in great Danger, hastily sent a Message for them not to come out, but as they had already started with La Butte, one of the Interpreters and some other French, they would not heed the Warning and passed on. When they came to a rising Ground, beyond which the Indians lay, the latter ran yelling towards them, as if they were prisoners running the Gauntlet, but Pontiac allayed the Tumult, and led them to a Lodge, where some few Words were spoken, but on their proposing to Return they found themselves Prisoners. They were quartered in the House of M. Meloche, near Parent Creek, and closely guarded, but otherwise well treated for the Present. Two Indians had been detained in the Fort a few Days before, and were still in the Hands of the English, which doubtless prevented the Savages from Acts of Violence at this Time.

On the 4th of July following, a Nephew of an Ojibwa Chief, was killed and scalped by a Party from the Fort. Upon hearing this News, the enraged Uncle ran to the House of Meloche, seized Major Campbell, bound him fast to a Fence and killed him with Arrows. He was afterwards shockingly mangled, and it was reported that his Heart was eaten by the Savages. Lieut. McDougall instantly fled, and succeeded in reaching the Fort in Safety. Some Authors have stated that the Murder of Major Campbell was approved by Pontiac, while others affirm that he was highly offended, and that the Murderer was obliged to escape beyond his Reach.— *Parkman's Pontiac*, 211, 260; *MSS. Sir Wm. Johnson*, vol. vii.

1763.
May,
11

as M. Bell Etre did, that was to say to take Provision enough with him to carry him to Niagara, but to leave all the Merchandise.¹³ To which the Commandant answer'd that he cou'd not come to any Terms with him until he sent back Capt. Campbell & Lieut. McDougal, for whom he wou'd give up the two Pottawattamies that he had detained for them. The Garrison lay on their Arms all Night as usual. We were at the same Time told by some French that they thought the best thing we cou'd do wou'd be to save ourselves in the Vessels, as there was 1000, some said 1500 Indians ready to fall upon all Sides of the Fort, but they got for Answer that if in case they were three times a numerous there was not an Officer or.¹⁴

12

In the Morning Pondiac sent another Message desiring the Fort to be given up, as before, to which the Commandant gave an equivocal Answer to gain Time, to get Provision, having for two Nights before employ'd some French Men to put some Corn and Pares Geese on board the Vessels unknown to the Indians. The twelfth in the Morning they surrounded the Fort & fired upon it and the Vessels for about four Hours very briskly, tho at so great a Distance that we had but one Man slightly wounded in the Fort and another on board one of the Vessels. We kill'd three or four of them and wounded nine or ten. We set fire to some out Houses from behind which they annoy'd us. The Garrison lay upon their Arms on the Rampart all Night, as they had done for three Nights before. The

---

[13] M. P. de Beletere was the last French Commandant at Detroit, before its Surrender to the English in the Autumn of 1760. He was sent with the other Prisoners under the Care of Lieut. Holmes and thirty Rangers to Philadelphia.—*Rogers's Journal*, p. 229.

[14] The Sentence in the Manuscript thus ends abruptly.

thirteenth

thirteenth in the Morning we heard that the Hurons had interfepted one Chapman,[15] with five Battoes or Canoes loaded with Merchandize, amongft which they got fixteen half Barrels of Powder and fome Rum, & that they were all drunk with it, upon which Hopkins,[16] with twenty-five Men, among whom were Mr. Starling, Mr. Watkins and McCormick, Volun[rs] went on board the Sloop in order to go oppofite the Huron Village,[17] and under the fire of her Cannon to land and burn it with their Booty and their Corn, the Wind being favorable to go up or down the River, but unluckily before he got Half way there the Wind fhifted and he was obliged to return, but by the Fire that the Huron kept while the Veffel was under Sail it did not appear that they were Drunk or off their Guard. They conftantly fired on the Fort & Veffels till dark, but without doing the leaft Damage. This Afternoon

---

[15] Chapman was a Trader, who, without fufpecting Hoftilities, was approaching Detroit. Heckewelder relates (*Hift. Ind. Nat.* 250), of a Man of this Name, and perhaps the Perfon here referred to, that after being kept fome Time by a Frenchman, the Indians refolved to burn him alive. He was bound to the Stake, and the Flames were kindled, when in the Agonies of that Moment an Indian handed him a Bowl of Broth. Upon touching it with his Lips, it was found boiling hot, and in an Inftant he threw the Difh and its Contents into the Face of the Savage. "He is mad! he is mad!" fhouted the Crowd, and haftily quenching the Fire, they relieved him from his horrid Fate and fet him at Liberty. The fuperftitious Awe with which the Natives regarded Lunatics and Idiots, has been often remarked by Hiftorians, and aids in explaining fome ftriking Incidents in their Annals. Chapman was brought in and furrendered July 12th, 1763.

[16] Captain Hopkins had Charge of a Company of Rangers, and in the numerous Skirmifhes and Sorties that occurred during the Siege, he is often mentioned as having had the Command.

[17] The Huron Village lay Eaft of the River, a fhort Diftance below Detroit. A Miffionary of the Order of Carthufian Friars, by Permiffion of the Bifhop of Canada refided there.—*Carver's Travels*, p. 92.

burn'd

1763.
May.
12

burn'd several out Houses from behind which they annoy'd us. The Garrison lay on Ramparts as usual.

The twelfth in the Evening Pondiac sent in another Message demanding the Fort, at the same Time saying that the firing shou'd cease until an Answer was sent; this was to get Time to bring of the Dead and Wounded that had fallen in the Morning as appear'd from about thirty or forty of them coming about the Fort without Arms immediately after the Messenger arrived, but not so near as to be taken; after this Messenger ariv'd we found that the Corn, Flower & Bare's Grease that we had put on board the Vessels & that we found in the Fort would last us for upwards of three Months.

The Answer to the above Message is in the Memorandum of the 16th.

14

The fourteenth[18] they began firing at about eleven o'Clock and continued till dark, not daring to approach nearer than the nearest Houses that cou'd cover them, which was upwards of two hundred Yards off. They fir'd a great deal but more upon the Vessels than on

---

[18] Major Gladwyn appears to have succeeded this Day in getting off a Letter to Gen. Amherst, as appears from an Epistle of the latter to Col. Bradstreet, Q. M. G., dated June 22, 1763:
* * * "Major Gladwyn writes me of the 14th May, that the Detroit was invested by a large Body of Indians; but that the Garrison was in high Spirits, and he was in Hopes of being able to defend the Place untill he received some Succours from Niagara; & Major Wilkins acquaints me he had, immediately on the Arrival of the Schooner from the Detroit, sent off a Reinforcement of fifty Men with a Lieutenant and non-commissioned Officers, which I trust will have arrived in Time to save the Place. I well know that you are always ready, however I think it necessary to acquaint you to be prepared for moving at a moment's Warning, as, if the Savages are not quickly reduced, I believe I shall employ you on a Command which I am certain will be agreeable to you."—*Bradstreet & Amherst Papers*, p. 140.

the

Pontiac's Siege of Detroit.

the Fort. We had this Day a Searjeant and one private Man wounded.

Last Night these Indians made a kind of Breastwork between the Fort and Mr. St. Martin House of some Pickets that he had for a Garden.[19] This Morning we cut two Embrasures through the Stockades for two four Pounders with which we intended to dislodge them in case they should return again. But instead of their coming to fire in the Manner they had done yesterday, there was only a few of them came and began firing scattering Shot at eleven o'Clock & continued so till the Evening which we did not mind. This Morning a Party went out and burn'd the remainder of the Houses that was near the Fort from behind which they annoy'd the Vessels. They day before yesterday we were informed that Mr. Rutherford,[20] who was with Capt. Robinson, was not kill'd but remains a Prisoner with the Indians.

The Garrison lay on their Arms to night as usual.

The Answer the Commandant sent to the verbal Message that Pondiac sent the 12th in the Evening was, That he was not sent here to give up the Fort to Indians, and advised Pondiac to disperse his People and take care of his Ammunition to hunt with.

This Morning at 11 o'Clock they began to fire scat-

---

[19] St. Martin, a French Interpreter, lived near the Fort, and his House was a convenient Point from whence the Indians might annoy the Garrison. The Owner appears to have been very kindly disposed toward the English, and on the 30th of June withdrew with his Family into the Fort.

[20] Mr. Samuel Rutherford was subsequently purchased by M. Cuefiere, from the Indians, for £80 worth in Goods, but Pontiac upon learning the Fact went with a Body of fifty Men and reclaimed him, saying it was not a good Precedent to sell Prisoners to the French. He escaped to the Fort on the first Day of August.—*Lanman's Hist. Michigan*, 108.

1763.
May.
16

tering Shot from Mr. S⁺ Martins House & Mr. Babies,[21] and continued till Evening, but without doing us any Damage.

The most of the Inhabitants assembled themselves to day to speake to Pondiac, who told them before he would give over his Design he wou'd send two Frenchmen and two Indians to the Illinois to inform himself whether what we had told him with regard to the Peace was true or not, & as to Capt. Campbelle & Lieut. McDougal he wou'd take care of them, and deliver them to the Commandant that he had sent for from the Illinois.

This Day a few Shot were fired as usual from Mr. Babies & Mr. S⁺ Martins Houses at the Vessels without doing any Execution. The Garrison lay on the Ramparts.

17

This Day there was not above a dozen Indians appeared within sight of the Fort, who did not fire above twenty Shot. The Garrison lay on the Rampart.

18

This Day a few Shot were fired from S⁺ Martins & Babie as usual without Damage. The Garrison lay on the Ramparts.

19

This Day we were very quiet, not having ten Shot fired at us. We were last Night inform'd that there was upwards of 150 Indians gone to the Mouth of the River to intersept some Party's that we expected from Niagara, upon which the Commandant ordered the Scooner to be got ready for Sea to send her down to cover t em in case they came safe to the Mouth of the River.

---

[21] M. Babie, a Frenchman in easy Circumstances, evinced the greatest Friendship to the English, and secretly furnished them with Provisions, at a Time when they were much needed. He came into the Fort with his Family, July 3, bringing such of his Goods as he could remove, and leaving the Remainder at the Mercy of the Indians. His House was burned by the English as a precautionary Measure on the 25th of August.

River. We alfo receiv'd fome Letters laft Night from Fort S.t Jofephs by an Indian that we had fent from here, every thing there feem'd quiet and the Indians declar'd great deal of Friendfhip for the Garrifon.

1763.
May.
20

This Evening a Man that was taken Prifoner fix Days ago by fome Ottawas and Mingoes in the Huron River ariv'd here by the Affiftance of two or three Frenchmen that were coming down that River. He inform'd us that he was hired with one Crawford a Trader who was on his way Home, that about 15 Indians met with them and laid down their Arms and call'd them Brothers, but after having reconnoiter'd them and finding they had a great quantity of Peltry fell upon them and took them all Prifoners and oblig'd them to return with them to a carrying Place on a fmall River that runs into the Miamis, from whence he made his Efcape as the Indians took him from a French Man, he fpeaking a little French.

The Garrifon lay on the Ramparts as ufual.

The 21. At eleven o'Clock the Scooner fail'd for the Mouth of the River with a N. E. Wind.[22] No Indians appear'd near the Fort to day till the Afternoon when a few came and fired fome Shot at the Sloop.

21

At fix in the Evening it was reported the Scooner was run aground, upon which all the Indians gather'd themfelves together to attack her, but the foremoft Cannoe having one Man kill'd by a Shot from her frightened the reft fo much that they put afhore again.

This Morning at 8 o'Clock we were inform'd that

22

---

[22] Other Accounts ftate that the Veffel which failed this Day for Niagara, was the *Gladwin*, the fmaller of the two, and rated at about eighty tons. Carver records the Fact that fhe was afterwards loft on Lake Erie with all her Crew, through the Obftinacy of her Commander, who could not be prevailed upon to take in fufficient Ballaft.—*Carver's Travels*, p. 99.

after

1763.
May.
22

after the Indians had attempted to attack the Schooner she carryed out an Anchor and hall'd off and this Morning arriv'd at the Mouth of the River.

At 9 o'Clock Mr. St Martin came with a Message from the Hurons, who desir'd him to tell the Commandant that they had been forc'd into the War by the Ottawas, that they had taken Chapman & his Merchandize, as also a Cannoe with five Englishmen coming from Sandusky yesterday, among whom were Mr. Smallman & two Jews, who must have all fallen into worse hands if they had not taken them, as they had not killed any of them; they desired to know what Opinion the Commandant had of them, that if he wou'd make Peace with them they wou'd give up their Prisoners and pay Chapman for the Part of his Merchandise that fell to their Lot in the Division of them with the other Indians; to which the Commandant desir'd the Interpreter, Mr. St Martin, to answer that upon these Conditions he wou'd take it upon himself to make Peace with them for the Present and recommend them to the General,[23] who he made no doubt wou'd make it a lasting one if their future behavior should merit it. They also offer'd to get themselves entrench'd on a small Island at the Mouth of the River and protect all Merchants Boats from the other Nations that should arive there. But the Commandant did not ask that of them for several good Reasons, but would rather they shou'd perform their Promises & remain quiet, or use their Endeavors to separate Pondiac & his followers, who at this Time had cut off all Communication between us and our Outposts, as also lay in wait at different Places to intercept all Merchants that might be on their way hither.

[23] Sir Jeffrey Amherst, then Commander-in-Chief of the British forces in North America.

He

He reign'd at this Time with moſt deſpotic Sway over the French, making ſeveral of them plow Land for him to put Corn in the Ground, and after they had done wou'd kill their Cattle. Three Days ago he ſent ſix Frenchmen with ſome Indians amongſt ſome other Nations to advertiſe them of what he was doing and to bring him Word from the Illinois wheather what we had told him with regard to the Peace was true or not.[24]

1763.
May.
22

We had not one Shot fir'd at us to day, notwithſtanding which the Garriſon lay on the Ramparts as uſual.

This Morning Pondiac being inform'd that the Scooner was on Ground, forc'd Capt. Campbelle to croſs the River with him in order to put him on board of a Cannoe to go and tell the Commander of her to give her to the Indians, but when he ariv'd at the Huron Village he was again inform'd that ſhe was in the Lake, upon which he return'd. When Pondiac propoſed this to Capt. Campbelle, he told him he might put him to death for he wou'd not go, but Pondiac told him he would not put him to death, but he would oblige him to go, and forc'd him.[25]

2

We had not one Shot fir'd at us to day.

The Huron; promiſ'd to remain neuter for five or

[24] The Commandant at the Illinois was at this Time M. de Neyon, who was ſtationed at Fort Chartres, the principal Poſt of the French in that Region. This was located near Kaſkaſkia, on the Miſſiſſippi, in the preſent County of Randolph, Ill. It was built in 1720, under the Auſpices of the Miſſiſſippi Company. The Capitulation of Montreal did not include the Remote French Poſts beyond the great Lakes.—*Brown's Hiſt. Ill.*, 165.

[25] Other Accounts ſtate that the Schooner lay becalmed, upon diſcovering which the Indians came out in their Canoes, with Major Campbell in the Prow of the foremoſt as a Shield againſt the Fire of the Engliſh. The brave old Officer called out to the Crew to do their Duty regardleſs of the Conſequences to him—*Parkman's Pontiac*, 230.

1763. May.

six Days to try if they cou'd not by some Means get Pondiac to separate his People, at the Expiration of which Time they expected some of the Delaware & Shawany Chiefs who was to join with them & oblige Pondiac to come to their Terms.

The Garrison lay upon the Ramparts as usual.

24 At about seven in the Evening the Indians surrounded us and began to fire on the Sloop and continued till about ten o'Clock, when the People on board observ'd a great Number firing from one Place they pointed a six Pounder and fir'd it, after which they did not fire ten Shot tho they had fir'd upwards of a thousand before; at eleven they began to fire from Mr. S[t] Martins House upon the Flag Bastion where we are inform'd there was about two hundred who brought Combustibles to set fire to the Fort, but none of them dare approach nearer than where they cou'd be cover'd, they kept a very hot Fire till after one, which we did not mind, hardly ever returning a Shot, till hearing one of them speaking louder than the rest and a great many answering him, the Commandant pointed a four Pounder at the Place loaded with a Ball & Grape & fir'd it, soon after which they went off, not firing twenty Shot after it, tho they had fir'd very briskly from 11. By the death Song that they sung two or three times we imagine there was some kill'd or wounded. The Garrison lay upon the Ramparts.

25 This Morning every thing was quiet till the Afternoon all which Time we employ'd in making a kind of Cavalier[26] to flank the Bank between Mr. S[t] Martins House from whence they much annoy'd us, but at

---

[26] A Mound of Earth, usually built in the Gorge of a Bastion, and several Feet higher. It is used to defilade the Works from the Fire of an Enemy on an adjacent Height, or to command the Trenches of the Besiegers.—*Brande's Dictionary.*

four

four in the Afternoon they furrounded us with Combuftibles as yefterday, which prevented our raifing the Cavalier, inftead of which Mr. Watkins was fent out to take with five Men to take Poffeffion of that Part of the Bank that the Enemy annoy'd us from the yefterday, which not only prevented them from approaching but drove them away, fo that from 9 at Night we had not a Shot fir'd at us. The Garrifon on the Ramparts.

This Morning early we put up the Cavalier. At 9 o'Clock we were inform'd that laft Night a Party of Ottawas ariv'd from Sandufky who brought Enfign Paulle,[27] the Commandant Prifoner having enter'd the Fort with a few that he thought were his Friends, who fiez'd him and put the Garrifon to death. The Ottawas that went there told the Hurons that this Place was taken & that their Brothers and the reft of the Hurons had taken up the Hatchet againft us, notwithftanding which the Hurons would not confent for three Days.

This Afternoon we were inform'd that Pondiac having underftood that the Veffel was ftill at the Mouth of the River, took Capt. Campbelle by Force as before, with an Intent to oblige him to go with them in order to take her by Treachery. They alfo took M. La

---

[27] Enfign Chriftopher Paully, of Sandufky, on the 16th of May was treacheroufly feized while in Converfation with feven Indians, difarmed and made Prifoner, moft of the Garrifon under his Command killed, the Fort burned, and himfelf thruft into a Canoe and taken on to Detroit. On the Way he was threatened with being burned alive, and upon arriving at Pontiac's Camp he was affailed with the barbarous Treatment ufually beftowed upon Prifoners. An old Woman, whofe Hufband had died, chofe to adopt him in Place of the deceafed Warrior, and he accepted the Alternative to fave his Life, but watching the firft Opportunity efcaped and reached the Fort at Detroit, July 4th. He had been commiffioned an Enfign in the 60th Regiment, Feb. 8, 1761.—*Parkman's Pontiac*, 238, 260.

Bute

1763.
May.
27

Bute the Interpretor & a Frenchman that could speake Englifh. The Garrifon lay on the Ramparts.

This Morning at Day light we fir'd two Cannon to advertife the Veffel that they might not be deceived as Pondiac intended in making them believe it was Peace. Every thing was quiet laft Night.

At 3 in the Afternoon Pondiac return'd with Capt. Campbelle, and faid that he had demanded the Veffell, but the Commandant wou'd not give her up, upon which Pondiac told him they wou'd come & attak him, & he anfwer'd they might. Then he went & encamp'd on a neighboring Ifland, but the Veffel weighed Anchor & went off before Day. This Pondiac fays.

A few Shot fir'd as ufual at the Veffel to day and a few at the Fort. The Garrifon lay on the Ramparts.

We were inform'd to night by M. St Martin that the Hurons were ftill refolv'd to remain Neuter, & that in cafe the Ottawas oblig'd them to take up Arms they wou'd go off into the Woods.

That if the reft of their Nation which were at Sandufky wou'd not defift they wou'd difarm them.

28

Nothing of Confequence to day. Some Councils were held between the French and Indians about their Cattle. Some few Shots as ufual were fir'd at the Veffel and Fort. The Garrifon lay on the Ramparts.

29

This Morning we were inform'd that there was about 50 Ottawas who lay in Ambufh in a Hollow way behind M. St Martins Houfe all Day yefterday, immagining that we fhould make a Sortee as we had done two or three Days before to burn fome Logs that they had made a Breaftwork of. This we fuppofe was in confequence of what fome of the French told them.

At 10 o'clock we were inform'd that two Batteaus were cut off in the River Huron with 19 Soldiers & a Woman which we fuppofe muft have been Serjeant
Shaw

Shaw who went from this with Provisions to Michilimackinac, the 17th April.

At 3 in the Afternoon Mr. Sterling[28] rec^d a Letter from Mr. Rutherford informing him that on the 8th Instant they were inform'd that by some French People in the River Huron that the Indians were ill inclin'd & beg'd them to go no further, but Sir Robert [Davers] and Capt. Robinson did not give much Credit to it and went on, that on turning a Point at the Entrance of the Lake they were fir'd upon by some Indians who kill'd Sir Robert, Capt. Robinson & two Soldiers the first Shot, the rest they took Prisoners. This Evening a few Shot were fir'd at the Vessel and Fort as usual, without doing any Damage. The Garrison lay on their Arms.

This Morning at 8 o'Clock we had the disagreeable Sight of eight Battoes with Provisions that a Party of Indians had taken belonging to a Party commanded by Lieut. Scuyler,[29] the [28th] Instant, about 14 Miles

1763.
May.
29

30

---

[28] Mr. Sterling was an English Trader then at Detroit. After the Receipt of the Treaty by which Canada was confirmed to the English, he was appointed to take Charge of the French who were in the Fort.

[29] This should have been written *Cuyler*. He had left Fort Niagara May 14th, with 96 Men in eighteen Boats, and a plentiful Supply of Provisions and military Stores. He had met neither Friend nor Foe until he landed on the 28th at Point Pelée to encamp. The Party was surprized by a great Number of Indians in Ambush. The Men threw down their Arms and fled to their Boats, five of which pushed off, but only two of which escaped. The following Letter from Niagara gave the first Intelligence of this Event to the Superintendent of Indian Affairs in America:

NIAGARA, 6th June, 1763.

Honoured Sir: By My Letter of yesterday you'll be fully informed of every thing that come to my Hands since my last of the Month of May.[1] I shall only signify to you at Present what Accounts have come here since last Night: first, that the Queen's Independents upon their way to the Detroit, and a Serjeant and twenty

[1] This Letter relates the infolent Demands of the Indians for Rum, but no Hostilities had then been heard of.

from

1763.
May.
from the Mouth of the River; as the Affair happen'd in the Night we have no juſt Accounts of the kill'd & Priſoners, but Lieut. Scuyler with two Batteaus made their Eſcape. When they were paſſing the Fort at about 600 Yards Diſtance we call'd to them, as their was but a few Indians in ſome of them, & told them to puſh off towards the Veſſel & ſhe would cover them with her Fire, upon which the foremoſt, having four Soldiers & two Indians[30] in it put off, the Soldiers ſiezing the Indians & throwing them overboard and gain'd the Veſſel notwithſtanding the Fire of the Indians from the Shore. The Batteau had ſeven Barrels of Pork & one of Flower on board. One of the Soldiers fell overboard with the Indians whome after a great Struggle they tomahawk'd.

At three in the Afternoon the remainder of the Party that was at the Lake return'd and brought two or three Traders Batteaus, which they lay in weight for, being inform'd

Men of the 60th Reg't within 25 Miles of that Place, at 11 o'Clock at Night were attacked by a Party of Indians and out of 76 of the Independents only 36 return'd here.

That the Old Betts Daughter has been informed this Day by a Seneca Chachim to quit this Place, as they have rec'd a Belt from the Indians about Pittſbourg to take up the bloody Hatchet, and that all the ſurrounding Indians in them Parts are abſolutely determined thereupon. An Anſwer the Senecas have not given to thoſe who ſent the Belt till ſuch Times as all the Shachims muſt be firſt made acquainted of their Proceedings the likewiſe have ſent with the Belt one Scalp that they took in or about Pittſbourg. You may depend upon me to give you the moſt timely Notice of every thing that pertains to his Majeſty's Service in the moſt diſtinct Manner that my Capacity will permit & never ſhall fail meriting Honor'd Sir to be your faithful Servant.

De Couagne.

The Honourable Sir Wm. Johnſon.
—MSS. of Sir William Johnſon, vol. vii.

[30] Other Accounts ſtate the Number of Indians in this Boat as *three*. The Soldier that periſhed was drawn overboard by the Indian he was throwing out, and ſome Authorities relate that they periſhed in each other's Embrace. Another Writer affirms that the Indian ſwam aſhore.
—*Parkman's Pontiac*, 233.

inform'd they were coming by the Prisoners they took of Mr. Cuylers Party. The Garrison lay on the Ramparts as usual.

1763. May,

This Morning two drunken Indians came up to the Fort without Arms, being hot brave, to set Fire to it, but were fir'd upon one of which fell on the Spot and the other ran away but fell in our Sight, and we since hear is dead. The Indians have been so drunk this two Days past that they did not fire five Shot at us. The Garrison lay on the Ramparts.

31

This Morning at about 3 o'Clock two Men call'd from the Hill behind the Fort who told us they were two Traders that had made their Escape from the Indians who we let in at a small Port. A Quarter of an Hour after a Man call'd to the Vessel for a Boat from the other Side of the River, but thinking it might be a Decoy, we got two Frenchmen in a Cannoe who went brought over a Man of Capt. Hopkins Company who made his Escape from the Indians after Mr. Cuyler Defeat and cross'd the Country from Lake; he brought his Arms with him. This Day some Indian Cannoes went down the River as we suppose to cut off some more Traders Boats that is expected from Niagara. The Garrison lay on the Ramparts.

June 1.

This Morning about fifteen Cannoes went down the River as we imagine to intercept some more Traders that are on the way between Niagara and this Place.

2

In the Afternoon a Frenchman brought in a Letter that was enclos'd to me from Niagara which Capt. Campbelle gave in, by which we were inform'd that the definitive Treaty was sign'd at London the 20th February. Not a Shot was fired to day. The Garrison lay on the Ramparts.

This Afternoon a few Shots were fir'd at the Fort & Vessel as usual. The Garrison lay upon the Ramparts as usual. This

3

1763.
June.
4

This Morning Mr. Cuefiere purchaf'd Mr. Rutherford from the Indians on Condition that he fhou'd keep himfelf. A few Shot were fired at the Fort and Veffel as ufual.

This Evening fome Indians ariv'd with four Prifoners and fome Scalps & reported that Miamee was taken,[31] & that the Shawanees & Delawares had commenc'd Hoftilities at Fort Pitt.[32]

5

This Afternoon about fifty Indians fired for an Hour or two at the Fort & Veffel without doing any Execution. The Garrifon lay on the Ramparts.

6

This Day we were inform'd that the Commandant of Fort St Jofeph was Prifoner with the Puttawattamies; we imagine that he was oblig'd to evacuate his Poft not having more than a hundred weight of Flour the 12 May and in attempting to come here was taken.[33] It

---

[31] Fort Miami, on the Maumee, under the Command of Enfign Holmes, was treacheroufly captured on the 27th of May. Holmes was enticed away from the Fort by a young Indian Girl who lived with him, and reprefented that a Squaw lay dangeroufly ill in a Wigwam not far off. He was fhot; the Sergeant who came out to learn the Caufe of the firing, was taken Prifoner, and the Remainder furrendered at Difcretion.—*Parkman's Pontiac*, 244.

A fimilar Verfion of this Affair is recorded in this Diary for June 8, and a further Statement June 15th.

[32] On the 27th of May a Party of Indians approached Fort Pitt and encamped. The next Day they came to the Fort with Pack Horfes laden with valuable Furs, with which to purchafe Ammunition. Tidings of murders and burning were foon after brought in, and the Country around was fpeedily vifited by a diftreffing warfare in which many Perfons were killed, and Communication with the reft of the Province was entirely cut off. On the 28th of July it was vigoroufly befieged, but on the 1ft of Auguft the Enemy withdrew to Attack Gen. Bouquet, by whom they were defeated in the memorable Fight at Bufhy Run.—*Parkman's Pontiac*, 359.

[33] The Poft at St. Jofeph in Charge of Enfign Schloffer with fourteen Men, was furprifed on the Morning of May 25th, by a large Number of Pottawattamies, who came into the Fort in an infolent and diforderly Manner. At a given
was

was also reported that Miamees was taken, but it was reported so many different ways that we did not believe it. Some Days ago Mr. Cuesiere purchas'd Mr. Rutherford from the Indians, but a Missisagy Indian ariving the Day before yesterday and informing Pondiac that they nor the Six Nations had not struck nor would not strike if the Peace was made, alarm'd him, upon which he went with fifty Men & took back the Prisoner, saying that it was not a good President[34] to sell their Prisoners, that when things come to be accommodated they cou'd exchange them or give them up as they saw occasion. Every thing quiet to day. The Garrison lay on the Ramparts.

This Day the Indian Chiefs had a Council at the Puttawattamees but for what end we know not. A few Shot were fir'd at the Vessel & Fort as usual. The Garrison lay on the Ramparts.

Yesterday Pondiac took two Prisoners from Mr. Babie that he had purchas'd from the Indians, telling him the same that he told Cuesiere.

The Council held yesterday as we are inform'd was to conclude upon a Method to attack the Vessel, which they intend by fiting up eight Batteaux and lining them, with which they are to fall down the Stream and board her, while a great Number keeps a hot Fire upon the Fort. This to be done in a very dark Night. All quiet to day except a few Shot from St Martins House. The Garrison lay on the Ramparts.

This Afternoon three Batteaux pass'd up the River that were taken by the Chippawas near the Place Mr.

Signal, those within rushed to the Gate, killed the Sentinel and ten other Men, and took the Commandant and the three surviving Men Prisoners. He was exchanged at Detroit, on 15th of June.—*Parkman's Pontiac*, 240.

Schlosser's Statement is recorded in this Diary for June 15th.

[34] Precedent.

Cuyler

1763.
June.
9

Cuyler was defeated. There was eleven Perfons in them, two of whom were kill'd, the reft they brought here Prifoners.

We were alfo well affured that the Miamee was taken, as a Frenchman fpoke to the Corporal of that Garrifon who was Prifoner with the Indians, who told him that Mr. Holmes had been inform'd of the Defigns of the Indians & that he had fhut the Gates of the Fort, which the Indians feeing found they cou'd not take it but by Treachery, accordingly they employ'd a Squaw that Mr. Holmes kept to bring him out of the Fort to bleed her Sifter who was fick in a Caban, and as foon as he came there three or four Ottawas who had hid themfelves on purpofe fired at him and kill'd him, then took one Welch whome they had Prifoner and went to the Fort & made him tell the Men if they would lay down their Arms they fhould be all fav'd, upon which they open'd the Gates. We hear they have carried them towards the Illinois. The Garrifon lay on their Arms.

10

This Day the Puttawattamies fent Mr. Gamelin with a Meffage to the Commandant defiring to change Mr. Schloffer for one of the Indians we have in Cuftody. To which the Commandant anfwer'd that they muft firft let him know how many Prifoners they had taken & what they had done with them, and gave leave to four of the Chiefs with Mr. Gamelin to come within thirty Yards of the Fort to fpeake to the two we had in Cuftody, at their Requeft. In a Hour afterwards the whole Nation came to Mr. S[t] Martins Houfe (when the Garrifon was order'd on the Ramparts), where they halted and fent forward four Chiefs, who told they were led into the War by Pondiac, &c.; to which the Commandant anfwer'd he believ'd it, & therefore advifed them to difperfe & mind their hunting & planting

planting, for if they perfifted it wou'd end in their utter Ruin. To which they hung their Heads & one of them faid he believ'd it. They faid they had fourteen Prifoners & Mr. Schloffer, all of whome the Commandant demanded, as one of the Indians we had in Cuftody was one of the firft Men in the Nation. To which they did not give a pofitive Anfwer but went to hold a Council.

Every thing quiet to day. The Garrifon lay on the Ramparts.

This Day we permitted fome more of the Puttawattamees to fpeak to the two we had in Cuftody.

All quiet to day. The Garrifon lay on the Ramparts.

Yefterday one Cavalier ariv'd from Montreal who inform'd us that at Grand River, within thirty Miles of the End of Lake Erie, feven Englifh Battoes with Merchandize was attack'd by fome Indians, five of which were taken, the other two made their efcape; that there was one Lafcelle with him from Montreal at the fame Time who return'd to Niagara.

At five o'Clock about thirty Indians ariv'd at Pondiacs Camp from Saggina, who made with what he had in Camp 168 Indians befides 250 that went down the River a few Days ago as it was faid to cut off the Communication at Niagara. Neither Cavalier nor young Lafcelle, who ariv'd two Days before him, are yet come into the Fort altho Lafcelle ariv'd two Days before the other, they fay the Indians have threatened to kill them if they come nearer than a certain Diftance.

All quiet to day. The Day before yefterday and to day made Sorties and burnt fome out Houfes and Gardens. The Garrifon lay on the Ramparts.

Yefterday and to day we buried five Corps that we took up in the River, two of whom we knew but the reft

1763.
June.

13

rest was so mangled that it was impossible for any body to have the least Knowledge of them.

Nothing extraordinary to day. Three of the Puttawattamees came and spoke with the two we had in Custody, who declar'd to us that they knew nothing of this Affair till they ariv'd at their Village below the Fort, when much to their Surprize they heard a great firing. That they never had any Message sent to them about it, nor was they consulted in any Manner whatever, but was forc'd into it by the Ottawas. Upon which the Commandant ask'd them if they were the Slaves of Pondiac, at which they hung their Heads; he then told them what he had told them before with regard to their disperfing, and that they wou'd see in the End that the Ottawas wou'd kill Pondiac for bringing them into such an Undertaking, for that they, and every one that join'd heartily with them, wou'd be ruined; as they wou'd forfeit their Lands and be depriv'd of all the Necessaries of Life. Upon which they promis'd to go to their Camps and send in their Corn, &c. The Garrison lay on the Ramparts.

14

Yesterday we heard that Ouattanon was cut off and the Garrison taken to the Illinois.[35]

Every thing quiet to day. The Garrison lay on the Ramparts.

15

This Morning between eleven and twelve o'Clock one of the Chiefs of the Puttawattamees (named Washee) who took St. Josephs, came with four or five others to change some of their Prisoners for the two that we had

---

[35] Ouatanon was a Fort on the Wabash, a little below the present Town of Lafayette. It was then under the Command of Lt. Edward Jenkins, who was taken on the first of June, by Stratagem, with several of his Men, when the Remainder of the Garrison yielded without Resistance. The Indians, however, apologized for their Conduct, by saying that they acted under the Influence of other Tribes and against their own better Judgments.—*Parkman's Pontiac*, 243.

Pontiac's Siege of Detroit.

in Custody, and after talking near two hours, the Commandant got them to consent to give Mr. Schlosser and two Soldiers that they brought with them for one of them that he had, and promis'd them that when they brought the rest of the Prisoners he wou'd give them the other. They did not seem to be well contented as they expected the Man of the most Consequence in return for the Officer, but the Commandant was almost sure that if he gave him up they would not give above one of the eleven that remain'd with them for the other, and therefore detain'd him. The Account Mr. Schlosser gives of the way he was taken is, that about seventeen Puttawattamees came into his Fort under a Pretence of holding a Council, after they had engag'd the young Men of the Nation about him to join with them, to whom they promis'd all the Plunder after they were in the Fort, Washashe the Puttawattamy Chief went into his Room with three or four others, to whom he had presented a Belt, as he cou'd speak a little of their Language himself, for they had detain'd his Interpreter on the other Side of the River till every thing was ready, but before they had made him an Answer a Frenchman came in and told him their Design, upon which the cry was given in the Fort & they siez'd him immediately & the young Men that agreed to join him rush'd into the Fort, knocking down the Centinel and before the Men cou'd get to their Arms put ten of them to death, which Washshe tryed to prevent but in vain, the remaining three and himself they took Prisoners. After this was done all the Chiefs of the St Joseph Indians came to Mr. Schlosser and told him that they knew nothing of the Affair, that their young Men cross'd the River in the Night unknown to them, & desir'd him to acquaint the Commandant here that they were not concern'd in the War, nor would not be.

1763.
June.
One of the Soldiers we got to day was taken at Miamee who gives the same Account of its being taken as we have already heard, with this Difference, that the Serj. after he heard the Shots that were fir'd at Mr. Holmes went out to see what it was & was taken Prisoner, after which they brought one Walch whome they had Prisoner to tell them what has been already mentioned, upon which they deliver'd up the Fort, and French Colours was immediately hoisted in it, but does not know wheather it was the French or Indians that hoisted them. This Evening we were inform'd from good Authority that Saggina Indians had been with Mr. Labute to desire him to speake to the Commandant to make Peace with them, that they had not yet enter'd into the War, that is they had neither kill'd any body nor did they take any Merchants. To which Mr. Labute answer'd they knew well enough he dared not go to the Fort, that if Pondiac knew he spoke to the English he would put him to death, and told them they must come themselves.

All quiet to day. The Garrison lay on the Ramparts. We are assured that all the Chiefs of the Hurons are peacibly inclin'd but there is a Band of 25 young Men that they cant bring over Part of whome are gone to Niagara with the Ottawas.

16   This Day at twelve o'Clock Washshe with two other Puttawattame Chiefs, & two Saggina Indians[37] came with a Flag to speake to the Commandant. After they enter'd the Fort one of the Puttawattamees got up with a String of Wampam & desir'd to be heard. That what they had already told him was true, & that what they were going to say was from their Hearts, upon which he presented the Wampam.

---

[37] One of the latter was Mindoghquay. He returned to the Fort Dec. 12th, tendering his Friendship.

He

He then took another String and told the Commandant that the two Saggina Indians were sent in the Name of all their Chiefs, that they were Brothers, and their Hearts inclin'd the same way. That they the Puttawattamees knew nothing of the Commencement of the War, but were hurried into it by the Ottawas, but they had now buried the Hatchet and it shou'd never rise again. Upon which they presented the Wampam. Then took another String & said they had sent Messengers for the rest of their Prisoners who shou'd be all deliver'd up as soon as they came in. Then one of the Saggina Indians got up with a String of Wampam & said he was sent in the Name of their Chief and desir'd he might be heard. That their Hands and ours had always been join'd since we took Possession of this Country, and they never shou'd be parted; that they had not enter'd into the War at all, that their Hearts were the same as the Puttawattamees, and intended to remain so; that he spoke the real Sentiments of the Hearts of all their Chiefs, which he desir'd we shou'd believe, knowing that if he told lies the great God wou'd be offended at him, upon which he presented the Wampam. Then the Commandant took a small Belt and desir'd to know before he gave them an Answer, wheather the Puttawattamee Chiefs that were there spoke only for their Bands in particular or for the whole Nation, to which they answer'd for the whole Nation. He then told them that he was glad they had open'd their Eyes and did not intend to persist in a thing that must end in their Ruin, that the only thing they cou'd do to convince him of their good Intentions wou'd be to give up the rest of their Prisoners and go to their Villages and tend their Corn & hunt. That he wou'd then recommend them to the General, and that they wou'd find every thing he told them was true.

1763. June. true. That the Peace was actually made between the French and us, and if they perſiſted in a Thing of this kind we ſhould not only fight againſt them, but the Canadians (the People they thought they were fighting for) wou'd alſo take Arms againſt them as we were all one. That he knew they were made to believe there was no Peace & that there was an Army coming from the Illinois, but thoſe that told them ſo, told lies, & were their Enemies, which they wou'd ſoon ſee. That if they took his Advice & did as he deſir'd them they might live for the Future in Tranquility as they had done before, and ſee the Ottawas ſtarving in the Woods for want of the Neceſſaries of Life that they cou'd no ways get but from us. Then preſented the Belt.

The Saggina Indians further ſaid that the Michilimackinac Indians wou'd not ſtrike and if Pondiac attempted to go towards that Poſt they would prevent him.

The Commandant then took another String and told the Saggina that he was glad to hear they were ſo well inclin'd & that they had more ſenſe than to be lead into a thing by the Ottawas (that wou'd be their Ruin). That he never intended any thing but Peace with them, that the Ottawas began the War without any Reaſon, that he was well pleaſ'd with their Behavior and would alſo recommend them to the General if they continued at their Villages in the ſame Tranquility that they ſaid they were then in. That they might be ſure every thing he ſaid was true which they wou'd find in the End, and deſir'd them not to give Ear to any Lies that might be ſpread amongſt them. Then gave the Wampam. Upon which the Saggina Indian ſaid he was glad to receive it, that the Chiefs wou'd believe when they ſaw his Mouth (as he call'd the Wampam) they were pitied. All quiet to day. The Garriſon lay on the Ramparts. All

Pontiac's Siege of Detroit.

All quiet to day. This Evening we was told that a Cannon was heard at the Mouth of the River about 11 o'Clock this Morning, which muſt have been the Veſſel; a little after Sunſet we fir'd another to anſwer her. Upon the Report of the Cannon in the Morning ſeveral Indians were ſent off to ſee if ſhe was there or not. The Garriſon lay on the Ramparts.

Since the firſt Information that we had of the Indian Intention of attacking the Veſſell with Batteaux, Capt. Hopkins lay on board of her every Night.

This Day the Jeſuiſt ariv'd from Michilimackinac, with the diſagreeable News of its being cut off by Treachery. The Particulars not yet come to Hand. All quiet to day. The Garriſon lay on the Ramparts.

This Day the Jeſuiſt came into the Fort, and brought a Letter[38] from Capt. Etherington by which we were inform'd, That the 2d June the Chippawas were playing at Croſſ[39] at Michilimackinac (three Days after they had a Council with him and profeſſ'd a great deal of Friendſhip. That upon the arrival of a Canoe from Saggina, one Mr. Tracy a Merchant went to the Water-ſide to ſpeak to them which the Indians ſeeing ſaid to

1763.
June.
17

18

19

---

[38] This Letter, dated June 12th, is publiſhed in *Parkman's Pontiac*, p. 596, from the Original, as preſerved in the State Paper Office of London. It is ſubſtantially the ſame as that of Capt. Claus, given on the following Pages. The Jeſuit referred to was Father Jonois, then ſtationed at L'Arbre Croche.

[39] The Game of La Croſſe, or Baggattway, is played with a Bat and Ball; two Poſts are planted in the Ground, about a Mile apart, and each Party having its Poſt, the object is to propel the Ball, which is placed in the Centre, toward the Poſt of the Adverſary. In the Ardor of Conteſt, if the Ball can not be driven to the deſired Goal, it is ſtruck in any Direction by which it can be diverted from that deſigned by the oppoſite Party.

A Game much ſimilar is ſtill played by the Iroquois of New York and Canada.—*Carver's Travels*, 201; *Smith's Hiſt. Wiſconſin*, i, 137; *N. Y. Senate Doc.*, 1850, *No.* 75, p. 81.

themſelves

1763.
June.

themselves now is the Time, for if these People enter the Fort they will tell our Design, upon which they tomahawk'd Mr. Tracy and gave the Cry, & in an instant siez'd Capt. Etherington & Lieut. Leslley who were at the Gate of the Fort looking at them playing, forc'd by the Centry and enter'd the Fort where they found their Squaws (who had been previously plac'd with their Tomahawks) with which they forc'd the Guard before they cou'd get under Arms, kill'd thirteen Men on the Spot with Lieut. Jamet who fought with his Sword against five for a long Time, but after receiving thirty-six Wounds fell in their Hands after which they cut off his Head and kill'd six of their Prisoners; they pillag'd all the Merchants and got fifty Barrels of Powder with Lead in Proportion. The Ottawas took the Officers and eleven of their Prisoners from them whome they keep at the Priests House. Capt. Etherington then gave a written Authority to Mr. Langlad[40] to Com^d in the Fort till further Orders, and recommended him Mr. Langlad and one Mr. Farli to the Commandant

[40] Sieur Augustine du Langlade, about 1750, became the Owner of most of the Lands around Green Bay, and his Descendants still reside there. He was a Man of Character and Education, and retained the polished Manners of the French Metropolis. His Son, Charles Langlade, was a Native of this Country and in 1760 was commissioned by Louis XV, and appointed Second in Command at Michillimackinack, where he was residing at the Time of the Massacre. The Narrative of Alexander Henry, the Trader, gives an unfavorable impression with regard to the Humanity of M. Langlade.

At the Time of the Attack, as the Indians were pursuing the English from one Retreat to another, Henry rushed into his House and besought him to afford an Asylum. The Frenchman, who stood at his Window watching the Slaughter, looked at him a Moment and then turned again to the Window, shrugging his Shoulders and remarking, *Que voudriez-vous que j'en serais?* "*What would you have me do?*" He afterwards willingly submitted the Keys of his House to allow the Savages to search his Premises for English.—*Smith's Hist. Wisconsin*, i, 346; *Henry's Travels*.

here

here as good Men & who did all in their Power for the good of the Service, as also the Jesuit who has a great deal to say among the Indians.⁴¹

All quiet to day. The Garrison lay on the Ramparts.

1763. June.

---

⁴¹ The Circumstances attending the Attack upon Michillimackinack and its Capture by the Indians, on the 4th of June are also set forth in the following Extract from a Letter written at Montreal by Capt. Daniel Claus to Sir William Johnson:

"* * * 6th Aug. Whilst I am writing this, my Landlord tells me that Capt. [George] Etherington and Lieut. [James] Lessley passed the Door coming from Missilimak^k who I heare with all the Traders except one Trasey [Tracy] who was killed by the Enemy Ind^ns were escorted here by the Ottawas as living near that Place. I followed them immediately to the Govr, and there learned the News of them Parts, which is that a Parcell of Chippeways to the Number of 100 assembled near the Fort as customary in the Beginning of Summer, and diverted themselves playing Football, and Capt Ethrington and Mr. Lessley (not suspecting the least Treachery, having then not heard a Word of Detroit being besieged by the Enemy Indians) stood out of the Fort to see the Indians Play: that on a Signal given by a Yell, they both were seized and bound, and that the same Instant the Centries were tomahawked, likewise Mr. James, who was Officer of the Day in the Fort, together with 18 Soldiers killed and taken. Then the Traders were plundered and taken Prisoners; that afterwards themselves were dragged to the Chippeways' Encampment where the Spoil was divided, and a Council held, in what Manner the Officers were to be put to Death. In the mean Time the News reached the Ottawa Town 30 Miles from Missilimakinak, who without any Delay sat off armed to Missilimakinak, and inquired into the Reason of the Chippeways Behaviour. The latter had nothing to say but that a few Days before the Blow, they received Belts of Wamp^m from Pontiac, the Ottawas' Chief at Detroit, in conjunction with ye Chiefs of their Nation living there, informing them of the Rupture with the English, and desiring them to cut off Missilim^k. The Ottawas were surprised and chagreend and insisted upon the Chipways delivering up the Pris^rs, &c.

The latter to reconcile themselves with the Ottawas, made up a Heap of Goods and put Mr. Lassley & 2 Soldiers by them as their Share of the Prey, but they would not accept of it, and demanded all the Pris^rs. The Chipways at last gave way and delivered over Mr. Lassley and the Soldiers and demanded a Ransom for the Traders, which they agreed to, and being every one exchanged they took them into their

This

Pontiac's Siege of Detroit.

1763.
June.
20

This Morning the Commanding Officer gave the Jesuit some Memorandum of what he should say to the Indians & French at Michilimackinac, as also to Capt. Etherington, as he did not choose to carry a Letter saying that if he was ask'd by the Indians if he had any he would be oblig'd to say yes, as he never told a lie in his life. He gave him a Belt to give to the Ottawas there, desiring him to tell them that he was very well pleas'd with their not meddling in an Affair that must end in their Ruin.

That if they send their Prisoners to Montreal, it will convince the General of their good Intentions for which they will be probably well rewarded.

To give his Compliments to Mr. Langlad and Mr. Farli and thank them for their good Offices which he exhorts them to continue. To desire them to try and prevent as much as possible all Commerce with our

Care and afterwards escorted them safe to this Place. The Officers and Traders can not say enough of the good Behaviour of these Ottawas and Gen¹ Gage is resolved to use and reward them well for their Behaviour. As Capt. Etherington is going to Gen. Amherst, you will doubtless hear the Particulars of the whole Affair. By what I can find none but the Chipeways at Missilim^k and those of the same Nation & Ottawas at Detroit, are concerned in the present Breach. All the rest of the western Nations, and even some Chipways living at the Falls of St. Mary would not engage or receive the Belts sent by Pontiac, and on the contrary are very well inclined to our Interest, in particular the Nations living at La Bay, and the Sioux, who are always at War with the Chipways; and if the Ind^ns now here (among whom there are some other Nat^s as they come here in behalf of 8 Nat^s to the westward who assure us of their Friendship) leave this satisfied; it may be of infinite Service wch I intend to represent to Gen. Gage, and I believe you will approve of making them handsome Presents as an Encouragement for their good Behaviour, and the only Means of chastising those villainous Nations who are the Occasion of this unhappy Event. * * *"—*MSS. of Sir William Johnson*, vol. vii.

The Circumstances of the Capture of Michillimackinack, have been related with great Minuteness by Alexander Henry, an Eye witness, who narrowly escaped the Massacre.—*Henry's Travels.*

Enemies

Enemies, above all Ammunition & Arms. That he authorizes Mr. Langlad to Command in the Fort according to the Orders given him by Capt. Etherington till further Orders.

To defire Capt. Etherington to try to advertife the Governor of Montreal of what has happened as foon as poffible, and to fend back all Merchants that may be on the way, Englifh or French, if they find from Circumftances of Affairs it is neceffary. To tell him all the News that he has heard from us that might be depended upon regarding the Pofts that has been furpriz'd and murdered, and that the diffinitive Treaty was fign'd at London the 20th of February according to the Articles of the Sceffation of Arms.

This Day we heard that fome Shawanees were ariv'd at the Hurons who fay that all this Nation (except a few who watch the Motions of the Army near Fort Pitt) are feveral Leagues below on the Ohio, who remain there to intercept the Army that is coming from Foit Pitt.

That upon their receiving the Belt, they were order'd to ftrike againft the Englifh, upon which they commenc'd by killing fifteen Merchants that was amongft them in different Towns.

Yefterday a Saggina that was in the Fort with the Puttawattamees was here & rec^d a Belt from the commanding Officer which he was to prefent to the Nation to tell them that it was his Advice that they fhould remain quiet as they faid they had done, as thofe that enter'd in the War wou'd furely be ruined in the End. Some few Shots fir'd to day at the Veffel at a great Diftance. A Sortie was made to day to cut down & burn fome Pickets between Mr. Babies & the Fort. The Garrifon lay upon their Arms.

This Morning fir'd two Guns down the River, being

1763. ing inform'd that the Veſſel was there. Made a Sortie
June. and pull'd down a good many Pickets and cut an
Orchard that was near the Fort.

At eleven o'Clock about fifty Indians came to Mr. Babies and fir'd briſkly at the Veſſel and Fort, they kill'd one Man on board the Veſſel & wounded another.

Two Hours after which they went over the River and the Hurons join'd them & the Puttawattamies to attack the Veſſel, but we do not know yet whether the Veſſel is there, or wheather that was their real Deſign. The Garriſon lay on the Ramparts.

23 This Day a few Shot were fir'd at the Fort and Veſſel as uſual.

This Evening we were inform'd that the Veſſel was not at the Mouth of the River, but that the Indians thought ſhe was and went & made a kind of an Entrench^t at the Iſle au Deinde[42] where the Channel is narrow in order to fire upon her as ſhe paſſ'd. The Garriſon lay on the Ramparts.

24 Some few Shots were fir'd at the Fort this Morning. Capt. Hopkins with twenty Men made a Sortie this Afternoon, imagining there was ſome few Indians in the neighbouring Houſes but did not find any. The Garriſon lay on the Ramparts.

25 A few Shot fir'd as uſual at the Veſſel & Fort to day. The Garriſon lay on the Ramparts.

26 [Sunday.] This Day Pondiac went to Maſs on the other Side of the River & after it was over he took three Chairs that belong'd to the People for himſelf and his Guard to ride in to look for Proviſion making the French his Chair men. He gave Billets to the People for their Cattle ſign'd with his Mark, with the Imita-

---

[42] Turkey Iſland, on the eaſt Side of the main Channel, and now included in Canada.

tion

tion of a Coon drawn on the Top of each Billet.⁴³ Nothing Extraordinary. The Garrison lay on the Ramparts.

Pondiac sent another Message to the Commandant telling him there was nine hundred Indians assembled at Michilimackinac, and that as he had Compassion on him desir'd him to surrender himself, that the Garrison wou'd be well us'd, but if he waited till those Indians ariv'd he wou'd not be answerable for the Consequences. That the Roads were all shut up round us and we cou'd receive no Succour.

To which the Commandant answer'd as he had done before, that he wou'd not give him an Answer to any thing he ask'd till he sent back Capt. Campbelle and Lieut. McDougal, whome he kept contrary to all the Laws of even Savages. That he might save himself the Trouble of sending any more for he wou'd not answer to any thing till these two Gentlemen were return'd. Soon after Pondiac sent Word by one that was passing, that he had too great a Regard for Capt. Campbell & McDougal than to send them to the Fort, for if he did that, as the Kettle was on the Fire he shou'd be oblig'd to boil them with the rest.

A few Shot fir'd at the Fort and Vessell as usual. The Garrison lay on the Ramparts.

This Afternoon at five o'Clock we were inform'd that the Scooner⁴⁴ enter'd the River at 10 this Morn-

---

⁴³ These Bills of Credit were drawn on Birch bark, and were promptly redeemed by Pontiac. Rogers states that they bore the figure of an Otter. The great Indian Chieftain was evidently assisted to the Idea by some of the Canadians. The Contributions were all collected at the House of Meloche near Parent's Creek, and a vain and conceited old Frenchman, named Quilleriez, acted as Commissary.—*Parkman's Pontiac*, 225.

⁴⁴ This was the Schooner *Gladwyn* that had sailed for Niagara on the 21st of May, and was now returning with Lieut. Cuyler and the

ing

1763.
June.

ing; at 6 she came in Sight after passing the Isle au Deinde where there was at least 160 Indians hid in Holes who fir'd upon her all the while at a little Distance, as the Channel is not above a hundred Yards wide. The Wind failing her she drop'd Anchor about four Miles from the Fort.

A few Shot were fir'd to day at the Vessel & Fort as usual. The Garrison lay on the Ramparts.

As it was imagin'd the Indians wou'd attack the Scooner, the Commanding Officer made a Feignt as if he wou'd land some Troops in Batteaux which the Indians hearing so alarm'd them that they guarded the Edge of the River and dropp'd their Intention of attacking the Scooner.

29 The Wind contrary all Day till about 6 o'Clock, when it came a little favorable for about Half an Hour, of which the Scooner profited, weighing Anchor and coming in Sight of the Fort beyond the Huron Village.

This Day we heard that the Indians that went from this about twenty Days ago had taken Presque Isle, that they lost three Men there, that the Way they took it was by setting fire to a small House that was close to the Fort & which communicated the Fire to it, that they kill'd but three, & the Officer with several Prisoners was given to the Nations near that Place.[45]

remainder of his Company, together with such Troops as could be spared from Niagara, in all numbering about fifty Men. To encourage an open Attack from the Indians who swarmed upon the Shores of the River and the Islands which divided its Channel, the greater Portion of her Men were kept out of Sight, ready to appear at a moment's Notice.—*Parkman's Pontiac*, 253.

[45] The Fort at Presque Isle, was a large Block-house of solid Timber, the upper Story projecting on all Sides and roofed with Shingles. It stood on the Shore of Lake Erie, a little below the present business Part of Erie, Pa. It was assailed on the Morning of June 15th, by 200 Indians, chiefly from around Detroit, and after a Resistance of three Days, which presents few Parallels in despe-

This

Pontiac's Siege of Detroit. 37

This Day a few Shot fir'd from over the River, &c., as usual. The Indians guarded the River side to night fearing a Sortie. The twenty-fifth at Night it was so Cold here that there was a very white Frost. The Garrison lay on the Ramparts.

1763. June.

At 12 o'Clock the Wind sprung up favourable for the Scooner when she weigh'd Anchor and reach'd this about 3, with a Detachment of twenty-two Men from the 30th Reg^t and Lieut. Cuyler and twenty-eight Men of Capt. Hopkins's Comp^y of Rangers, with 150 Barrels of Provision and some Ammunition. Lieut. Cuyler informs us that Presque Isle was burn'd the 22d Instant after being attacked three Days.

30

We were inform'd this Evening that Pondiac had been demanding of the Inhabitants to assemble to dig Trenches, that if they refus'd it he wou'd put them to the Sword. The Hurons fir'd upon the Scooner all the while she was passing and a great Number from Pondiacs Camp assembled at Mr. Babies & fir'd at the Boats that went & came from her after she came to an Anchor.

One Serjeant and four Men were wounded in the Scooner a coming up the River. The Garrison lay on the Ramparts, except those that came in the Scooner, who lay in their Quarters.

The Garrison was employ'd this Morning in unloading & puting Ballast on board the Scooner. Mr. St. Martin & his Family came into the Fort to day, he being inform'd that the Hurons intended to take him to their Town to interpret for them. This Afternoon

July 1.

rate Labor and unavailing Courage, the little Garrison under Ensign Christie surrendered on Condition that they should be allowed to withdraw to the nearest Post. With Characteristick disregard of this Treaty, the unfortunate Men were seized and sent Prisoners to Detroit.

Christie was brought in by the Hurons and surrendered with several other Prisoners, July 9th.

the

1763. July.

the Puttawattamees came with a Flag to speake about giving up their Prisoners, five of whom they said they had at their Village and whom they promis'd to bring in the next Day.

The Commandant recommended to them to bring them in as soon as possible & retire to their Villages, as he should now make Sorties with great Bodies of Men, and if he should meet with them should treat them as Ennemies as it was not possible for him to distinguish the Nations one from another.

A few Shot were fir'd to day at the Fort & Vessels. The Garrison lay on the Ramparts.

2   At three o'Clock this Morning Lieut. McDougal with an Albany Trader ariv'd at the Fort, having made their Escape from the Indians; about Half an Hour afterwards, another Prisoner ariv'd at the Scooner that made his Escape from the Hurons, who had been taken with one Crawford a Trader some Time ago.[46] Lieut. McDougal inform'd us that the Council the Indians held yesterday to demand the French to join them & make Trenches, which was promis'd by one in the Name of all the young People. A Party was sent out to Mr. St. Martins House to cover a working Party near the Fort, which the Indians came to fire upon, and upon our sending out a Reinforcement all the Hurons cross'd the River & came running up as far as Mr. Gamelins and after firing a few Shot at the Fort went back.

This Morning took Post in the two Block Houses on the Hight that commands the Fort, and from which a Chief of the Saggina's was wounded in passing by the Edge of the Woods an Hour after.

This Evening we were inform'd that Pondiac had

[46] Crawford's Capture is related in this Diary for May 20. See p. 11.

taken

taken away Mr. Navarre, Mr. Hecotte and all the Heads of Familys on that Side of the Fort, but no body knew for what.

This Evening threw a Shell to try a Mortar that we had enlarg'd about Half an Inch. All the Garrison except the old Guard lay on the Ramparts.

This Day Mr. Navarre wrote a Line to the Commandant informing him that the Inhabitants were oblig'd to write to him in Pondiacs Name for the laſt Time to ſurrender the Fort, and to let him know that if he wou'd not give it up they wou'd oblige all the Inhabitants to take up Arms. Accordingly Mr. Louis Campo came in with the Meſſage in the Evening, and at the ſame Time aſk'd Permiſſion to come into the Fort, which the Commandant agreed not only to him but every one that cou'd bring Proviſion with them. Mr. Babie & Mr. Recme who liv'd oppoſite the Fort came in with their Familys between eleven & twelve at Night, abandoning all they had except a few Moveables that they brought with them.

All the Garriſon lay on the Ramparts except twenty Men that were finiſhing a ſmall Ditch round the Fort.

This Day the Commandant collect'd the Inhabitants of the Fort and read the Articles of Peace to them & ſent a Copy of it over to the Prieſt on the other Side of the River.

This Morning early made a Sortie with thirty Men to cover a Party to bring in ſome Powder & Lead that was in Mr. Babies Houſe, after which we deſtroy'd an Entrenchment that the Indians had made, from which they annoy'd us. The Indians being advertiſ'd that we was out came down and Capt. Hopkins was ſent out with a Party of twenty Men more, who with nine or ten Frenchmen and the Party that was firſt out, purſued them as far as it was ſafe; we took one Scalp and

1763.
July.
and wounded two or three more,[47] we had one Man wounded. While we were at Dinner Dr. Paulli enter'd the Fort having made his Escape in open Day light, by whome we were inform'd that the Indian we kill'd this Morning was the Son of the most considerable Chiefs of the Chippewas, and that we only wounded another. That upon their Arrival at the Camp he was inform'd that they were gone to look for Capt. Campbelle to kill him, upon which he form'd a Resolution to attempt to save himself. He was dress'd so like an Indian, his Hair being cut and painted in their Fashion that no body knew him when he was brought in. This Evening we were inform'd that there was 140 Frenchmen gathered at the Hurons who had made an Agreement to defend one another against all Ennemies. Mr. Navarre published the Articles of Peace both to the French & Indians.

The French were assembled to day by orderd of the Commandant, who all rejoic'd to take up Arms to the Amount of about forty, and chose Mr. Sterling to com^d them.

The Garrison lay on the Ramparts. Yesterday we wounded an Indian with a Grape shot from the Vessel behind the Breastwork at Mr. Babies House.

5 This Morning Mr. Labute came into the Fort, and inform'd us that as soon as the Chippewas were inform'd that we had kill'd the Son of their great Chief they went to Pondiac and told him that he was the Cause of all their ill look, that he caus'd them to enter

---

[47] The Sortie of this Day was led by Lieut. Hay. One of his Men had long been a Prisoner with the Indians and had acquired in some Degree their ferocious Habits. Coming up to a wounded Savage, he tore off his Scalp and shook it with an exulting Cry towards the Enemy. This Act cost the unfortunate Major Campbell his Life.— *Parkman's Pontiac*, p. 260.

into

into the War and did nothing himself, that he was very brave in taking a Loaf of Bread or a Beef from a Frenchman who made no Resistance, but it was them that had all the Men kill'd and wounded every Day, & for that Reason they wou'd take that from him which he intended to save himself by in the End, then went and took Capt. Campbelle, strip'd him, & carried him to their Camp, where they kill'd him, took out his Heart & eat it reaking from his Body, cut off his Head, and the rest of his Body they divided into small Pieces.

He likewise inform'd us that in a Quarter of an Hour after Mr. Paulle made his Escape upwards of a hundred Ottawas left their Camp in search of him.

This Evening we were inform'd that the Ottawas found one of their Men dead in the Edge of the Woods opposite the Fort, who we supposed must have been kill'd from one of the Cavaliers. The Garrison lay on the Ramparts.

This Morning we were inform'd that we kill'd three Indians and wounded one in the Affair of yesterday.

At 12 o'Clock the Commandant sent the Sloop up to Pondiacs Camp under the com^d of Capt. Hopkins and Ensign Paulli, but the Wind being very weak they had Time to remove almost all their things out of their Cabans & send their Women and Children away before she ariv'd, however they fir'd near fifty Cannon at those that were there, and threw several Shells amongst them, we have not heard what Number was kill'd or wounded.

The Puttawattamees came with a Flag while the Sloop was battering their Camp, and after telling the Comm^t that they had heard the Peace between the French and us proclaim'd, & that they believ'd it, and the several Chiefs with their Bands were gone & going

1763.
July.

to leave Pondiac, they afk'd him to give them the Indian we had for two of our Prifoners that they wou'd bring in. Upon which the Commandant told them that he wou'd ftill ftand to what he had told them before with regard to changing Prifoners, that notwithftanding all they had promif'd the laft Time they were with him, they went down the River and fir'd againft the Scooner when fhe was coming up, and a few Days before ftole two Horfes from him, notwithftanding all which, to fhow that he pitied them if they wou'd bring in all their Prifoners & the Horfes, & promife not to do any more Mifchief either to the French or Englifh, as we were now one, he wou'd give up the Indian he had, and wou'd recommend them to the General, but if they made the leaft Difficulty in it he wou'd not hear them any more and they muft take the Confequences of his Difpleafure, upon which they hung their Heads and faid they found every thing that he had told them to be true, and could not deny what they were accuf'd with, and not only promif'd to do all he afk'd of them, but that none of their Nation was to come nearer the Fort than Mr. Campo's Mill, about a Mile from it.

Pondiac who always told the French that we were all dead Men that were in the Fort, cou'd not help acknowledging to day that we were come to life & that he was ruin'd. The Garrifon lay on their Arms.

7

This Day the Puttawattamees came with a Flag for a Belt of Wampam that the Commandant promif'd them to carry to the reft of their Nation at St. Jofephs & to the Miamees to tell them what they had done & how much they were pitied by the Commandant whofe Advife they muft always follow; which Belt they got with a Letter to the Interpreter there defiring to tell the Indians what he had promif'd the Puttawattamees here as they were the firft that offer'd to make Peace,

viz.

viz. if they continued quiet for the Future and minded their hunting he would recommend them to the General, who he made no doubt wou'd forgive them, as he believ'd they had no hand in the War, further than that some of their young men were led into it before they knew what they were doing.

The Hurons came at the same Time and told the Commandant that neither they nor the Puttawattamees knew any thing of this Affair at the Commencement, for Pondiac never consulted them about it until he had got such a Number of Men together that overpower them both, and then he told them his Design & threatened them that if they would not join with him he would cut them to pieces. That notwithstanding which they never did any thing but fire one Day against the Fort except a Band or two of their young Men whome they cou'd not then command.

The Commandant told them he believ'd it, and ask'd them if they did not now see that every thing he told them was true, which they cou'd not deny. He then promis'd them the same he had done to the Puttawattamees, if they would give up all their Prisoners & behave well for the Future. He told them he cou'd not make Peace with them, but as he told the Puttawattamees wou'd recommend them to the General.

They promis'd to do all he desir'd of them, but told him it wou'd take them two or three Days, as all the Prisoners that were adopted in the Room of the People they had lost must be given up by the Consent of those that had them, as they were given to them by the Nation.

We imagine that the Reason of the Hurons coming to day was in Consequence of the Commandants sending the Sloop yesterday to batter the Camp of the Ottawas & Chippewas, by which they saw how much
they

1763.
July.
8

they were in our Power. The Garrison lay on the Ramparts.

All quiet to day except a few Shot being fir'd as usual at the Fort & Vessel at a great Distance. Several of the principal Inhabitants brought in their Goods yesterday & to day, and one Maisonville brought five Pittiaugers[48] loaded with 10,000 weight of Lead & Peltry into the Fort tho the Indians knew he was coming with it; if it had fallen into their hands it wou'd have been a fine Prize, but he being resolute & acquainted with their Manners & Customs took such Opportunitys that he ariv'd safe. He was at Outattanon when it was taken. The Garrison lay on the Ramparts.

9

This Morning six of the Huron Chiefs came in and brought Ensign Christie, a Soldier of the R. A. Rangers, a Woman & Child and five other Prisoners, and after telling the Commandant that they were drawn into the War before they knew where they were and many things to the same Purpose of what they had told him the 7th Instant, they ask'd him if it was not advisable for them to retire until such Time as we receiv'd Succours enough to assist them in case they should be attack'd, which he told them to do, and when the Army ariv'd desir'd them to come back that they might show their Sincerity.

They intended to go and join the Puttawattamees & build a kind of Stockade upon the River Huron to defend themselves against the Ottawas in case they should declare War against them. All quiet to day. The Garrison lay on the Ramparts.

10

Last Night at twelve o'Clock the Enemy made a large Float with Four Batteaus, which they fill'd with Faggots, Birtch Bark & Tar, and other Combustibles

---

[48] Perigua, a narrow Ferry boat, carrying two Masts and a Leeboard.—*Webster's Dict.*

which

which they brought into the Middle of the Stream about 1763.
a Half a Mile above the Veſſels & ſet on Fire, but the July.
Veſſels being properly moor'd let go one of their Cables and ſheer'd off from it, letting it paſs at about a
hundred & fifty Yards Diſtance.

This we ſuppoſe was not entirely the Invention & Work of Indians.

At 4 o'Clock ſome of the Miamee Indians came within three hundred Yards of the Fort with a Flag, with an Intention to ſpeake to the Commandant about one Levy they had Priſoner, but not daring to come any nearer they ſent in a Liſt of Things by a Frenchman that he had promiſ'd them if they wou'd give him up. But the Commandant ſent them Word he wou'd not give them any thing.

The Garriſon lay on the Ramparts. Not a Shot fir'd to day.

This Day the Hurons brought in the Goods (that had fallen to the Share of three or four Bands) that belong'd to Chapman & Levy & others, as alſo a Panee that had been adopted in the Family of one Babi, which was a very extraordinary thing, as they ſeldom give up a Priſoner that is adopted.

Yeſterday Pondiac was at the Huron Village with fifteen of his beſt Warriors compleatly arm'd to frighten them, but it had no effect with Babi & Theata & two or three other Chiefs as appeared from their Teſtimony to day. They told the Commandant that they had not yet brought the reſt of the Nation to Reaſon, but hop'd in a little Time to do it, when they wou'd give up their Priſoners & their Merchandiſe; they alſo told the Commandant the Name of a Frenchman who had bought a gold Watch of them for 2000 Wampam.

The Commandant told them that if they cou'd not bring the reſt of the Nation to do as they did they
muſt

1763. muſt abandon them, as by & by when the Army came
July. it wou'd be too late for them to make any offers.

We heard to day that the Miamee Indians were gone off with Mr. Levy.

This Night & between 12 & one o'Clock the Indians ſent down another large fire Float which paſſ'd without doing any Damage. They had made two, but Capt. Hopkins, who was on board the Sloop, fir'd a Cannon at them as ſoon as he perceiv'd the firſt & frightened them ſo that they jump'd out of their Cannoes & let the other go without being light'd, which we tow'd on ſhore. The Garriſon lay on the Ramparts.

12   This Morning the Puttawattamees came again with Mr. Chapman, one Crawford & another Priſoner of Capt. Hopkin's Company, & promiſ'd to bring the reſt as ſoon as they arriv'd. Accordingly at 4 in the Afternoon they came with four Royal Americans two of the Rangers & one of Mr. Crawford's Men, & demanded their Brother, but the Commandant told them what he told them before, that when they brought in all the Priſoners he would let him out, knowing by our Priſoners that they had ſome more, they promiſ'd to bring them the next Day or as ſoon as they cou'd be got together, & wou'd bury every thing that had paſſed in their next Speech.

They brought an Ottawa with them which the Commandant was inform'd of, and upon enquiry found that he came to ſee where the Fort was moſt acceſſable, that they might ſet Fire to it, upon which he told the Puttawattamees that they had an Ottawa with them. They then ſeeing he was diſcover'd ſaid he was left with them by a Band that was gone home, to bring them the News of the finiſhing their Peace with us, but the Command^t told them if he let him out again

the

the Ottawas would laugh at him & defir'd them to afk him in cafe he fhou'd fend one of his to their Camp if they thought their Chiefs wou'd not do the fame.

He then defir'd the Interpreter to tell them that he wou'd not ufe him as they had done Capt. Campbelle & the reft of our Prifoners, but would guard him for the Security of the reft until they brought them all in.

At 4 o'Clock this Afternoon the Scooner fet fail for Niagara, but the Wind failing fhe drop'd Anchor about 4 Miles off.

Since the Proclamation of the Peace, the French that were in the Fort were put under the Command of Mr. Sterling. The Garrifon lay on the Ramparts.

This Morning at about Half paft two, our outlying Centrys fir'd upon two or three Indians that were cralling to the Fort, but one of them being a Frenchman & afraid got up and run away, calling out Je fuis François, at which Time the Indians fir'd at them & fhot him through the Body, but he is not yet dead.

At one o'Clock the Puttawattamees came in with a white Belt and made many Profeffions of Friendfhip, but their chief Errant was to try to get the Ottawa that the Commandant detain'd yefterday. But the Commandant told them they wou'd do better if they wou'd not even fpeake to that Nation, as they only fought their Ruin.

They promif'd to bring in all the Prifoners they had to the Number of fix belonging to their Village if the Commandant would give them their Man, which he told them he would do, as he thought they were fincere.

They gave him a white Belt as a Token of their Fidelity & Friendfhip & he promif'd them another when they came back, as he had not any then made that was proper. The Garrifon lay upon the Ramparts.

This

1763.
July.

14 This Day an Ottawa from Michilimackinac came into the Fort and after a long Story was going to say something about the Indian that the Commandant detain'd the 12 Inftant, but he finding what he was going to say told him fomething that ftop'd him from making any Demands. All quiet. The Garrifon lay on the Ramparts.

15 This Day one Clermont who was formerly Major in the Militia came into the Fort and inform'd the Commandant that moft of the young Men in his Departm^t were going to Illinois, and afk'd if he thought proper to fend an Order to them not to leave the Settlement without his Permiffion (though he had already given a general one) which the Commandant did with Power to him or any of the Officers of Militia to bring them back with a Party of Men in cafe they fhould go off. This Day we were inform'd that the Ottawas & Chippawas had quarrel'd and were going to feparate.

16 All quiet. The Garrifon lay on their Arms.

The 13 Inftant the Wind blew frefh at N. W. and continued till the 14th when it was eafterly till the Evening fhe came about wefterly and blew frefh all the next Day and to day S. W. fo that we imagin'd the Scooner muft have been at Niagara fome Time laft Night, or at furtheft to day.

17 All quiet to day. We heard this Morning that the Ottawas were encamp'd on a Plain about a League off. The Garrifon lay on the Ramparts.

This Afternoon we were inform'd that the Indians had broke down two Barns to make fix large Rafts, which they were to tie together to burn the Veffel but they did not fend them. At 11 o'Clock two Frenchmen came to the Fort for Arms & Flints, informing us that the Jefuift had fent Word from the other Side of the River that the Hurons & Puttawattamees intend

tend to fall upon the French on the south-weſt Side of the Fort. But they did not. The Garriſon lay on the Ramparts.

Yeſterday the Wind S. W. to day N. E. This Day we were inform'd that the Float they were making was 300 Foot long. We were alſo inform'd that all the young Men towards the Groſs Point intended to go off to the Illinois as they were afraid of being hang'd.

At about 11 o'Clock ſome Ottawas came down oppoſite the Sloop and call'd out to them ſeveral Times to go over to them with ſome Rum, &c. which they anſwer'd. When the Garriſon call'd all was well, they were very angry & fir'd over the River, which the People on board obſerving fir'd three or four Muſquets in return, & by Accident wounded one of them. The Garriſon lay on the Ramparts.

This Day about ſixty Indians as neer as we cou'd gueſs, came within about 350 Yards of the Fort in ſome Orchards and fir'd upon the Fort. We threw a Shell amongſt them but unluckily it did not break, which gave them great Joy by their crying; however we prepar'd another, and while they were taking the firſt one up we fir'd it & it fell directly amongſt them & burſt about three foot from the Ground, and as they run away fir'd another after them, but have not yet heard wheather any of them was kill'd or wounded, tho every body imagin'd there was, as they went off without making one Cry.

This Evening we were inform'd that the Enemy were making twenty-four Rafts of about 30 Foot long each, four of which were finiſh'd. The Garriſon lay on the Ramparts.

This Day we fited up a large Batteau with a Pattararoe that carried a three pound Ball.

We were inform'd that there was one Indian wounded with

1763.
July.
21

with the Shell yesterday. The Garrison lay on the Ramparts. The Wind westerly & fresh.

This Day fitted up a second Batteau as the one mentioned yesterday. The Wind S. W. all Day & pretty fresh. The Garrison lay on the Ramparts.

22 This Morning Mr. L. Campo inform'd us that about the Middle of June the Ottawas of Michilimackinac brought off the Garrison at LaBay,[49] without doing any further harm than killing one Man, who was kill'd by the Chippewas; the Renards[50] and Folls a voines[51] Nations came with them to Michilimackinac, but finding them well dispos'd turn'd back.

The Ottawas of Michilimackinac say that they brought off Mr. Gorrel & his Garrison fearing the Chippewas wou'd kill them. The Wind S. W. all Day & pretty fresh. The Garrison lay on the Ramparts.

23 The Wind S. W. and fresh the most part of the Day. The Commandant & several Officers went out of the Fort, some on Horseback & some on Foot, at whom

---

[49] The Post at Green Bay, was then garrisoned by Lieut. Gorell, who, upon receiving a Letter from Captain Etherington of Michillimackinack, informing him of the Events at that Place, and advising him to withdraw and join him, summoned the neighboring Indians, stated to them that the public Service required him to leave them for a while, and committing the Fort to their Care during his Absence, he departed.

The Dacotahs were hereditary Enemies to the Ojibwas, and in Case of Hostility would have been active Auxiliaries of the English.—*Parkman's Pontiac*, 321.

[50] Renards, the Foxes. This Tribe belonged to the Ottawa Confederacy and numbered about 320 Warriors.—*Sir William Johnson's Report*, 1763.

[51] The Folles Avoines (Wild Oat) Tribe, according to Sir Wm. Johnson's Report to the Board of Trade, dated Nov. 18th of this Year, numbered 110 Warriors, and formed a Part of the Ottawa Confederacy. In 1736, they numbered 160 Warriors, resided North of Lake Michigan and bore as their armorial Device the large tailed Bear, the Stag and a Kilion (a Species of Eagle), perched on a Cross.—*N. Y. Col. Hist.*, vii, 582, ix, 1055.

the

the Indians fir'd a good many Shot but without doing Execution. The Garrison lay on the Ramparts.

The Wind S. & S. W. the most part of the Day. This Day the two Batteaux were sent up the River to look at the Situation of the Enemys Camp & try to bring off any Cannoes or Fire Floats that might be convenient, but there was none to be come at without running a Risk of losing more Men than they were worth; however they oblig'd them to throw away their Ammunition, as they lin'd the Sides of the River & fir'd very briskly from each Side without even wounding a Man. The Batteaux now falling down with the Stream & then rowing up again, on purpose to draw their fire, as we were well inform'd they had not much Ammunition.

This Day we were inform'd that there was about 70 Chippawas ariv'd from Michilimackinac, among whome were 5 of the Foles a voines but not one Ottawas. The Garrison lay on the Ramparts.

The Wind S. & S. westerly all Day, but not strong. Nothing Extraordinary to day. The Garrison lay on the Ramparts.

This Morning Mr. Nauvarre sent in some Letters that were brought from the Illinois in consequence of some that were wrote by the Inhabitants of this Place some Time in May. The Messengers also brought some for Pondiac.

This Morning were inform'd that yesterday there was a Council at the Huron Village with the Shawanees that are come; that one Andrew, a Huron who undertook to go to Fort Pitt some Time ago, came with them & says he was hinder'd by them to go on, that he was at Venango when it was taken & that all the Garrison was put to death without Exception; it was taken in the same Manner with the rest, fifteen went in to speak to the Commandant & forty remain'd without

1763. July.

without, & while they were in Council the forty rush'd in & put the Garrison to death.⁵² The Wind westerly.

The People in general seem'd to be a little cast down on the Return of their Messengers from the Illinois, from which we imagin'd they had not receiv'd such Answers as they expected. The Letters they wrote were sent from this about the Middle of May, unknown to the Commandant. The Garrison lay on the Ramparts.

27 This Morning André the Huron came into the Fort, who told us that he was not at the taking of Venango & that the Reason he said to the Ottawas that he was there, was because they would suspect him, but that all the Indians that he saw near the Ohio told him so. That he was stop'd upwards of twenty Days by different Party's of Indians and that in trying to cross a River to get from one of them, he lost his Letters, that he did not dare to go into the Fort as he wou'd have nothing to show, & knowing that the Indians had commenc'd Hostility's there, altho he was on the opposite Side of the River. He likewise inform'd us that the Delawares had kill'd all their Prisoners in consequence of the Prophecy's of one of their Nation who pretended that he had been to Heaven and was told by God that they must put all the English to death, but not to burn any as was sometimes their Custom, otherwise we shou'd overcome them. He also inform'd us that all the Hurons except the Bands of Babi, Theata & another Chief, with Part of the Put-

---

⁵² Venango was garrisoned by a small Party under Lieut. Gordon, and as every Man within it perished, we have no History of the Details except the Narrative of Indians, and the Traces of its Ruins. The Men were all slaughtered on the first Attack, except Lieut. Gordon, who was reserved for the most refined Tortures by Fire that Savage Ingenuity could invent. This done, they burnt the Place and departed. —*Parkman's Pontiac*, 337.

tawattamees

tawattamees had sung the War Song again, but that the Hurons, or Wiandots told the Ottawas that notwithstanding that, they wou'd not fight.

He also told the Commandant that as he was suspected, being so long away & not being at Fort Pitt, if he would give him Letters again he wou'd go & return in twenty Days. Upon which the Commandant told him he did not suspect him, and as Proof wou'd send him again & desir'd him to come the next Day in the Evening & he wou'd have every thing ready for him, tho at the same Time he cou'd not be otherwise than suspected, but as he was a very knowing fellow & had a good deal to say among the Indians it was thought best by the Interpreter and every body that was present to try him again, as he might change seeing the Confidence we put in him, tho he had been acting the Knave before. The Wind southerly.

This Day we were inform'd by Mr. Sterling that Madamoiselle Cuersiere told him that Godfoy told Pondiac when he return'd from the Illinois that he cou'd not send him any Succours yet as they had heard by a Spanish Vessel that the Peace was made, but that as soon as his Couriers ariv'd that he had sent to New Orleans if he found the News to be false he wou'd see what he cou'd do, & desir'd that the Inhabitants shou'd not appear in it at all, but keep themselves quiet.

This Morning six Frenchmen set off in a burch Canoe for Niagara with Letters from the Commandant. This Evening Andre came in & took the Commandants Letters for Fort Pitt. The Wind southerly.

This Morning at Half past four o'Clock, it being very foggy, we heard the Report of several Musquets & now and then as we thought Swivels at the Huron Village, which we [thought] to be some Indians firing at the Scooner, as she might have come that far up the
River

1763.
July.
River without our seeing her in the Night, but in about Half an Hour to our great Surprize, we saw about twenty Batteaux, which upon their coming near we found to be English Boats, with a Detach^t of about 260 Men under the Comm^d of Capt. Dalyel.[53] They came the south Side of the Lake & burn'd a small Indian Village near Sandusky that the Indians had abandoned. They had fourteen Men wounded in passing the Huron Village.

In the Evening we saw some Fires at the Huron Town which was said to be some Cannoes that they set on fire as they were gone away. It was given out by the French to Pondiac (as we were inform'd) that it was not a new Detachment, but that the Commandant had sent out his young Men as they cou'd under the Cover of the Fogg, and row'd up the River again to make them believe it was Succours that ariv'd. The Wind S. westerly all Day.

30 The Wind S. westerly. This Morning André set off for Fort Pitt. Nothing Extraordinary to day. Two Prisoners sav'd themselves to night from the Indians.

31 This Morning at three Quarters after two a Detachment of 247 Men under the Command of Capt. Dalyel march'd out with an Intention to surprize the Indian Camp about three Miles & a half from the Fort.[54]

---

[53] James Dalyell (sometimes written Dalzell) had been appointed a Lieutenant in the 60th Regiment or Royal Americans, early in 1756, and in 1760 obtained a Company in the 2d Battalion of the Royals, or the 1st Regiment of Foot. He perished in a brave but indiscreet Attack upon the Enemy soon after his Arrival at Detroit, as stated in the following Pages.

[54] The following Paragraph had been written in the MSS. next following this, and erased:

"It was given out yesterday Morning by the French that we intended to attack them, but they But

But whether the Enemy were inform'd of it or discover'd them in marching out is not known, but when they were within a Half of Mile of their Camp they were fir'd upon by a great Number of Indians from behind Orchards, Fences & Entrenchments that they had posted themselves in for that Purpose, which put them a little in Confusion at first, but they soon recover'd their Disorder and forc'd the Enemy from their Lodgements. They then finding that their Scheme cou'd not be put in Execution, they thought of making the best retreat they cou'd, the Enemy being twice as numerous as they were, and knowing they cou'd not expect any more Succours from the Garrison, for which purpose they took Post in several Houses that was most advantagious for to prevent the Enemy as much as possible from getting between them and the Fort. Capt. Dalyel, who behav'd with all the Bravery in the World, was unluckily kill'd; after receiving the fire from the Enemy, tho' Capt. Grant beg'd of him either to push on immediately, make a retreat without loss of Time, he remain'd almost in the same Place for at least three Quarters of an Hour, soon after which he was kill'd, and Capt. Grant then with the Assistance of the two row Galleys made as good a retreat as was possible for any body to do, after sending off all the Wounded & all the Dead except seven.

did not know when. Their Reason for thinking so was, because we were mending some old Canoes, but we gave out we should not want them in less than four or five Days, imagining that News would be carried to their Camp with everything else, as we never could do anything in the Fort without their knowing; for even if the Gates were shut and nobody permitted to go out, yet they knew everything we did, as one may see from the other Side of the River every movement made inside of the Fort. The Detachment was three Quarters of an Hour from the Fort before we heard any firing, when it commenced and continued four to five Minutes very heavy, at which Time our People were approaching the Bridge on the Side of the River."

We

1763.
July.

We loft in this Affair, Capt. Dalyel kill'd, Capt. Gray, Lieut. Luke & Lieut. Brown of the 35th wounded, one Serjeant & 13 Rank & File kill'd and one Drum^r and 25 wounded. 60 Reg^t one Private kill'd & feven wounded. 80 Reg^t two kill'd & three wounded. 2 R. A. Rangers 2 kill'd & one wounded, & a Traders Servant wounded. Total, Officers included, kill'd & wounded, 61. The Indians fay they had five kill'd and eleven wounded.[55]

Auguft 1

Laft Night about ten o'Clock a Prifoner was brought in that was wounded at Mr. Cuylers Affair.

The Wind S. & S. wefterly all Day, and at Night chang'd all round the Compafs.

This Day we were inform'd that Part of the Hurons were Encamp'd on the upper End of the Grofs Ifle,[56] where they had fome Corn, that they had fent their Chief who was wounded in yefterday's Affair to the Grand River with a Belt to defire the Puttawattamees to join them.

This Morning about two o'Clock Mr. Rutherford ariv'd at the Sloop, having made his Efcape from the Indians about nine Mile from the Fort, feven of which he came by Land, when finding a Cannoe he embark'd in it & came to the Veffel.

Young Mr. Campo brought in the Body of poor Capt. Dalyel about three o'Clock to day, which was

[55] Parents Creek, ever fince this memorable Affair called *Bloody Run*, enters the Detroit River about a Mile and a Half above the Site of the Fort, and near its Mouth was croffed by a narrow wooden Bridge. The Surface beyond was broken by Ridges parallel with the Stream, and Pontiac, forewarned by Canadians in his Intereft, had ample Time to remove his Camp, and conceal his Warriors along every Hollow and behind every Building and Tree along the Route of the devoted Band.

[56] An Ifland about twelve Miles below Detroit and ftill known by this Name. It is feven Miles long and about two wide at the wideft Part.

mangled

Pontiac's Siege of Detroit.

mangled in such a horrid Manner that it was shocking to human nature; the Indians wip'd his Heart about the Faces of our Prisoners.

1763. August.

Since the Detachment ariv'd the Garrison has been less fatigued than before, as instead of every body lying [upon] the Works, a Capt. Picket of 80 Men & three Subalterns took their Place every Night.

The Wind wavering to day, but mostly S. and southwesterly.

2

Since the last Sortie the People have brought in several Cattle for the King, & offer'd any thing they had, which we imagine was partly owing to some Disorders that the Soldirs committed the 31st in the Morning by plundering several Houses, and partly as they see we are so strong that we can defend ourselves both against the Indians & them, that is to say to maintain the Post without their Assistance.

The Commandant has not yet been able to get a Copy of the Letter that the Inhabitants wrote to the Illinois, nor a Copy of the Answer that Mr. Noiyon sent back to them, by which it appears they had a great Share in the Affair, tho they try to hide it.

The [Wind] N. Easterly and pretty fresh. This Day we began to fit up another Batteau for a four Pownder.

3

Since the Sortie there has been every Night as we are inform'd at least two hundred and fifty Indians disperf'd in Partys round the Fort to watch our Motions. About two o'Clock about fifteen were seen at a House about a Quarter of a Mile from the Fort, upon which a Party was sent out, but whether they were seen in going out or no we cant tell, but the Indians went off immediately.

4

This Morning at Half an Hour past three o'Clock, Capt. Grant with sixty Men of the Picket was sent out

5

1763. August.

to take Poſt in ſome Houſes near the Fort that the Indians made a Practice of coming to in the Day time, where he reſted till one o'Clock, but none came near enough for him to hurt them.

The Wind S. Eaſterly & pretty freſh. At four this Afternoon the Scooner appear'd in Sight.

6

This Morning at 8 o'Clock the Scooner anchor'd before the Fort; ſhe brought but eighty Barrels of Proviſion, a good deal of Naval Stores, & ſome Merchandiſe.

At 3 in the Afternoon a Frenchman came in from Michilimackinac which he left 15 Days ago and informs us that Capt. Etherington & his Garriſon, with that of Fort Wm. Auguſtus[57] and all the Engliſh Merchants were gone down to Montreal guarded by the Ottawas, a Detachment of one Subaltern, four Serjeants, four Corporals, one Drummer & .... as alſo Commodore Lorain with ſixteen Sailors.

This Day unloaded the Scooner & made the Sloop ready to ſail.

7

This Day the Commandant rec'd a Letter from Capt. Etherington dated at Michilimackinac the 18 July, who with his Garriſon & that of Fort Wm. Auguſtus

---

[57] This Fort was near the Grand Portage on Lake Superior and ſubſequently became an important Station of the Northweſt Fur Company under the Name of Fort William. Another Fortreſs of this Name ſtood on an Iſland in the St. Lawrence, at the Foot of Sloop Navigation, three Miles below the preſent Village of Ogdenſburgh. This Iſland was named by the French Iſle Royal, and by the Indians Oraconenton. From the Ruins of its Barracks and other Buildings, it is now known as Chimney Iſland. This Iſland was fortified in 1759 under the Direction of Chevalier Levi, and from him was named Fort Levi.

In the Summer of 1760, while under the Command of M. Pouchot, it was attacked and reduced by Lord Amherſt and its Name changed to Fort William Auguſtus. This was the laſt Reſiſtance made by the French againſt the Engliſh in Canada.

was

was then going into the Boats to go to Montreal, as also all the English Merchants, for whome he had obtain'd Permission of the Indians to carry all their Merchandize.

1763. August.

This Morning at two o'Clock Capt. Hopkins and two Subalterns with 60 Volunteers went down in Boats with an Intent to surprize an Indian Caban at the Puttawattamee Village. We went down undiscover'd to the Place we intended to land, and in turning in the Boats to the Shore the Row Galley which was commanded by Lieut. Abbot being heavy did not follow so near as could be wish'd, by which Means, it being foggy & dark under the Land, she lost Sight of us and drop'd down with the Current so far that before Capt. Hopkins got her up again it was broad Day light & we was discover'd & oblig'd to return back without attempting any thing. The Fogg continued so thick that my Boat & the Row Galley was lost again; the Row Galley at last threw out her Anchor and lay there till it began to get clear, but the other Boats cou'd neither do that nor go to the Shore, as the Enemy follow'd us on each Side of the River. 8

The Wind has been up the River ever since the Vessel ariv'd that she cou'd not go from this. 9

Both Vessels were made ready to sail to day, fifteen of the Wounded were put on board the Sloop to be sent to Niagara as they cou'd be of no use here this Year, & it sav'd Provision, as also fourteen or fifteen Merchants that had been Prisoners with the Indians. 10

The Wind straight up the River alday. This Day we were inform'd that the Puttawattamees & Hurons were all coming back. 11

This Night one Jacob Taylor a Trader came in, having made his Escape from the Indians.

The Wind almost West, the Vessels cou'd not stir. 12

The

1763.
August.
13   The Wind a little to North of W., the Veſſels weigh'd Anchor at 10 o'Clock & in two Trips got below the Huron Point, from where they had a large Wind to Sanduſky.⁵⁸ The Indians did not fire one Gun at them.

14   This Morning the Wind W. and freſh.

15   The Wind Weſt and freſh all Day with a good deal

---

⁵⁸ The Arrival of theſe Veſſels was announced to Sir William Johnſon in the following Letter:

"NIAGARA, 24th Auguſt, 1763.

Sir: Being allways glad to ſelebrat all oppertunityes of giving you the earlyeſt Inteligence of any thing perticular intreduces me to trouble you with this.

The Commodore arrived here on the 22d Inſt. and allſo the Schooner and the Sloop from Detroit. By them we have the following Account of the grate Luck and ſafe Arrival of Capt. Duel [Dalyell] and his Armiment at Detroit being ſomewhat remarkable, as the Indians was lying in Ambuſh for him which he knew of, but the Night and Morning that he arived being fogee Weather he got in to the Garriſon without the Knowledge of the Indians, who were ſoon made acquainted with it, not only his Arrival but his Intentions, which was the next Morning he march'd about two Miles Diſtance from the Garriſon being informed of ſome Intrenchments they had there, where he was fired on very warmly by a Party of Indians, as he was croſſing a wooden Bridge which was behind ſome Pickquets, notwithſtanding which the brave and undaunted Capt. Duel [Dalyell] march'd the Men on to the Breſtwork or Trench which the Engliſh ſoon got Poſſeſſion of, and the Indians retreated to another Trench they had ſome Diſtance in the Rear of the Intrenchment where Capt. Duel behaved with the greateſt Courage and Reſolution imaginable, but ſoon told Capt. Grant he was wounded, notwithſtanding which his Bravery in the Command was the ſame as before, but ſome Time after Lieut. McDougle informed Capt. Gray, belonging 55th [35th], that Capt. Duel [Dalyell] was wounded again and dead. Then Capt. Gray took the Command and being informed that the Indians were ſurrounding them faſt by the Directions of their Sachem Pondeack and takeing Poſſeſſion of the French Houſes. Upon this News the Engliſh thought proper to Retreat. Some Partys were detached to drive them out and take Poſſeſſion from the Indians, which they ſoon did, at which Time Capt. Gray was wounded taking Poſſeſſion of a Mill, but hope he will recover. Alſo Lieut. Brown of the 55th was wounded at the ſame Time. Then Capt. Grant had the Command, who marched the Men very regular on the Retrait into the Fort. About fifteen Men with Major Rogers got in a Houſe who was to bring up

of Rain. This Day threw a Coehorn Shell to the other Side of the River. 1763. August.

The Wind westerly all Day with Rain. This Day we were inform'd that Pondiac had given out that the Commandant only sent the Vessels out into the Lake to make the Indians believe that they went to Niagara, but he knew better for they neither brought Provisions nor Men. That when they ariv'd opposite the Fort we always sent two or three Batteaux along side of them full of Men who were all hid except those that row'd, and as soon as they got on board huzza'd, by which Means we made them believe that we receiv'd Succours. 16

The Wind still westerly and N. W. with Rain. Last Night there was 150 of the Enemy within about three Quarters of a Mile of the Fort, 50 of whome were constantly Centry; the Night was extremely bad. They themselves say that two or three of them swimed down close to the Fort, but observing some Soldiers that was in a Batteaux anchor'd above the Fort with a Patteraroe[59] in it, to put up their Heads, they went back as fast as they cou'd. 17

the Reare and Cover the Retrate, which was soon surrounded by the Indians and had no other way to get clear of them but by showing them a clean pair of Heels, which he did, and a Corporal of the 55th had a fair Tryal for, and got safe in the Fort.

There is killed and wounded in this Engagement about thirty English, the Number of Indians is not known.

The have murdered Capt. Duel [Dalyell] in a barbarous Manner by Schelping him, cutting of one of his Arms and one Leg and takeing out his Bowels, his Body was brought in and buried in the Fort. Last Night arrived here seventy of the 46th Reg^t.

I am Sir
   Your most Hum^{ble} Serv't.
         T. DE COUAGNE.

P. S. By the Prisoners we have Account of the Seneckees, it is suspected that they have joyned the Dellawares.

[59] Paterero, or Pederero, a small Cannon mounted as a Swivel.

The

1763.
August.
18

The Wind N. W. Laſt Night & this Morning before Day the Ottawas chang'd their Camp from behind the Grand Marais to the River Rouge,[60] where they will be very convenient to harraſs any Party that may be coming up; or the Veſſels, as they will have early Intelligence of it, and Time to poſt themſelves in the moſt convenient Places for that Purpoſe.

Laſt Night Mr. Watkins with about eighteen Volunteers lay in Mr. Babi's Houſe as the Indians had paſt it two Nights before in order to try how near they cou'd come to the Fort. But he did not get an Oppertunity of firing upon any of them as there was Cry given as ſoon as he got there, which we imagine to have been one of their Centrys.

This Evening the Commandant rec'd a Letter from one Waſſong, the Chief of the Chippawas, to this Effect: That if he had a Mind to leave the Fort he might do it peacibly at preſent, but if not that the River would ſoon be ſtop'd up. That he had never yet fought againſt him, for that if he had the Fort wou'd have been burn'd long ago, with a great many threats & very inſolent Expreſſions. The Commandant ſent Word to the Indians that if they had any thing to ſay to come to the Fort; that he knew they cou'd not write & therefore might be impoſ'd on by thoſe that wrote for them, & deſir'd the Meſſenger to tell the French that the firſt that wrote another Letter of that Kind might expect to be hang'd; which we ſuppoſe was in conſequence of ſome Batteaux that were ſent up the River in the Morning to ſee what the Enemy were doing, as it was reported they were making a large Raft.

19   The Wind eaſterly, but not much of it. This Day finiſh'd another Batteau for a four pownder.

[60] The River Rouge empties into the Detroit River from the Weſt, four Miles below the Site of the Fort.

The Wind N. easterly in the Morning & westerly in the Afternoon, but not much of it.

This Morning at Half an Hour past three Capt. Hopkins, Ensign Perry & Ensign Kiggel and forty Men of the Piket, with Capt. Roger & four or five of his Men, & Mr. Watkins & Mr. Cornwell and some other Volunteers went to waylay the Road that the Indians generally take to pass from the Puttawattimy Village to the Camp up the River, to favour which the Commandant sent up four Batteaux, two with a four Pownder in each, and two with Patteraroes, they went as far as the upper End of the Isle au Cochon,[61] and drew a good many of the Indians that way, but Capt. Hopkins being discover'd return'd without being able to do any thing.

The Wind S. & S. easterly, but very little of it. This Day part of the Picket was out about four hundred Yards from the Fort lodg'd in Houses to try to catch or kill some Indians that daily came near the Fort, but their Intelligence was so good that they always knew of it and never came near enough. A Woman was wounded through the Arm by Accident at the Door of a House behind which were two Indians.

The Wind southerly in the Morning, from 12 till Night S. E. pretty fresh, then more southerly. This Day part of the Picket was out as yesterday and fir'd a great many Shot at the Enemy, but was so far off that they cou'd not do any Execution. On their going out they saw two Indians whom they follow'd in pursuit of whom we had one Man shot through the thigh, for the Indians ran away (as is their Custom) as soon as they saw our Men, and when they return'd the Indians return'd also and generally got a Shot at our Men without exposing themselves, however we heard

[61] Nearly five Miles from the Fort.

that

1763. that one of the two that ran away this Morning was
August. ſhot through the Body.

At Half paſt nine this Evening a Negro made his Eſcape from one Marſacks who had bought him from the Indians.

23 The Wind S. & S. weſterly all Day. This Morning we were inform'd that one of the Indians died laſt Night that was wounded yeſterday & that two others are wounded.

This Day the Picket was at Mr. Barrois & a little beyond it ſkirmiſhing with the Indians the moſt Part of the Day, we fir'd a good many Shells in the Garden where ſome of them was & fir'd ſeveral Shot through the Houſes they were in, ſo that we imagine they receiv'd a good deal of Damage. About Half an Hour before Sunſet the Party was order'd in, and as ſoon as the Rear of the Party was well in the Fort they were impudent enough to come to Mr. St. Martins Houſe and fir'd ſeveral Shot in at the Gate & ſet Fire to two or three little out Houſes that we had Poſſeſſion of all Day, which the Commandant thought ſo inſolent that he ſent out Major Rogers with the Picket to take Poſſeſſion again, and upon his appearing the Indians run away & he remain'd there all Night. We had three Men wounded to day.

24 The [Wind] S. & S. weſterly but not much of it; in the Afternoon Rain, the Wind changing all round the Compaſs.

This Night the Commandant ſent out an Officer & thirty Men of the Picket to keep Poſſeſſion of Mr. Brarrois's Houſe & Barn to protect it & Mr. St. Martins, which the Indians ſaid they wou'd burn, which he intended to do till they had thraſh'd their Corn, &c. This Day we had two Men wounded, but one of them very ſlightly.

This

This Day a Bennickee[62] Indian came into the Fort for a Pafs to go to Montreal, being the third time within this five Days; he faid he had been at War againft the Cherokees, & that his Brother who came with him laft Winter with Mr. Ferguſon went a hunting when he went away and he had not heard of him fince.   But one ―――― an Albany Trader who was taken with one Meldrum between Miamee & Ouiattanon, came in this Evening and inform'd us that he had been four Days in the Woods without any thing to eat, having made his Efcape from one of the Puttawattamee Villages about forty Miles off, where he heard the Indians fay that in Capt. Dalyels Affair there was fix Ottawas, two Chippewas and one Bennickee Indian kill'd, which Bennickee we fuppofe to be the Brother of this one that is in the Fort.

1763. Auguft.

At ten this Night the Indians fet Fire to a fmall Houfe that we had Poffeffion of all Day from which we gall'd them. It was too far from the other Houfes that we had Poffeffion of to keep Men in, as they were always liable to be cut off.

This Day in the Afternoon the Indians came to their Poft & fir'd a good deal at our Men that keep'd Poffeffion of Mr. Barrois Houfe &c., but without doing any Harm.

25

This Morning Mr. Cecote & Mr. Forville came to the commanding Officer in the Name of four of the moft principal Chiefs of the Ottawas to afk Mr. Labute to come to fpeak to them, but Mr. Labute did not choofe to go, & the Commandant wou'd not order him. In the Afternoon they fir'd a great deal & expof'd themfelves more than ufual. At four o'Clock they fet Fire to Mr. Babi's Houfe which burn'd to the Ground in

26

---

[62] Abenaque.

1763.
August.

27 a few Minutes. This Day we had one Man wounded. The Wind S. & S. westerly.

The Wind S. This Morning we were inform'd that there was one Indian kill'd yesterday & three wounded. This Day did not fire so much as yesterday, wounded one Indian.

28 The [Wind] S. W. Very little firing to day at the advanc'd Post.

29 The Wind weavering from S. S. E. to W. N. W. This Day by Accident found two Keys that had been lately made, one of which open'd one of our small Gates & the other a large one. Yesterday about fifty Indians ariv'd here, 30 of whom had been opposite to the landing Place 9 Mile up the River, & say they saw a great many English carry'g Provision on their Backs and otherwise, are likewise inform'd that the Indians that [went] to Montreal with Mr. Lerond by Pondiacs leave are come back, who met Cap. Etherington & Garrison about 25 Leagues from thence.

30 The Wind chang'd all Day from S. E. to S. & S. S. W. This Evening we were inform'd that four Hurons ariv'd from Sandusky to inform the Indians here that there was an Army of two thousand Men between that & Fort Pitt on their way hither, that the Indians had been neer enough to fire upon them, & the English returning the fire kill'd seven of the Miamee Nation.

The Indians fir'd a good deal from their Breastwork at the outlying Picket to day.

31 The Wind chang'd all round the Compass. This Morning we were inform'd that a Chief of the Missesagys was badly wounded yesterday.

Sept. 1 The Wind almost due East all Day. This Day we were inform'd that the Chief of Missesagys who was wounded the 30 August died yesterday. This Day the Nephew of a great Chief of the Ottawas was kill'd

at

Pontiac's Siege of Detroit.

at their Retrench[t] that they were trying to open again, as Mr. Brehm deftroy'd it yefterday Morning.

The Wind Eaft & a little to the fouthward of Eaft all Day. The Indians fir'd a good deal to day at the advanc'd Picket.

The Wind a little to the fouthward of Eaft. This Morning we were inform'd that the Scooner was in the River near the lowermoft inhabitants & that there was fome Mohawks in her, as four of them had landed and fent for Babi[63] & Theata of the Hurons to come & fpeake with them & then went on board again.

At one o'Clock the Indians came and fet Fire to a Windmill about three hundred Yards from the Fort. At Half an Hour apaft 2 one Mr. Petet & another Frenchman ariv'd from the Illinois by way of Fort St. Jofeph, who inform'd us that 28 Days ago Mr. Neyon the Commandant there had not rec[d] the acc[t] of the Peace from Authority but expected it every Day. He had heard it from New Orleans by an Englifh Merchant that was ariv'd there from Martinico.

That the Oueattanon Indians had been with Mr. Neyon for Ammunition and he had given them about three Barrels of Powder & Lead in Proportion, enough to keep them from ftarving a little while.

The Wind Eaft the moft of the Day. Laft Night at about 9 o'Clock 340 Indians embark'd in Cannoes and went to board the Scooner. The Merchants were on Shore. The Channel where the Veffel lay not being very wide and Rufhes growing on each Side of it, they came within a little more than a hundred Yards of her before they were difcover'd & then rufh'd in at once upon her furrounding her with Cannoes & Bat-

1763.
Sept.
2

3

4

---

[63] Babie, the Huron Chief, figned the Treaty at Fort Niagara, July 18, 1764. His Indian Name was Odinghquanooron, and he appears to have poffeffed confiderable Influence among his Tribe.

teaux

1763.
Sept.

teaux and under a very brisk fire attempted to cut holes in her Stern & the Cable. The Cable they cut, but notwithstanding there was but twelve on board, two of whome Mr. Horsey and another was kill'd & four wounded at the beginning, they never was able to board her, but oblig'd to fly with the loss (as the French tell us) of eight kill'd & twenty wounded. When the Commanding Officer was inform'd that there was Indians on board and but twelve Men, he sent off an Express with a Letter to Mr. Horsey, but they did not get down till the Attack began, and consequently cou'd not get on board, and this Morning, the fifth, when we were inform'd that she had been attack'd, the Commandant sent down four Row Galleys.

5   The Wind S. E. At 9 o'Clock the Row Galleys return'd, Capt. Hopkins & about twenty Men including some Volunteers remain'd on board.

At 11 the Wind spring up a little & the Schooner came in Sight and at Half apast three cast Anchor opposite the Fort. She brought 47 Barrals of Flour & 160 of Pork.

6   The Wind S. W. This Day we heard that the Indians were watching near the Mouth of the River to pick up those that were kill'd. The Mohawks say that the Hurons kept them Prisoners after they went on Shore, but from all Appearance they are great Rascals & came with an Intent to betray the People in the Vessels.

7   The Wind S. W. This Day we were inform'd that seven Indians died of their Wounds. The Commandant being inform'd by the People in the Schooner that there was two more Indians coming in the Sloop, who with those that came in the Schooner might have laid a Scheme to come on board with other Indians as Friends and endeavour to take her by Treachery, thought

Pontiac's Siege of Detroit.   69

thought proper to send a Man with a Letter to the 1763.
River Cannard (as if he was going a hunting) with Sept.
Orders to remain there till the Sloop came into the
River, and then to go on board of her and give the
Letter to the Commander, to whom he gave Orders
for preventing any Treachery that they might think to
practice against him.

This Morning the Commandant was inform'd that   8
it was realy the Intention of the Mohawks to betray the
Sloop if they cou'd & for that Purpose they were gone
to the Mouth of the River, upon which the Wind
coming about he order'd the Schooner to make ready
to sail, and wrote a short Letter to the General telling
him the Reason of his being oblig'd to send her away
before he had Time to write all that he intended, and
wrote a Letter to the Commander of the Sloop with
Orders & Directions how to behave in coming up the
River. The Wind N. W. when the Schooner sail'd at
Half past one and continued so till about Half after
four, when it came about to East and continued all
Night.

The Wind E. Last Night at about 11 o'Clock the   9
Indians burn'd the Barn of Mr. Reaume[64] on the other
Side of the River with about 1000 Bushels of Wheat
in it, some Peas & some Hay.

This Morning we were inform'd that seventy Puttawattamys ariv'd from St. Josephs.

The Wind S. W. Nothing Extraordinary to day.   10
The Wind westerly all Day, & at Night blew pretty   11
fresh.
The Wind westerly.   12

---

[64] In 1777, one Pierre Reaume was a prominent Settler at Detroit, and the next Year Charles Reaume was a Captain in the British Indian Department at that Place. The lat- ter settled at Green Bay in 1790, and after holding a civil Office many Years died between 1818 and 1824. —*First An. Rep. State Hist. Soc. Wisconsin*, 61.

The

1763.
Sept.
13

The Wind S. & S. West. This Day we were inform'd that there was a Vessel seen at the Mouth of the River yesterday Morning.

One of the Sailors that was wounded in the Scooner told us yesterday that the Sloop was going to land 200 Men and Provision at Presque Isle & was then to return to Niagara for Provision for this Place, which if true is very surprizing, as they knew we had but six Weeks Provision in Store when she went away, and the Scooner was sent loaded with Pork, all to about forty Barrels of Flour.

14 The Wind S. W. This Day we were inform'd that forty Puttawattmys were gone to their Village at St. Josephs.

15 The Wind W. & S. W. For two or three Days past we have had Accts of the Vessels being at the Mouth of the River & of Boats being at Sandusky.

16 The Wind westerly. To day we heard that the Indians were making ready their Cannoes to go off.

17 The Wind S. & S. W. Last Night a Soldier that was taken the 29th May coming from Michilimackinac & a Merchant made their Escape & came into the Fort. The Soldier says that he was told by a Frenchman that the Reason that the People ask Billets or Certificates from Pondiac for their Cattle was because the People in Canada were to pay Half their Losses. That he spoke with Aaron the Mohawk, who told him he was sent here by Sir William Johnston to find who were the Cause of the War.

18 The Wind S. & S. W. This Day we were inform'd that the Ottawas, Puttawattamys & Wiandots were to go off to morrow. That a Cannoe with some Hurons was ariv'd from the East End of Lake Erie who said that they saw a Number of Troops embark'd on board the Sloop and a great Number of Batteaux on their way hither. The

1763. Sept.

19. The Wind W. & N. W. Very fresh all Day & last Night from 8 o'Clock it blew very hard Squawls from the same Quarter with a great deal of Rain.
This Day we were inform'd that the Puttawattamys were all gone, & that the Ottawas were angry at Pondiac for proposing to go, & they chose one Manitoo for their Chief in his Place.

20. The Wind W. & N. W., very fresh all Day and very cold for the Season. Last Night twelve Frenchmen got a Pass for Montreal & took some Letters with them.

21. The Wind W & N. W. and very Cold. We were inform'd a few Days ago by Monsr Fortville that Baptiste Deriverre with his Party who came from the Illinois with Monsr Sabole fought in Conjunction with the Indians against the Vessel when Mr. Horsey was kill'd.

22. The Wind West till 12 o'Clock when it changed to the Eastward of South, and continued all Day a light Breeze, the Air not being so cold as it had been for two or three Days before. Yesterday the Indians sent word to all the Inhabitants not to offer to go into the Fort for three Days, and if any came out of the Fort they were to tell them to go back & inform those within not come out during that Time, under Pain of having their Houses & Barns burnt.

23. The Wind S. & a little to the Eastward of S.

24. The Wind S. E. and E. S. E. all Day. Last Night at about a Quarter after eight o'Clock Serjeant Fisher in passing from the Fort to Mr. St. Martins House was fir'd upon by two Indians as we suppose & was kill'd, which gave Reason for us to think that it was Scheme laid by the French & Indians to get an Officer Prisoner, as they knew the Commandant and many of the Officers walk'd there (since we took Post at Mr. Barrois's

1763.
July.
Barrois's) after Night, and for that Reason the French was neither to come in nor go out of the Fort; as otherwise they might fire upon some of them instead of us.

This Day at about one o'Clock Baby the Huron came into the Fort but brought nothing extraordinary. He said that the most of his Errant was to see the Major & pay him his Respects, it being the first Oppertunity he had since he was in before, as the Ottawas & Puttawattamys were always being along the Road to watch our Motions.

25 The Wind S. & S. E. till twelve of Clock then chang'd to the West with Rain.

This Evening we were inform'd that the Enemy intended to attempt to surprise the advanc'd Post. The Night was very bad, it raining very hard & the Wind shifting with hard Squawls from South to West.

26 The Wind pretty fresh from the West with Rain. This Day we were inform'd that some Indians came in last Night that had been to see whether there was an Army on the Lake or no, who reported that there was a vast Number of Boats between this & Sandusky which they imagin'd wou'd be here this Night or to morrow.

27 The Wind westerly all Day with Rain. This Day Aron the Mohawk sent word to the Commandant that he would come into the Fort to night or to morrow night.

28 The Wind N. W. & N. all Day.

29 The Wind W. all Day, hazy weather. Last Night at seven o'Clock Aron the Huron [Mohawk] came into the Fort with his Pass from Sir William [Johnson] & five other Mohawks who were to join Capt. Dalyell, who said that he was sent to find out the Reason of the War, and that he was convinc'd the French were great Rascals,

Rafcals, yet the firft Belts came from the Five Nations, and that the Mr. Horfey fent him afhore before the Schooner was attack'd, Contrary to his own Judgment, to buy Vegetables; that the Veffel was attack'd in Confequence of the Intelligence that was given the Indians by the two Frenchmen that went on board of her, & not from any that he or his People gave, and that the People on that Side of the River furnifh'd them with Cannoes & every thing they wanted. That many of the Inhabitants were going off to the Miffifippi with Quantitys of Merchandize that they had bought of the Indians, that they had taken from our Merch^{ts}. He promif'd to return in three or four Days.

The Wind S. to N. E. 30

The Wind N. & N. E. & fome Part of the Day Oct. 1
N. W.

This Morning a Frenchman crofs'd the River a little above the Fort with his Goods on his way to a Houfe down the River that he had hir'd, but being call'd to, to come in Shore, and not obeying was fir'd upon, which he did not mind but went on. The Commandant then ordered a Boat to bring them back, which they feeing coming after them oblig'd them to put in Shore oppofite the Fort. But as no Enemy was to be feen, the Boat went in under the Bank to bring her off, but before they got thirty Yards from the Shore two Indians came running down and fir'd upon them & kill'd one Man.

The Wind N. E. This Morning, at 10 o'Clock, Lieut. 2
Brehm, Lieut. Abbot, Enf^{n} Riggell & myfelf were fent up the River with four arm'd Batteaux to Reconnoitre an Ifland in the Mouth of Lake St. Clair to fee if it was poffible to bring Wood from it for the Garrifon & to try to bring off a Ships Boat that the Indians took from Capt. Robinfon, when we were about four

Miles

1763.
Oct.

Miles from the Fort the Indians began to fire upon us from Holes they had made on the Side of the River, and two or three Times attempted to put off in a Batteaux & two or three Cannoes as we imagined to cross the River to fire upon us from each Shore, but we drove them ashore as soon as they were well on board, but at last seeing we only lost Time with them, push'd on to perform what we were sent about, when we had gain'd the upper End of the Hogg Island we saw them push off with nineteen Cannoes & Batteaux & seem'd to follow us, & when we were in the narrow Part of the River surrounded us under a brisk Fire from each Shore; upon which we turn'd to attack them, they still pushing on with great Bravery all open to our Fire, making a great Hallowing; at length Lieut. Brehm got a good Shot at some of them with a four Pownder charg'd with Grape at about forty or fifty Yards Distance, which he so disabled that out of about 15 or 16 that were in it we cou'd not see but two that paddled. They then put on Shore some on one Side of the River and some on the other, & cry'd two death Hollows; we then rowed up and down in the same Part of the River & call'd to them to put off again, that we were waiting for them. But they were then very quiet & did not Hollow as in the Beginning, & chose rather to fire few straggling Shot from Shore than attempt coming off again. Then finding it too late to proceed we return'd to the Fort. We had one Man kill'd & three wounded, two of which were very slight. We have not yet heard what Number of them were kill'd or wounded. Upon our Return we were inform'd that one of the Vessels were in the Mouth of the River.

3   At 12 o'Clock, the Wind being almost South, heard firing of Cannon & small Arms down the River, & at one or Half past, the Schooner came in Sight; about Half

Half past three she arriv'd at the Fort, in which came Capt. Montresor, who inform'd us that the Sloop was lost the 28th of August between Presque Isle & Niagara,[65] the Provision and Guns were all lost except 185 Barrells, which they brought in the Schooner; the Rigging was all carried to Niagara.

The Wind S. W., pretty fresh with Showers of Rain. Last Night the Enemy set Fire to a Barn about sixty Yards from the Post occupied by our outlying Picket, and crawl'd about the whole Night to try to get a Prisoner & kill a Centry, but they did not succeed if that was their Design, but on the Contrary had one Man kill'd as our People fir'd at every thing they saw move. Another had a speer run through his Body by one of their own People, and we hear is like to die.

The Wind West & very fresh. This Day the

---

[65] Letters to Sir William Johnson:
NIAGARA, 8th Sep^r, 1763.

S^r: In my last I wrote you that ye Sloop was lost upon Lake Erie, since ye have been on Shore they have been attacked by a few stragling Indians, we have lost three Men in ye Breastwork and one out that was scalped. Danl & ye Rest of the Indians behaved very well.
DE COUAGNE.
CAT FISH CREEK, 9th Sept^m 1763.
14 Mills on Lak Eria.
Dr: According to Daniel Oughnour's Desire I now take the Freedom to write to you. The 8th ult^m we have been cast away at this Place which detained him from Proseiding to Detroit, but he says he'll go forward and deliver your Belts and bring you an Answer from the different Nations according to your Directions. The 3d Inst we had 3 Men kill by a small Partey of Indians. Daniel spoke to them at little Distance from the Breastwork but they would not tell what Nation they were, he says he believes they are Cinices [Senecas]. We expect the Scooner from Detroit dayly. Aaron & 5 Indians went in her to Detroit. Daniel gives his Comp^s to you & Familey and desire the Favour of you in case you see his Wife to tell her that he is well. Sir excuse my Freedom in writing in such a maner for I have had the Fever & Eague those several Days.
I am Sir your most
ob^t Humb^l Servant,
COLLIN ANDREWS.
P. S Capt. Coghran gives his Complements to you, he has used Daniel extremely well.—*MSS. of Sir William Johnson*, vol. vii.

This

1763.
Oct.
Schooner was made ready to fail. This Day we were inform'd that there was two hundred Indians & twenty five Cannoes when they attack'd the Boats.

6 The Wind West. Aron the Mohawk came in to day to fee his Comrades that came in the Schooner, who told us that there was three Chippewas kill'd & feven wounded the fecond Inftant. That the Hurons were fickly with a bad Feever. That feven or eight had died within five or fix Days paft.

7 The Wind E. & N. E. The Schooner fail'd at twelve o'Clock, in which went Capt. Grey, Lieut. Brown & Lieut. McDonald.

This Day Mr. Campo came to the Commandant in the Name of Wabicommigot a Toronto Chief to know his Sentiments about a Peace, to which the Major gave no direct Anfwer, but told Mr. Campo that he might bring him to the Fort & he wou'd fpeake to him. He ariv'd here laft Sunday with twenty four Men as he fays not to make War, but to try to accommodate Affairs.

8 The Wind E. & N. Eaft. This Day 60 Miamees ariv'd; we hear that the Chippewas are preparing all the Boats & Cannoes they can to attack the arm'd Boats when they go up the River again.

9 The Wind Weft & N. W. Laft Night a Soldier, a Trader and a Cherokee that was Prifoner with the Indians made their Efcape & came into the Fort.

This Day we were inform'd that the Indians had taken all the Cannoes they cou'd get from the Inhabitants but know not for what End.

10 The Wind E. to N. E. in the Morning, in the Afternoon wefterly.

12 The Wind wefterly. Yefterday was held a Council with the Miffifagues, and this Day another with the fame.

The

1763.
Oct. 13.

The Wind from W. to N. W., pretty fresh all Day.

The Wind West & a little to the North of West all Day & pretty fresh.

14
15

The Wind W. & N. W. with Snow in the Morning.

16

The Wind chang'd from one Point to another all Day with now & then Snow.

17
18

The Wind S. & S. E.

The Wind Easterly.

19

The Wind Easterly. The Councils that has been held these few Days past has been attended with this good Effect, that we have been able to get in some Wheat & some little Flower, without which we shou'd not have an Ounce of Flower in the Garrison ten Days past, as the Men for upwards of seven Weeks past have had only five Pounds of Flower p^r Week, & for the other two Pounds Half a Gallon of Wheat each.

25

This Day a Soldier sav'd himself by running off from a Chibbawa who brought him to Cuesieres to sell.

29

This Morning Capt. Grant with a Party of 150 Men was sent to the Isle au Couchon to cut Wood for the Garrison, the Commandant not choosing to let more Time pass in waiting for the Troops that he expected some Time ago.

30

Last Night Mons. Dequendse a Cadette ariv'd from the Illinois and was in Council with Pondiac and the Chiefs of all the Nations here, and this Morning brought a Letter to the Commandant from Mon^r Daneyon Commandant of the Illinois Country, with a Speech which he sent addreſſ'd to all Indians with three Belts of Wampum & four Pipes of Peace, which he distributed to the Nations as he came along. In the Speech he let them know that Peace was made between England & France & exhorted them to live in

Peace

1763.
Oct.

Peace with us, telling them that fighting againſt us at Preſent was fighting againſt them, and deſiring them to eſteem their Brothers the French that remain'd amongſt us, as they wou'd never be abandoned by them. That they chang'd their Situation as the King order'd, & that they had given up thoſe Parts of the Country that belong'd to the King & not theirs, and deſir'd an Anſwer to his Speech telling them they ſhou'd allways receive Succours from them at ſuch & ſuch Places. That their Villages would be full of Amunition & Merchandize. Upon which Pondiac ſent in Word to the Commandant that their Hatchet was buried & deſir'd to have his Anſwer in writing. To which the Commandant anſwer'd that if he had begun the War it wou'd be in his Power to end it; but as it was him, he muſt wait the Pleaſure of the General, to whome he wou'd write & inform him of his pacific Inclination in caſe he committed no more Hoſtilities. Pondiac then ſaid he wou'd not commit any more & wou'd come when he was ſent for.

The News of the diffinitive Treaty ariv'd at the Illinois the 27 of September. In another Letter to the Inhabitants of the Peace being concluded, he mark'd five Places on the South Side of the Miſſipi that any of the Inhabitants might retire to that had an Inclination where they wou'd receive all the Succour that was in his Power to give them. From which one may imagine that if one word cou'd prevent all the Nations from committing further Hoſtilities it was in their Power with a very few to do all they have done & that they will always remain in their Intereſt as long as they have any Footing on the Continent from whence they can ſuccour them.

31

[66] This Day Mr. Jadeau was in the Fort & in talk-

[66] The following Extract from a Letter of Wm. Edgar at Detroit,
ing

ing with Major Gladwin about Provision, he told him that ever since the Beginning of this Affair, the Inhabitants in his District had receiv'd Orders to give Pondiac a Bushel of Peas or Wheat pr. Family, under Pain of disobey'ng the greatest of Orders, & that when the Indians were ask'd who gave them the Orders they said sometimes Mons. Cecotte & sometimes Baptist Campo. Once in particular one of the Inhabitants upon being told that it was Cecotte that gave the Order tore it & told him he did not mind the Order nor Cecotte and then went away. The next Day the Indians came & it was much as all the rest of the Inhabitants cou'd do to prevent them from taking every thing he had in the World & pulling down his House.

1763.
Oct.

The following Names are those People who went from the Settlement & from his District within these three Weeks without Leave:

    Grenon, an Inhabitant.
    Millehomme Do.
    Brisar & his Family.
    De Roen.
    Jean Faies.
    Des Cheine, Labourer, & one Lizott Do.

Three Days ago Aron went from the River Huron on his way to Fort Pitt with Letters.

Nov. 10

dated Novr 1st, 1763, states the Progress of pacific Overtures as then understood:

"I have lately rec^d a Letter from Hornlach, which came by an Officer from Illinois, who brought a Belt & Letter to the Savages, with the Account of the Peace between England & France which neither the Savages nor the French, *here* believed till now. In Consequence of which, our most implacable Enemies, the Ottawas who were the only Nation here disposed for continuing the War (all the rest having begged Forgiveness for what they have done of our worthy Commandant) are now with the others, suing for Peace, in the most abject Manner.

Mr. Prentice is very well at Sandusky, as is Mr. Winston at St. Joseph's, and from the present Disposition of the Savages I apprehend they will soon bring them *in*."

This

1763.
Nov.

This Day by the Returns from the Commissary it appear'd that we had upwards of 9000 weight of Flour & Wheat equal to about 23000 more, which would have been enough for to keep 250 Men here all the Winter, as the Commandant had given over any thoughts of Boats coming & imagin'd the Vessel was lost, as she had been gone from this upwards of thirty Days.

This Evening Mr. Jadeau came in with a Letter from the Schooner dated at Isle au Boisblond, informing us that the Troops had left Niagara the 20th October.

Mr. Jadeau in Conversation happen'd to tell before Mr. Duquindse that Pondiac had said he was going with 9 of his Men to the Illinois with him, & that he, Pondiac, had been inform'd that Mr. Dequindse was to take a good many French with him, which a little shock'd Mr. Duquindse as he had given out that he was to pass by St. Josephs.

At three o'Clock the Schooner ariv'd, in which came Mr. Willero of the 80th, who brought us the disagreeable Acc't of a Party of about 70 Men being cut off at the Carrying Place at Niagara by a large Body of Indians, as also the loss of most of the Carriages & Bullocks, which undoubtedly prevented the Army from coming so soon as they otherwise wou'd have done.[67]

---

[67] The Affair here alluded to, is the Surprise and Massacre at the Devil's Hole, three Miles below Niagara Falls and on the Road then recently constructed from Fort Niagara to Fort Schlosser.

In September, twenty-five Wagons loaded with Provisions and Supplies for Detroit, and escorted by fifty Soldiers and their Officers, were ambuscaded at this Point by Seneca Indians, and with two exceptions the whole were killed, or driven off a frightful Precipice of a hundred and eighty feet. The Wagons and their Contents, with the ox Teams attached, were also hurled down the Chasm. William Stedman, the Contractor, narrowly escaped on horseback, and a drummer Boy, named Matthews, was caught by his Belt in the Limbs of a Tree, which broke the Force of his Fall, and he fell in the River

This

This Morning two Indians ariv'd from Point au Pain, with a Letter one Half wrote in Erse & the other in English, from Major Montcrife, giving an Account of the Batteau being cast away the seventh Instant at the Highlands beyond the said Point, where they lost 20 Boats & 50 Barrels of Provisions, with two Officers and a Surgeon drown'd, as also 70 Men,

near the Shore. He lived many Years afterwards near Queenston.

The following Letters, addressed to Sir William Johnson, relate to these Events on the Niagara Frontier:

NIAGARA, October 17th, 1763.

Sir: I have acquainted you of the sad Usage of the Savages to the Detachment of our Forces that turned out at lower Landing sometime past, where the Officers and Men were almost totally destroyed by them together with the King's working Cattle. Our Endeavor since in transporting Provisions to little Niagara, intended for Detroit, has been safely hurried on without their offering to disturb the Troops, but a few Days ago they killed a Man on the Race that dropped behind and scalped him. There are four Men more of the Flankers missed, all this without the Noise of a Gun. The Man that was scalped was between Starlings House and the Fort. They gave one fire at the Troops, Fort, or in the Air, uncertain, none being hurt or any Damage done. I have no more to acquaint you of but conclude Sir,

Your most obt Servt,

DE COUAGNE.

I forgot there were some Cattle sent here from Ontario since which we had up at Work and now they are all taken, stole by the Savages or straying in the Woods.

NIAGARA, Novr 11th, 1763.

Honble Sirs:

My last to you was to acquaint you of Daniel, &c., which I hope came safe to your Hands, since which a small Party went out from the Lower Landing to cut Wood, when a Body of Indians surrounded them & killd & scalped nine, one of which had his Head cut off within Sight of that Post, it is supposed that the Indian who did this Murder was wounded from the Fort, as he was seen go off lame with the Head in his Hand, all which happen'd on the fifth Instant.

I am in hopes of a Line from you the first Oppertunity wherein should be glad to know how Affairs go down the Country, I mean in regard to the Indians, &c.

I am Sir

Your obdt Humle Ser.

DE COUAGNE.

P. S. Sir here is two Sisters of Silver Heells at this Place who would be glad to know where he is. One of them is the lame one, the other is the young one. Neither of them dare go to the Castle.

1763. Nov.
& that all their Amunition, even the Mens Cartridges, were wet, & that they had wisely (not knowing our Circumstances) take na Resolution to turn back to Niagara. But from the Steps Major Gladwin had taken some Time before he was in a Situation to keep a tolerable Garrison here with Provision till the Month of May, & was in a good way of getting in enough till the Month of July, tho at the Expence of listening to the Demands of Peace the Indians had some Time before made, which notwithstanding he did not grant them. But put them off by telling them they must wait the Generals Pleasure, &c., as will appear from the Councils he held commencing about the Middle of October.

Dec. 5. This Day two Mohawks went from this by Land to Niagara with Letters; they came from Sandusky to this Place, having come with a Pass from Sir William Johnston when the Schooner was attack'd.

7 This Day Andrew the Huron got 6000 of Wampam & a good deal of Vermillion for the Voyage he made last to Fort Pitt. The Reason he took so much of these Commoditys was (as he s^d) to send the young Men of Sandusky to War against the Cherokees.

Mr. Jadeau told Major Gladwin that Lafontaine, an Inhabitant near his House, told the People that the Peace was not yet made, and that the Army was only come to save the 200 Men who departed from hence under the Command of Major Rogers to reinforce the Garrison at Quebec, he likewise took the Oppertunity of robbing the Merchants Batteaux that were brought in by the Indians when they were Drunk. He declar'd before Mon. Legrand that he had no more than 17 Yards of Chapmans Linnen, but Mr. Jadeau has found that he had 69 Yards. He broke open some Cases and stole a Box with silver Trinkets which the Indians afterwards got from him.   Prud'homme

Prud'homme Senr is a dangerous Man & animates the Savages. He underſtands their Language & told them not to go off, for if they did the Engliſh wou'd hang the French, and as for Proviſion they (the Savages) ſhould never want.

Michael Campeau told the Indians of two Barrels of Powder that were hid in Mr. Jadeaux Houſe, he likewiſe animated the Indians very much. Buxton, an Ottawa Chief lodg'd in his Houſe.

St Louis, an Officer of the Militia on the South Side of the River, ſaid, when Mr. Jadeau was in Council with the Hurons, engaging them not to ſtrike againſt the Engliſh, and gave them three Days to conſider of it. What! ſaid St Louis, four Days? it muſt be reſolv'd immediately; ſhall we let our Throats be cut for the Sake of the Engliſh? which ſignified, ſays Mr. Jadeau, that they ſhou'd rather ſtrike againſt the Engliſh than have the ill will of the Savages. He alſo ſaid it wou'd be a luckier thing for them to be with the Indians than the Engliſh. Another Time he told the Informer that he did not know what Dominion he was under.

This Day Mindoghquay (a Chief of the Sagginaws who was in the Fort the 16 June & aſk'd the Commandants Friendſhip, &c. as he had not enter'd into the War) ariv'd here with three Priſoners of the 60 Reg^t & one Sailor who was brought from the Chibbawas by one Beaulieu, and demanded the Continuation of the Commandants Friendſhip as he had promiſ'd in the Summer and gave him a Pipe of Peace & ſeveral large Belts. He was very well rec^d by the Commandant, as he had obey'd all his Orders from the firſt Time he came into the Fort, retiring with his People and not committing Hoſtillities as others did.

Laſt Night one Mackoy ariv'd here, having made his

1763.
Dec.
his Escape from the Puttawattamees about fifteen Ligues from this.

23 This Day Mr. Cicotte came to the Fort & told the Commandant that the Puttawamees intended to have brought the Man in that made his Escape two or three Days ago, and that they intended to come in hoping he wou'd pity them.

25 This Day Mr. Marsac inform'd us that he was asur'd that there was four or five of the Puttawattamys of Naintaws Family that intended to come and take a Scalp if possible, & desir'd the Commandant wou'd not let any body go out of the Fort, as some of the Merchants had straggled out in the Country some Days before.

27 This Day a Mohawk with one David Vanderhiden ariv'd Express from Niagara, which they left two Days after the Arival of Major Rogers, who was only six Days in going from the Detroit River to the Niagara.

31 This Day six Indians (originally of the Saqui[68] Nation) but at present of the Puttawattame came in with a Prisoner, & told the Commandant that they came in Hopes of receiving Mercy. That if they pretended entirely to excuse themselves from being concern'd in the late War they wou'd lye, but that did not signify, tho' they were living amongst the Puttawattamys they were not of that Nation, nor like them. That what offence they committed was through fear, as they had been oblig'd to ask liberty to live amongst them, having been oblig'd anciently to fly from other Nations, who had this Summer made War against their Brothers.

That they knew their Brothers the Putts had lied, & even come & spoke to their Brother & the same Day fir'd against his Fort, but begg'd he wou'd not

[68] Sacs.

think

think that they had an Inclination to do the fame, but that they fpoke from their Hearts, & came to offer one of his Flesh which had fallen to them by Lot, & to demand Mercy. That their Familys were ftarving. That they cou'd not come into the Fort in the Summer as the Fort was every Day on fire. That in fine they beg'd that they might live in the fame Friendfhip with their Brother that they had done when he took Poffeffion of the Country. That they hop'd, nor they wou'd not return Home fhamefully, fuppofe their Brothers did not liften to them, as what they did was their Duty & which they wou'd have done before but had not an Oppertunity. That notwithftanding they were Orphans & had no Chiefs, & knew that the other Indians wou'd laugh at them, & afk'd them how their Brother rec^d them at his Fort, they wou'd not be afham'd as it was their Duty they were doing, but neverthelefs expected their Brother wou'd take them in Compaffion.

The Prifoner being afk'd if he knew of their going from Home during the Summer faid they always ftay'd upon their Land the whole Time, except the two that was at Prefq Ifle where he was taken, & they never went abroad to War after he came amongft them, but once in the Summer came as far as Mr. Gamelins with him to give him up, & the other Nations told them not to go to the Fort as they wou'd be kill'd.

This Day Baby & Theata with four or five more of their Relations came in to wifh the Commandant a happy new Year, as is their Cuftom, whom he rec^d very well.

This Day fome of the Puttawattamys came to the Settlement & fent in Word by Mr. Cicotte that they wanted to come & fee their Brother the Command^t but Mr. Cecotte was told that the Command^t had nothing

1763. Dec.

1764. Jan. 10.

11

to

1764.
Jan.

to say to them & they wou'd do much better to stay at their hunting Ground.

12 This Day Vanderhiden & Jacob the Mohawk left this for Niagara with Letters.

13 This Day one of the Chibbaways came to the Settlement & sent for Mr. Labute to desire him to ask the Commandant leave to come in & see him, which Mr. Labute inform'd him of, but the Commandant told Mr. Labute not to make him any Answer, but let him, the Indian, return as he said he intended to do the next Morning.

14 This Day the Huron Chiefs (Baby, Theata & the Doctors Son) went to see the Command^t before they went away, & after talking of the Beginning of this Indian War, &c., Mr. St. Martin said it was sure that it took its rise from the Belts that pass'd amongst the Indians two Years ago, & that it was commenc'd in Consequence of the Succours that the Indians were made to believe they might expect from the Illinois. That one Sibbold that came here last Winter with his Wife from the Illinois, had told at Mr. Cuellierrey's that they might expect a French Army in this Spring, & that, that Report took rise from him. That the Day Capt. Campbelle & Lt. McDougal was detain'd by the Indians, Mr. Cuellierry accepted of their Offer of being made Commandant, if this Place was taken, to which he spoke to Mr. Cuellierry about and ask'd him if he knew what he was doing, to which Mr. Cuellierry told him I am almost distracted, they are like so many Dogs about me, to which Mr. St. Martin made him no Answer.

20 This Day two Michilimackinac Chiefs came in to see the Commandant, with one or two Washtinon Chiefs from the Grand River who were here in the Beginning of the Summer about fifteen Days, but went away

away. They brought in a Prisonner that was given to them by the Ottawas. — 1764. Feb. 1

This Day Wabagommigot, a Chief of the Toronto Indians who came in last Fall, return'd and ask'd a Certificate which the Commandant at that time promis'd him of his Behavior, which he gave him.

This Day some of the Saky's came in with the other Prisoner they promis'd to bring in the last Time they were in the Fort. — 14

This Evening Aron the Mohawk ariv'd from Fort Pitt with Letters from the General.

This Day some of the Ottawas of the Grand Rivierre ariv'd with a Prisoner whom they bought from some other Indians. — 20

This Morning the Gunner going his Rounds found a Brand's end that had been set up against the Magazine Door the Night before, which appear'd to have been on fire but was gone out. — Mar. 12

This Day a Cow belonging to one Moran came in from the Woods with ten Arrows sticking in her, which were suppos'd to be shot by some Party of Indians that was lying about the Fort. — 14

This Day two or three Frenchmen saw a small Party of Indians back of the Fort going loaded with Meat, which must be the Cattle that was kill'd & missing for two or three Days past. — 18

There has been a Party of Puttawattamys in the Settlement every Night since the 15th Instant.

This Day the Commanding Officer was inform'd that one Mintiwaby, an Ottawa Chief of the Grand River, was to come in under a Pretence of Trade & endeavour to surprize him & put all the Officers to Death. M. Informer. — 21

This Day two Saky's came in and inform'd the Commandant that the Chibbaways of the Isles about Michilimackinac — 23

1764. March. Michilimackinac had fent Belts this Winter to their Nation, to the Folavin & Puante, to ftrike againft us this Spring, but they wou'd not receive them. That Waffong & Mafhoquife had tried to prevent that Party from coming from towards St. Jofeph that was here fome Time ago, but they wou'd not be advif'd, they faid they had loft a Man laft Year & they wou'd have Revenge. That if they had known it fooner they wou'd have advif'd us of it before they arriv'd, but they [knew] nothing of it till they were gone.

That the Delawares & Shawanys had fent Belts during the Winter towards St. Jofeph & La Bay to invite the Nations thereabout to take up Arms againft us in the Spring.

27 This Day France Ruiard fet off with two other Frenchmen Exprefs to Niagara.

29 This Day the Commandant being inform'd that there was thirteen Indians in the Woods behind the Settlement, who were come to make War, fent out a Party commanded by Lt. M'Dougal of twenty Men to try to fall upon them by furprize; they fet off a little after Dark & went through the Fields guided by a Frenchman to the Place where their Fire had been feen, but not finding them there, they return'd towards a Houfe that they had been at the Night before, & fell in with them on their way, but the Indians finding they were difcover'd run off, after receiving the Fire of the moft of the Party, but it was fo dark that they cou'd not fee to ajuft their Firelocks & don't know whether they kill'd any or no.

30 This Day an Indian was feen at the Edge of the Woods behind the Fort.

April 12 This Morning at ten o'Clock the Schooner fail'd for Niagara, in which were fent the two French Prifoners, as the Commandant was inform'd that the Indians

dians had said they shou'd not long be Prisoners, and as it was imagin'd if any thing was intended by them, it was through the Influence of the Friends of these two.

1764.
April.

Last Night at about 8 o'Clock [a] Prisoner came in from Sagginaw who reported that the Day before he came away the Indians kill'd and eat a young Girl they had Prisoner & that he was to been kill'd that Day himself, but they sent him out to bring in some Wood & he run off; he was eight Days a coming, but when he was ask'd if he was hungry he said no, that for the first two or three Days he was fainty, but since he found no great alteration though he had not eat a mouthfull of any thing the whole eight Days.

15

This Day Andrew a Huron & two others from Sandusky brought in one Mr. Prentice whom they had Prisoner since last May. They told the Commandant they were not sent by any Chief, but as he (the one that spoke) looked upon Mr. Prentice as his real Brother, he told him in the Winter he wou'd bring him in, for he chose to see him content at this Place than discontent with him, which was the Reason he brought him in. But he imagined that Mr. Prentice cou'd have other no Reason for leaving them, than because he cou'd not get Bread amongst them.

27

Mr. Prentice said that he never wanted for any thing they had during the whole Winter, & notwithstanding this Man never got any of the Plunder that the Indians took from him when they made him Prisoner, he gave him two Packs of Beaver & twenty Dollars when he gave him up.

This Day a four in the Afternoon the Commandant thought he heard a Cannon down the River & fir'd another.

28

This Morning at Half past four Mr. Jadeau ariv'd from the Vessel with Letters and inform'd us that they fir'd

29

1764.
April.

fir'd a Gun from the Veſſel about the Time the Commandant thought he heard one.

This Afternoon eight Huron Chiefs & two or three young Men came to ſpeak to the Commandant. Theata ſpeaks:

My Brother, we beg you may take Pity upon us & hear us, that the Words we now ſay may be as a Carpet for your Succeſſor to walk upon.

Brother, we beg you to have Pity upon us and be aſſured of our good Intentions, as we have moſt faithfully repented of all the Ill we may have done, & do ſincerely promiſe never to be guilty of any bad Thing for the Future, having thrown ourſelves into the Hands of God, if any Evil happens to us it muſt be from him, as you may be perſuaded let the Earth turn how it will, we ſhall never be adviſ'd to a bad Thing again.

This, Brother, we beg you will inform the General of the firſt Oppertunity. Gave a large white Belt.

Another Chief got up with a ſtring of Wampum and ſaid:

Brother, ever ſince the Engliſh have had Poſſeſſion of this Place we have been uſ'd very tenderly, agreeable to the Promiſe you made us when you firſt came here, for which Reaſon we hope our Brother will grant us the ſmall favour we are going to aſk.

Brother, as Wood & Bark is very unhandy to us at our old Village we hope you will give us leave to make a new one up a ſmall Creek near the Bottom of the Settlement, where every thing will be more convenient. Granted.

Brother, when you firſt came here you told us you had conquer'd our Father & ſent him over the Great Lake, & that all that then belong'd to him was yours, but that we ſhou'd remain in our former Poſſeſſions

and

and be allowed the Jesuist, and now as we are going to alter our Village we hope you will not prevent him going with us. Gave a string of Wampum. 1764. May.

Granted by the Commandant.

This Evening four Indians sent by Sir William Johnston ariv'd here with a Speech to the Nations hereabout. 6

This Day we were inform'd by Mr. Jadeau that one Rainbeau & his Family with one L'esperence went off to the Illinois. 8

This Morning at Half past six the Schooner sail'd for Niagara, in which went Peter & the three other Indians that came here with a Speech from Sir William Johnson. 15

This Afternoon some of the Saky's came in and inform'd us that one Lagesse and four other Puttawattamees were some where in the Woods near the Fort, and intended to try to take a Scalp.

This Morning the Schooner anchor'd off the Fort after having been kept at the Mouth of the River three Days with contrary Winds. June 2.

This Morning a Band of Chippawas who were at the Gross Point dividing themselves amongst the Inhabitants, ask'd at several Places for Provision, &c., one of them being refus'd a Cock by a Farmer had a Dispute with him, & because he wou'd not let him have it fir'd at him and shot him through the Body.

This Day the Band of Chippewas who fir'd at the Frenchman headed by a Chief they call'd the Great Spoon, came with a Belt & Pipe to Mr. Marsack, telling him they were very sorry for what they had done, which Belt & Pipe he brought to the Commandant next Day with a Prisoner they had sold him who was taken at Presq'Isle. The Man they fir'd at died of his Wounds last Night. 3

They

1764.
June.

They then sent in a Frenchman to tell the Commandant they had always been Fools, but that their Senses were now come to them and beg'd he might receive them, to which he sent them Word that when they return'd the Goods that Mr. Marsac gave them for the Prisoner & brought in the rest as they had promis'd the Fall before, he wou'd see them, but not till then.

4 Being his Majesties Birthday, the Garrison was under Arms at 1 o'Clock & fir'd three Volleys with three Discharges of the Cannon in the Fort & one of those in the Schooner; after which His Majesties Health was drunk upon the Parade by all the Officers & several Frenchmen who were ask'd there by the Commandant who afterwards din'd & sup'd with all the Officers of the Garrison together. At nine at Night almost the whole Town was eluminated.

6 Mr. Marsack after going to the Priests came in haste to the Commandant to tell him that the Indians had return'd him his Merchandise that he had given for the Prisoner two or three Days before, & wanted to come in. To which the Commandant sent the same Answer as he had done two or three Days before, that when they brought in all the rest of the Prisoners & their Chiefs came in a proper Manner, he wou'd receive them.

7 This Morning Mr. Marsack came in and inform'd the Commandant that there was a small Band of Chippawas from beyond Saggina to come in, who came with a Belt & Pipe of Peace, and after they had smok'd & told the Commandant they were come to open a new Road between him & their Nation, as the old one had been shut up for some Time; he enquir'd what they were & who sent them, & found that they were from the same Place & Village with those that sold the Prisoner to Marsack a few Days before, and had no Authority

thority for coming nor had no Chief with them, but
they were Part of a Party that came to the Settlement
about seven or eight Days before, consisting of forty
Men, who told the Inhabitants they did not come to
make Peace but to make War. All which they could
not deny. The Commandant then took a String &
Wampum & told them to take that to their Chiefs &
tell them when they brought in the other Prisoner they
had in Possession & came & ask'd Peace in a proper
Manner he wou'd hear them, and until then one of
them must stay with him, as perhaps they might to sell
the rest, & at the same Time told them to tell their
Chiefs if any thing happen'd to his People amongst
them, he knew what to do with those he had. When
they saw this a second offer'd to stay to keep the first
one Company; he is a Son of

The Coll. then ask'd them if he had three or four of
his Nation Prisoners, & wou'd send two or three of his
People to their Village wheather they would not keep
them, to which they said they wou'd. Then said he
you wou'd undoubtedly think me a Fool to let you all
go when you have Prisoners of mine. They then s'd
perhaps it wou'd be hard for them to get those Prisoners, as they did not belong to their Relations. Yes,
but said the Commandant, if they have an inclination
for Peace as you told me a few Minutes ago, they will
bring them in without any Difficulty. They then s'd
they were a little Band of six or seven, every one for
himself; then s^d the Interpreter how came you here to
make a new Road for the whole Nation and fight in
alliance with them all last Summer; to which they
hung their Heads & cou'd not say any thing.

10 This Day the Schooner sail'd with a head Wind for
Niagara and got below the Hurons Point.

11 This Day the Schooner return'd the Wind being
fresh

1764. June.

fresh ahead, and as Teata the Indian Chief ariv'd at their Village with Aron & two other Mohawks who came into the Fort and gave the following Intelligence annex'd in two Sheets of Paper:

DETROIT, June 9th 1764.

This Day a small Party of Puttawattamees ariv'd here who inform'd, that an Indian was come from the Illinois to St. Josephs who inform'd them that he was in Council with Pondiac there.

That Mr. Deneyon told him he was glad to see him & hoped that his Senses were come to him.

Pondiac then took a large Belt and laid it before him saying, my Father the Reason of my Journey is to get you and all your Allies to joyn with me to go against the English, upon which Deneyon took the the Belt & told him, your Speech much surprizes me, as I doubt not but you have receiv'd my Message wherein I inform'd you that the French and English were but one, then return'd the Belt. Pondiac took the Belt again and importun'd Mr. Deneyon on the same Subject. At last Mr. Deneyon grew angry & kick'd it from him, asking him if he had not already heard what he s'd to him. He then address'd himself to the Illinois Indians & told them they saw him that Day in the Fort, but perhaps they wou'd see their Brothers the English the next, and exhorted them to live in amity with them, which he made no doubt of as their Sentiments were very good.

Pondiac then ask'd for Rum & Deneyon gave him a small Barrel, which he took to one of the Illinois Villages & with a red Belt exhorted them to sing the War Song with him, which some of them did, but were sorry for it when they were Sober. The Indian that brought this Account says that before he left the Illinois he saw three English Officers who were sent on before,

before, the Army being but a little way behind with a large Body of Indians.

DETROIT, June 10th 1764.

This Day Teata a Wiandott Chief ariv'd here from Sandufky, where he had been to carry Sir William Johnfon's Speech, who fays that after he deliver'd it and left it to their deliberation, the great Chief Bigg Jaco got up and thank'd him for the Trouble he had been at to bring it, and immediately the whole went out. After he had deliver'd the Speech he fays he advif'd them to come to their Senfes, but in cafe they did not it was their Affair. Aron fays they made great Game of Teata on faying fo to them.

Four Days after, they came back and afk'd Teata to come and hear what they had to fay in Anfwer. The firft Belt they gave him was a Repetition of Sir Williams Speech. Then they took another faying, Sir William afks the Reafon why we ftruck againft the Englifh, we think he ought to know better than any body; yes, faid they, it is Sir William that ought to know, but fince the Senecas have made Peace with him & the Englifh, tell him it was them that firft embroil'd the Earth, & were the firft Caufe of what has been done. Gave the Belt.

They then took another Belt & faid, Sir William & the Six Nations want that we fhould own our Folly & find words to excufe ourfelves that we may be again fet right. You'll tell him by this Belt, which you are charg'd to deliver to him, that for what is paft, its paft, that we have yet done no Harm fince laft Summer, we have kept our young Men quiet, for which Reafon we think the Breach may be eafily mended; and tell him alfo we fhall keep them quiet this Summer, when we think we fhall be reconcil'd.

The two Mohawks who are come with Teata, fay that

1764.
June.
that they were told by the Hurons of Sandusky, that they wou'd not tell Teata the Result of a Council they had had with the Shawanies, which was that they were to try to take Fort Pitt by Treachery, & if they fail'd there were to go ag^t the Inhabitants on the Frontiers. That the Onondagoes that Sir William sent against the Shawanies came to one of their Villages, where they were ask'd what they came for, they said we come to scalp you; then one Kayoughshoutong said here, take these, giving them two old Scalps that he had newly painted, go home & tell Sir William you have scalp'd some Shawanies. Upon which they return'd; that the above mentioned Indian was the Cause of their not striking against the Shawanies. But it was not so with the Tuscroras, for they lost three Men.

One of them further says that before he left the Delaware Towns he saw thirty small Partys go out who were all intended to go to our Frontiers. They both say, also, that the Hurons at Sandusky laugh'd at Teata behind his Back, & call'd him a Fool for believing what Sir William sayd and bringing such a Message.

That tho' he said they wou'd be Friends, it can never be until all the English, except Traders go from this Place, meaning Detroit, & then we believe we shall agree. That their God tells them they must make War & Peace for seven Years, at the End of which by force of Treachery during that Time, all the English will be drove away & then they will have Peace and not till then.

That the Delawares & Shawanies and Hurons of Sandusky all say the English are Fools, that they can make Friends with us when they please, and next Day tomahawk us. That the English allways told them they had as many Men as there was Leaves on the Trees, but wee look upon one Indian as good as a thousand of them, and notwithstanding we are but Mice in comparison to them, we will bite as much as they can. The two Mohawks father says that the Hurons at Sandusky told them they were very sorry that Sir William was coming here, as they imagin'd by that he wanted to leave his Bones here.

They also say that while they were at the Shawanie Village the French from the Mississippi sent them a Present of Powder, of which he saw three Barrels.

Mr. St. Martin, Interpreter, told Coll. Gladwin that Hurons of this Place told him many Times that if a Peace was made with the Delawares, Shawanies & Hurons of Sandusky, that it would not be good, nor lasting.

The Schooner sail'd at about four in the Afternoon, and run out of Sight from the Fort before dark.

This Day Teata & several Hurons came to the Fort & ask'd the Commandant if they might not go once more to the Hurons of Sandusky, as perhaps tho' their Ears had always been stop'd till now yet they might be open at present.

The Commandant told them they might do as they pleas'd, that he had sent their Answer to Sir William Johnson with their Belts, that it was not intended to force a Peace down the Throats of the Indians, nor was it intended for any but those who had sincerely repented of what they had done, & was realy resolv'd to remain our Friends for the Future. That in his opinion they ought not to go, as they only laugh'd at the Message taken by Teata, & him for carrying it.

This Day a Huron promis'd to set off with his little Band of about twelve to bring in some Delaware or Shawany Scalps.

This Day Wabagommigot came in with some Chippawas & two Prisoners & after repeating a good deal of

1763.
June.
of what pass'd in Council last Fall, said that as the Commandant had desir'd him several Times go to his old Village & to see him yet here, would perhaps make him think that he had no Intention to do what he had order'd him, but the Reason was, that he had been trying to get all the Prisoners that was among his Nation & to gather his Band together, which he had now almost affect'd; he did not speak for the whole Nation, but for those who were with him who had heartily repented of what they had done & hop'd to be receiv'd as he himself was. That there were some whom he advertised of what he (the Commandant) had told him with regard to their quick Repentance & of the Council that was to be held at Niagara, but since they did not come in it was their Affair. He then ask'd for the two Prisoners, saying it was nothing, but this War, that sepperated him from the rest of the Nation, who were neverthelefs part of his Body, for which Reason hop'd they wou'd be given up, as he then wip'd away all the Blood that had been spilt with the two Prisoners he brought in. That he hop'd in going home to his old Village he might not hear it said that things went ill at the Detroit because Wabigommigot was refus'd that Favour. That since the Malefactors he then spoke for (meaning People he had with him) were come to their Senses, & heartily repented of what they had done, & as they were set on by the Six Nations, hop'd they wou'd be forgiven & no more thought of it.

The Commandant then ask'd him if he came in the Name of the whole Nation, he s'd no, but in Part. Then s'd he if you'l take my Advice you'l go to Niagara before the Council is over & make Peace for yourself & Band; you have no Time to lose as it will be over in twelve Days. And as to the Prisoners I shall

shall keep them till I get all mine in, as they belong to a Band that has not as yet ask'd for Peace nor brought in all my flesh. As to what he (Wabbigomigot) might hear of things going ill here, nothing cou'd go ill with us, but if any body did any thing that they ought not to do, it wou'd be them that wou'd suffer; that we were out of their Power. He then repeated to him that it was necessary he shou'd be at Niagara at the Council, for which Purpose he wou'd give me a Receipt, that he had deliver'd two Prisoners, &c.; that the Time was short & the sooner he went off the better.

The Frenchman that danc'd the War Dance at Sandusky this Spring with the Indians is named Thefault.

This Day Mindockquay came in with about 70 of his People & about thirty Chibbaways who brought in two Prisoners, being the last they had amongst them, for whom the Commandant gave them the two Indians he detain'd some Time ago.

The Puttawattamess after all the Promises did not go to Niagara, nor Wabbigomigot neither.

This Day the Schooner Victory return'd from Niagara with another new Schooner, the Boston.

This Evening at about ten o'Clock one Reaume, a Frenchman, ariv'd from Michilimackinac with 18 Cannoes of Savages who came from the Bay the 3d June to go to Montreal, but when they ariv'd at Michilimackinac they were inform'd that ten Cannoes that were going there and an Express with a Belt informing them that they shou'd go to Niagara where they wou'd meet a great English Chief, upon which they took their Route this way, & several Cannoes from the Nations thereabouts went across Lake Huron by way of Lake Ontario. They brought four Englishmen

1764.
July.

men with them with all their Packs, who had been amongſt them ſince laſt Spring was a Year.

3   This Day ſome of greateſt of the Huron Chiefs of Sanduſky came in with five Priſoners to throw themſelves at the Commandants Feet, as they ſaid, and after telling him that what they had done was in conſequence of what Meſſages and Lyes the Ottawas ſent them, ſaid that if he wou'd have pity on them, he wou'd ſee they were ſincere, as his Will was theirs.

The Commandant told them the only way they had to get a Peace, and if they did not benefit of what he ſaid, it was their Affair. He gave them a Certificate that they had deliver'd five Priſoner and that they had aſk'd for Peace, which they ſaid they wou'd take to Niagara with all the reſt of the Priſoners they had amongſt them.

This Afternoon the Michilimackinack Chiefs & Folle Avoines came in told the Commandant they came to take him by the Hand & let him know they were glad to ſee him, & wou'd come to morrow to ſpeake to him.

4   This Morning the above Indians came in to the Amount of fifty & told the Commandant that they, the Renards, the Sieus, the Saky's, Puants & Pians, were one Body & one Heart, and that, that Heart was as well intentioned as it had always been; that he 'knew himſelf from their Behavior laſt Year, that their & ours cou'd be but one; that they were invited by the General laſt Year to come to Montreal this Spring, but that when they were aſſembled at Michilimacinac they received a Belt from him, telling them that he ſtop'd up the Paſſage that way as the Small Pox was amongſt his People which they might catch & carry Home to the Deſtruction of their Wifes & Children, but if they wou'd go to Niagara they wou'd find all they

they were in need of, for which Reason they beg'd the Rivers & Lakes might be open to them as usual, shewing the Belt they receiv'd.

This Day some of the Hurons of this Village came in with the Chiefs of Hurons of Sandusky who were in the Day before yesterday & brought with them some Hurons that ariv'd the Day before to join their old Village & brought in five Prisoners, whom they said they wou'd not have brought in till their Chiefs return'd from Niagara,[60] had it not been to encourage those of Sandusky to do the same, as the Commandant knew he was always sure of them, but nevertheless, tho they had, had some of them since they suck'd, yet that the Chiefs from Sandusky might be witness of their good Intentions they brought them in sooner than they promis'd.

The Huron that went to strike against the Delawares & Shawanies return'd this day without doing any thing.

This Day Mr. Jadeau in repeating to the Commandant somethings that had pass'd between him and one Clermont (who had been sent with a Letter to the Illinois, but went no further than where the Ottawas are in the Miamee River) said that Clermont told him, you do very well in serving the English, but I have my Reasons for what I do, and you will soon be oblig'd to save yourself in the Fort. Another thing said he I'll tell you that you don't know, the English are all

---

[60] These Chiefs had gone to Niagara to hold a Treaty with Sir William Johnson. The Treaty was signed July 18, 1764, and bound the Hurons to deliver up all Prisoners, Deserters and Negroes or other Slaves among them; to maintain a friendly Alliance and to do their utmost to preserve His Britannic Majesty's Interests and promote Peace among the western Tribes. They were promised Pardon for all past Misdeeds, and a free, fair and open Privilege of Trade.—*N. Y. Col. Hist.*, vii, 650.

defeated

1764.
July.
defeated in the Mississippi and there will be fourteen hundred Men soon here, and all the Indians that are going to Niagara have agreed with the Ottawas to return with the Army, & the Ottawas are to meet them on the Lake & try to destroy them. That Merchandize & Powder was in the greatest plenty at the Miamee River.

That one Borgard who came from St. Josephs brought them a Barrel of Powder & some Corn, Flour, &c. That there was one Clincincourt a French Officer, who was sent by Mr. Deneyon with Letters for the Commandant here, was stop'd by the Ottawas, where they keep him, neither giving him Liberty to return nor come forward.

This Afternoon a Saggina Indian who had been sent by his Brother, as he said, to the Miamee River to see what pass'd came in and inform'd that while he was there a French Officer ariv'd there from the Illinois who was coming here with Letters, but the Ottawas stop'd him & took his Letters from him, and sent for Cusieres Son to read them. After which one of the Ottawa Chiefs told him that Cuessiere had told them that it was a Letter from their Father the French King, who desir'd his Brothers the English to make haste & go away from this Place, for he was coming in a great Body & had a great many of his Children with him, whose Inclination he was not Master of, & wou'd not answer for what harm they might do. The Officer they keep there & will neither let him go back or forward.

10 This Day Part of the four following Nations ariv'd here, the Saky's, the Renards, the Puants, and the Saulteux of Lake Superior, some of whom came from the Forks of the Mississippi (and from all Appearance, and what they said) they came in Expectation of getting Rum. They were upwards of two Months a coming;

coming; they brought upwards of sixty Packs of Beaver.

1764. July.

This Day at 2 o'Clock the two Schooners left this for the east End of Lake Erie. — 12

This Day Mr. Clinencourt ariv'd from the Miamee, who had been detain'd by the Ottawas. — 13

This Day at about 4 o'Clock in the Afternoon the Schooner Gladwin ariv'd from Niagara. — 14

This Day Waſſong, a Chief of the Chibbaways came in with a Prisoner that he had promiſ'd to bring in, in the Winter, but who had got Frost bit and was not able to come. After telling that he was not concern'd in the Beginning of the Insurrection and asking Pardon in a most submissive Manner said: he did not pretend to excuse himself, that as he had told Mr. LaBute in the Spring he would behave as a Dog that had offended his Master, that if he was puniſh'd & was miserable he had no body to blame but himself, and wou'd still fawn till he was taken into Favour again, for that he was as a Dog that had been beaten and was running round his Master with Fear & Respect, and wou'd continue till he was pardonned, having since last Fall resolv'd to die rather than disobey his Brothers Will. And asked what were the most salutary Means to be well received by the General, since he had not been inform'd that he shou'd have gone to Niagara. At the same Time begging Mercy in the most submissive Manner and said if his Brother cou'd see the Distress their Familys were in, he wou'd have Pity upon them & think they were puniſh'd enough. — 21

The Commandant told him the Reason of the Insurrection was because they had something then in their Power which they wou'd never have again, for if they had they wou'd act the same Part over again.

In the Evening we were inform'd that the Sloop Royal — 22

1763.
July.
Royal Charlotte was aground on this Side [of] the Whitewood; at 2 in the Morning a Detachment was sent with four Batteaux to lighten her & get her off, which they did next Day by four in the Afternoon, and the 24th she ariv'd here.

27　　The Schooner Boston arived from Niagara.

29　　This Morning at 11 o'Clock the Sloop Charlotte set Sail for Niagara with Wind at N. W.

In the Afternoon Manitoo, an Ottawa Chief, with five other Ottawas, four of whome were from the Miamee River, came in with three Prisoners. The Speaker said that God had been speaking with him a great deal this last Winter, & that what he y^n said was the Sentiments of all the Chiefs, and beg'd to be pitied & heard. He then beg'd Pardon for what they had done in a most submissive Manner; the Reason of their beginning he did not know, but he that set them on (Pondiac) was return'd from the Illinois, but was no more heard by any body in the Nation; that God had told him he had done wrong, that he had made this Earth for them & us to live quietly together in, & that Pondiac the Causer of its being disturbed wou'd not die but wou'd burn in Hell eternally, as all those wou'd do who did not follow the Advice & obey the Will of their Brother. God also told him he must not lie, steal, nor covet another Mans Wife, all which Commands they would strictly adhere to for the Future, and that their Brother should see that what they said was true & sincere in the End, & hop'd he wou'd have Pity upon them. That they wou'd return to Sandusky to where their Corn was planted, and after it was gather'd wou'd come and ask'd Liberty to stay there another Year, and that after that if their Brother was convinc'd of their Sincerity they hop'd he wou'd give them Liberty to come & settle their antient Village.

The

The Commandant told them if they did not know the
Reason of their beginning he would tell them. The
Reason was, said he, that you had at that Time something in your Power that you will never have again,
for if you had I am sure you would make the same
Use of it you have already done, but if you bring in
all those who set you on, black or white, I shall tell
the General what you say, and it may be a Step toward
your getting Peace, but it does not look as if you were
very sincere, since this is the first of your Appearance.
But I suppose the Reason of your coming is because
your vain Hopes of an Army from the Illinois is
vanish'd & you see yourselves without Succour.

To which the Speaker said the Reproaches their
Brother made them were very just, but it was not the
Chiefs Fault that they did not come sooner, but his,
for God had told him to remain quiet & not mind any
more bad Belts for that he wou'd be forgiven when
they prostrated themselves before their Brother. And
as a Proof of their sincerity they wou'd go and endeavour to bring in the People he mentioned.

This Day the Schooner Victory ariv'd from Niagara
loaded with Baggage for the 17th; she left Niagara
the 20th, but had very bad Weather. She sprung her
Bowsprit and broke her Gaft.

Yesterday some of the Hurons came to dance before
the Commandants Door, & after they had done were
going away, when one of them who stay'd a little behind was stop'd by a Royal American near Mr. St.
Martins House, where he coax'd him in and murder'd
him as it appears from all the Circumstances of the
Affair; the Soldier was immediately put in Irons, and
the Commandant was going to send for the Chiefs,
when two of them came into the Fort, having been inform'd of it by two other Indians who stay'd behind a
little

1764.
July.
little Time with him that was murder'd, who tho they did not see the Stroke, was near enough to hear it, as was also a Corporal of the Artillery.

Aug. 5   This Day *the little Chief* came in and inform'd Mr. Labute that Seckaho had deceived the Commandant, that he was gone back to the Miamee River to where his Corn was, & that after it was ripe, he heard that Seckaho & what People of his Band would go with him, with those of Pondiacs Band were going off to the Illinois.

8   This Day Mintiwaby from Saggina came in with six or seven of Mindochquays Band, and brought a Prisoner that he had had all the Winter, who Mindochquay told the Commandant in the Spring, would have then been brought in, but Mintiwaby was gone to Michilimackinac. He said that the Chippewas at Shaguomigan had sent a Pipe to Mindochquays Band, & desir'd him to send it to Machoquish who wou'd send it to the Shawnies & Delawares with the following Answer, to the Invitation they gave them to join with them to strike against the English last Fall as Mochoquish had sent the Belt from the Sha. & Dele. namely, That they had no Complaints against their Brothers the English, & they had a greater Regard for their Wives, Children & young Men, than to enter into so bad a Thing.

10   This Afternoon at about four o'Clock, the Sloop Charlotte & Schooner Gladwin ariv'd here, Commodore Loring & Capt. Grant came in the former.

11   This Day Mashoquish, a Puttawattamy Chief, sent in a Turkey & some Venison & desir'd the Commandant would except of it, as he was unworthy of coming into the Fort, but nevertheless he & the Chiefs of the Puttawattamees of St. Josephs were getting the Prisoners they had together to bring them in, in two or three

three Days in cafe they would be received. And that if the Commandant had not a Mind to ftarve him, he beg'd he wou'd fend him two or three Charges of Powder and Ball.

1764.
Aug.

This Day *the little Chief* told Mr. Labute that Pondiac continued his ufual Difcourfe & was as ill intentioned as ever; that he had tried to animate all the Nations about here, by telling them that there was abfolutely a French Army on the way here, from the Illinois, but that the Commandant there could not come with them untill he had received a Letter from their Father, which he expected every Day. That Seckaho had fent three young Men on to the Poft Vincent[69] to meet them & bring him News.

12

This Morning a Puttawattamy came to the Settlement & fent for Mr. Labute, to whome he told that he was fent by one of their Chiefs to put his Brother upon his Guard, as the Shawanees & Delawares were come to join Pondiac at the Miamee River, to come and attack this Place, that they were not yet arived, but one of their Chiefs had feen fome Runners that came before to inform they were coming.

14

Mr. Labute was further inform'd by the little Chief of the Chibbaways that Pondiac had much threatened the Ottawa Chiefs who brought in fome Prifoners a little Time ago & told them that his Father was on his way March & as foon as he came he would have them all hang'd that tried to make up a Thing that he (Pondiac) had begun.

The Sloop fail'd for Niagara.

15

The Schooner Bofton ariv'd in the Mouth of the River from Niagara.

17

This Day at about one o'Clock the Schooner Glad-

19

---

[69] Now Vincennes, on the Wa- bafh in Indiana.

win

1764.
Aug.

win fail'd for Niagara. At three o'Clock Mr. Marfack came in and inform'd that he had been told by fome Indians that fome of the Hurons of Sandufky were gone to meet the Army with the Belts that were fent them by the Six Nations to take up the Hatchet againft the Englifh, for that they might at leaft let the Englifh fight their own Battles, which they would tell them when they met them & defire them to return by the fame Belts that they defired them to take up the Hatchet. That they were all ready to receive the Englifh at Lake Sandufky.

20 This Morning Mr. Campeau came in & inform'd that he had overheard an Ottawa & two Folsavoines fpeaking about the Army, & the Ottawa afk'd where they were & which way they were coming; the others told him they were coming on the fouth Side of the Lake. What to do? f'd the Ottawa. To cut off the Hurons at Sandufky, f'd the others. O, faid the Ottawa, they are all ready to meet them, the Miamees & all the Puttawattamys are affembled there, & they have fent their Wives & Children back in the Woods, & have prepared their young Corn & Squafhes on purpofe that they may keep. That a Chibbaway was foon after fent off as he imagined to go to the Miamee.

Mr. M'Dougal was told this Morning by an Indian that most of the Chibbaways & all the Puttawattamys were on the Miamee River with the Ottawas & Miamees, and a good many other Indians.

This Day & laft Night all the Ottawas & Folsavoines, &c., that came from Michilimackinac this Spring to go to Niagara return'd.

21 This Afternoon the Schooner Bofton ariv'd. Laft Night Mr. Jadeau came with a Letter informing us that the Schooner Gladwin was aground near Ifle Bois Bland

Pontiac's Siege of Detroit.

Bland[70] upon which Mr. Grant was sent off with some Men to get her off. *1764. Aug.*

This Night Mr. Colville, one of the Masters of the Vessels, came up to get a Grapling and some other things for the Schooner Gladwin, as she had lost her Anchors in getting off.

Commodore Loring left this in the Barge to go on board the Schooner Boston at the Mouth of the River, for Niagara. *24*

This Afternoon the Army ariv'd under the Command of Coll. Broadstreet.[71] *27*

A Party of Men were sent to cut Timber upon Isle Cochon for Barracks, &c. *29*

All the Inhabitants were ordered to appear at nine next Morning from fifteen Years old upwards to renew their Oaths of Allegiance, which ran in the Terms following.[72]

This Morning the Schooner Victory sail'd for Niagara, with Coll. Gladwin on board. *31*

This Evening the Hurons came to see the new Commandant, and after their usual Compliments gave him the Name of the little Deer.

This Afternoon fifty-five Ottawas, including Women & Children, ariv'd here according to their Promise *Sept. 2*

---

[70] Isle Bois Blanc, or White-wood Island, lies in Front of Amherstburgh, on the Canadian Side of the Channel and 18 Miles below Detroit. It is a little over a Mile in length, and to one descending it is the last Island on the left-hand Side before entering Lake Erie.

[71] Col. John Bradstreet had served with great Reputation in the Wars with France in America. He received a Commission as Colonel in Feb. 1762, and held at this Time the Office of Quarter-Master General. In 1772 he was promoted to the Rank of Major-General. He died at New York, Sept. 25, 1774, aged 63 Years. *Mass. Hist. Coll.; Army Lists; Dunlop's Hist. N.Y.; Parkman's Pontiac.*

[72] A Blank here occurs in the MSS.

made

1764. Sept.

3 — made to Coll. Broadſtreet, when he left the Miamee River.

This Morning the Ottawas came to Coll. Broadſtreet to give him their Hands & told him they only came to tell him that the Chibbeways & Puttawattamys were to come in next Day & then they would ſpeake for the Whole. But without their ſaying any thing about making Peace, he told them that *if they were as well inclined for it as him* there would be one juſt at the Mouth of the Miſſiſſippi.

5 This Day a Council was held with the Ottawas and Chippawas, the Puttawattamees not having come in.

6 This Day the Puttawattamees ariv'd.

7 This Day the Ottawas, Chippawas, Puttawattamees, Miamees & Hurons ſign'd the Articles of Peace given them by Coll. Broadſtreet, the Contents of which is in the Book of Councils. Yeſterday the Sloop Charlotte, the Schooner Boſton & Schooner Gladwin enter'd the River.

10 This Day the Schooner Victory ariv'd from Niagara.

11 This Morning the Schooner Gladwin ſail'd for Michilimackinac.

13 This Morning Mr. Crofton arived from Niagara in a Batteaux with Deſpatches for Coll. Bradſtreet.

This Afternoon News came by Indians, that the Shawanies & Delawares would not make Peace, & that they had detain'd Mr Paulie & the People with him, & were reſolv'd to defend themſelves.

14 This Morning at 8 o'Clock the Army embark'd to go to Sanduſky.

16 This Morning the Schooner Victory ſet ſail for Sanduſky, where ſhe was to wait Coll. Bradſtreets Orders.

17 This Morning the Sloop ſail'd for Niagara.

This Evening Capt. Morris ariv'd here, having been ſent by Coll. Bradſtreet to try to go to the Illinois, but

Pontiac's Siege of Detroit.

but was ſtop'd by the Miamees who were going to burn him.   1764. Sept.

This Morning an Expreſs was ſent to overtake Coll. Bradſtreets with Letters from Coll. Cambell & Captain Morris.   18

The Schooner Victory return'd from Sanduſky for Proviſion; in which came Mr. Cheppoton with Orders from Coll. Bradſtreet.   27

This Morning the Schooner Boſton arived after laying four Days in the River with contrary Winds.   Oct. 6

This Morning Minecheſne arived from Coll. Bradſtreet with ſome Indians, who brought Orders for Mr. Cheppaton to ſpare no Expenſe in getting ſome Indians of each Nation to take up the Hatchet againſt the Shawanys & Delawares & for Minecheſne to bring the *little* Chief of the Chippawas in particular. As alſo Orders to Coll. Campbell to ſpeak to the Hurons to ſend as many of their People as poſſible; his Speech & Anſwer to it is in the Book of Councils of this Date.   8

This Morning the Schooner Boſton ſail'd for Fort Erie.

This Morning Mr. Cheppaton left this for Sanduſky with thirteen Indians, who had taken up the Hatchet againſt the Shawanies & Delawares.   11

This Morning Mini Cheſne left this with eight Indians who had taken up the Hatchet againſt the Delawares & Shawanies.   12

This Day we were inform'd by a Man who came from Lake St. Clair that Mr. St. Clair[73] enter'd Lake   16

---

[73] This was probably James St. Clair who was commiſſioned as a Captain in the 45th Regiment, March 10, 1761. Arthur St. Clair had previouſly been in the Regular Service but was then reſiding in Pennſylvania.

Huron

1764. Oct.	Huron the thirteenth with the Schooner Gladwin, & was soon out of Sight, the Wind being very good.
	This Morning the Sloop Charlotte arived from Fort Erie.
20	This Day the Sloop Charlote sail'd for Fort Erie, with 121 Packs of Peltry, being the laſt of 1464 Packs that were ſent from this ſince laſt April.
21	This Day ſome Indians with Maiſonville & J. Reaume arived from Sanduſky, who brought Letters informing us that the Army had left that Place the 18th Inſt.
22	This Day André the Huron arived from Sanduſky, who inform'd that he had been ſent out on a Party from Sanduſky with twenty Engliſhmen & nine Indians to cut off a Shawanie Village conſiſting of four Cabans. That the Morning after his firſt Days March, four of his Indians who were of the Six Nations choſe to ſtay awhile behind, and at mid day when he halted he enquired for them, & was told by one of the Engliſhmen who ſtay'd a little while with them that they were return'd to the Camp, upon which he puſh'd on without them. The fourth Day, knowing he was near the Village, he ſent two of his young People on before, who in a ſhort Time return'd & told him they ſaw two Indians coming on Horſeback, who ſoon after arived & told him they knew his Deſign, but that the Village was increaſed to ten Cabans, & if he went on would be cut to Pieces, & moreover that the Shawanies had aſk'd Peace from Coll. Boquet & were gone with all their Priſoners to meet him to the Amount of two hundred, upon which ſeeing they were apriz'd of his Deſign & were going to make Peace he ſent back his Party & took two Indians & proceeded to the Village, where he was inform'd that the four Indians that return'd from the Party inform'd a Huron Chief who had made Peace

Peace with Coll. Bradstreet, who immediately sent off an Express on Horseback to the Village, & that one of the two Indians that met him was the Brother of a Mohawk Chief. That he was sure in case that his Design had not been discovered, the Indians that were with him would not have fought. That in passing by the Head of the Sandusky River he saw a Huron of Sandusky who told him he was ariv'd from the Frontiers of Virginia where he had been at war with a Party of Shawanies & Delawares, who had taken thirty Scalps, and that if he would not believe him he would give him two, that were pretty fresh to show to his Father the Commandant at this Place, which Scalps he saw.

This Day the Militia return'd from Michilimackinac.

This Day the Schooner Boston ariv'd at the Mouth of the River after been eighteen Days from Niagara, & the Schooner Victory, who came out with her, they suppose was drove back.

This Morning Capt. St. Clair arived here from Michilimackinac after laying up the Schooner Gladwin in a small River near the Head of the River Huron.

This Evening the Sloop Charlotte, the Schooner Boston & Schooner Victory arived opposite the Fort.

This Morning André & five other Hurons left this on a scout against the Shawanies & Delawares & were to encamp at the River Rouge for to night.

This Afternoon a Soldier was kill'd and scalp'd on the Road between the River Rouge & the Fort.

This Morning a Soldier was kill'd & scalp'd behind the Fort near the Edge of the Woods.

Andrew return'd this Morning & promis'd (as he imagined it was Indians from Sandusky that took the two Scalps) that he would fall upon the first Indian he saw from the other side of Lake Erie.

1764.
Nov. 25   This Day we were inform'd that it was some St. Joseph Indians that took the Scalps as they had seen them.

26   This Day two Puttawattamies of this Place came in & inform'd that it was the St. Joseph Indians that took the Scalps at the Inftigation of a Saky who had been with them near twenty Years, & whose Son was kill'd this Time twelve Months at this Place.

This was confirm'd by many Informations from many Indians.

Dec. 14   This Day Machioquisse a Chief of the Puttawattamees of this Place arived from St. Josephs with a Letter from one Chevallier to the Commanding Officer, who inform'd the Commandant that Chevallier told him the King of France had sent over some Merchants, whom he had order'd to sell Things to the Indians at the following Rate, viz: if the English sold a Blanket for four Beaver they were to sell it for three; if they sold it for three, they were to sell it for two, & if the English sold it for two they were to sell it for one, and every thing else in Proportion. That there was five Cannoes of that Merchandize already at St. Josephs, as much at Ouiattanon & a good deal gone to the Shawanies & Delawares.

After a good deal of Discourse with the Commandant about the Scalps that was taken the 23d & 24th of Novem. he afk'd him in case the Murderers could be brought before him to make a proper Submission, wheather he would not forgive them; to which he said if they were brought before him & made proper Submissions he would not use them as they merited. Upon which Machioquisse promis'd to go and get some Sauteux & use all the Means in his Power to bring the Murderers in & with the English Prisoners that was at St. Josephs.

January

January 21st, 1764 [1765].

1765. Jan.

This Day Andrew the Huron arived from Fort Pitt, with Letters, for being inform'd that Peace was made with the Shawanies & Delawares, he proceeded to that Place inftead of ftriking againft them as he was directed when he left this. He faid the Shawanies & Delawares told him there was three Battoes & two Perriaugres arived at the Mouth of the Oenentois, from the Illinois, & they fent them a large Belt of Wampum defireing them to go immediately out of their River. That they had made Peace with their Father the Englifh, and would not have any more to do with the French.

Andrew the Huron left this for Fort Pitt with Maifonville. Feb. 27

A fmall Party from the Miamees took a Prifoner that had ftraggled from the Veffel at the River Rouge. Mar. 11

Mr. Jadot was fent from this to the Miamee to bring one Clermont & his Family & fome others to this Place, as we had been inform'd they fpirited up the Indians to ftrike here, but the Indians met him before he ariv'd there & difarm'd his Party, and fent him back. 17

Coll. Campbell fent them a Meffage by fome Chibbawas (who offer'd themfelves as Volunteers) to let them know if they did not give up every Prifoner they had & the Arms they took from Mr. Jadots Party, he would declare them his Enemys; & the Chibbawas who carried this Meffage had Orders from their Chief Seccaho, that in cafe they did not comply with this Demand they might look upon them as their Enemies as they wou'd immediately ftrike againft them. 15

The Schooner Victory fail'd for Niagara, in which went Lt. Stewart & Sir Edward Pickering.

This Day the Chibbawas return'd from the Miamee and May 8

1765.
May. and brought Word they wou'd foon be in with their Prifoners & defir'd their Father not to be impatient; but by private Intelligence we were inform'd quite otherwife.

16   This Day the Sloop Charlot ariv'd from Niagara, in which came Lt. M'Dougal.

17   This Day fome of the Ottawa Chiefs from the Miamee River came in & deliver'd a Meffage to the Commandant which they f'd they receiv'd from Colº Croghan, inviting them to Fort Pitt, begging he wou'd write to Colº Croghan & tell him in cafe they did not come at the Time appointed that it was becaufe they were emploied in trying to bring in the Miamees to make a proper Submiffion to ther Father & with their Prifoners.

And defiring if he their Father chofe they fhou'd go to the Miamee he wou'd get one or two of the Hurons Chiefs to go with them.

In the Afternoon one   a Mohawk who had been fent laft Fall by Sir Willm Johnfn as a Spy among the Indians came in with two Bennakees & inform'd the Commandant, that as their was frequent Reports at Sandufky that a Body of French & Indians were coming by way of the Miamee, they fent fome young Men as far as the Miamee to fee whether it was true, & as the above mentioned Indians were on their way here they met the Hurons returning from Miamee, who told them that the 9th Inft. Pondiac's Nephew ariv'd from the Illinois who inform'd them that while Pondiac & the great Saalteur from Michilimackinac was there, fix Englifhmen, with one Maifonville a Frenchman, a Delaware, a Mohawk & a Huron from this Place ariv'd there from Fort Pitt, whom Pondiac caufed to be feized and brought them as far as Ouiattanon, where they were all burnt but two whom he was

bringing

bringing to give to the Miamees. That Pondiac had
seven large Belts for to raise the St. Josephs, the Miamees, the Ouiattanons, the Pians, Mascoutons, and the
Illinois, who were to assemble with some Nations to the
northward & make what Efforts they could against this
Place the Beginning of next Month, for which Purpose Pondiac had besides the above Belts a very large
one which was for the Hatchet from the French. That
this undertaking was to be entirely by the Indians
without any Assistance.

1765.
May.

St. Vincent, one of the above Indians further says,
that being at the Shawanee Town about twenty Days
ago, a French Trader from the Illinois told him that
he had receiv'd a Letter from Maisonville when he was
going down the Ohio, who inform'd him that he had
been sent by the Commanding Officer at Fort Pitt, to
go to the Illinois with some Englishmen.

Three Chiefs of the Ottawas with some young Men
left this with a Message from the Commandant to the
Miamees and one for Pondiac.

20

This Morning the Sloop Charlotte sail'd for Niagara.

21

This Afternoon one of the Chibbawas who were sent
to the Miamee the 15th March, came here & brought
back the Belts which the Miamees would not receive &
told quite a different Story from what their Chief Seccaho told on the Return of the rest.

This Day the Indians from St. Josephs came to the
Settlement with a Prisoner, & a Belt from their Chiefs,
but the Commanding Officer wou'd not receive them
as there was no Chief with, and as they had not fulfil'd
their Promise.

24

The Prisoner they sent in by two Puttawattamy
Chiefs of this Place with the Belt, which the Commandant receiv'd & sent them Word, when their Chiefs
fulfill'd

1765.
May.

fulfill'd their Promise he wou'd receive them as his Children, but not till then. This Prisoner was gave to them by the Shawanies & Delawares two Years ago, whom we new nothing of, being one more than they s'd they had.

25 This Day the Huron Chiefs with two Onondagoes came in & told the Commandant that they came to speake to him upon the same Subject they had done the 17th Instant, saying they had since been inform'd by some people from towards the Illinois that they were in Danger, that the Indians the last Time had only taken up the Hatchet against the English, but that now they would take it up against the French & them, as they liv'd near the English and lik'd them; & that they should perish with them. They then desir'd they might give the Commandant a little Advice, which if found good he wou'd have Pitty upon them & do.

They then s'd that as the Indians depended entirely upon what they could get or take from the Inhabitants for Subsistance, they thought it advisable that they should joine in small Partys & gather together their Corn & Cattle & make at different Places small Stockades where eight or ten Families might secure themselves in, with their Effects; that in proposing this to them the Commandant would see whether they were inclin'd to be faithfull or not, for if they objected against it, they were certainly inclin'd to fight, as the Indians would render themselves Masters of them & would oblig'd them to do what they pleas'd & strip them of every thing, in case they remain'd in the undefensible Condition they were then. They beg'd the Commandant would desire the Inhabitants on the South Side of the River to join with them to make a Stockade at the Huron Point near the Priests House, that they

they might put their Wifes & Children in for Security, for notwitſtanding they were a ſmall Number they would then Laugh at any thing the other Nations cou'd do, but if they were to remain they would be in their Power & perhaps be oblig'd to do thing they had not Inclination to do, for ſaid they, what will not a Man do to ſave his Life, & when we ſee a Knife at our Throats we ſhall perhaps commit Faults, for theſe and many other Reaſons they beg'd the Commandant wou'd propoſe to the People to put themſelves in ſome kind of Defence. They further ſaid they new the Inhabitants would be very angry at them if they new they propoſ'd ſuch a thing, but they new on their Side that if they did not comply with it they wou'd ſoon repent it, and perhaps wou'd be very glad to take Refuge in their little Fort, in caſe they got one built. They ſaid there was no Time to looſe, the ſooner it was done the better.

1765. May.

In the Afternoon the Commandant ſent for the Officers of the Militia, and acquainted them of the News he had heard & propoſed to them to put themſelves in the beſt ſtate of Defence they cou'd, agreeable to which he gave them ſome Propoſals in Writing, a Copy of which is amongſt the Orders iſſued to the Militia.

This Day the Schooner Victory ariv'd, having been ſent from Niagara with Capt. Simpſon of the Artillery to take up the Cannon left by Colo Bradſtreet laſt Fall near the River au Roche, but was oblig'd to put in here for Want of Proviſion, having had a great deal of bad Weather & not being able to go to the Place. The Veſſell in very bad Condition.

26

The Schooner Victory.

June 6

[The Diary thus ends abruptly in the Middle of a Page in the Manuſcript.]

JOURNAL

OF THE

SIEGE OF DETROIT,

BY

Major ROBERT ROGERS.

INTRODUCTION.

MAJOR Rogers arrived at Detroit on the 29th of July, 1763, with the Detachment under the Command of Capt. Dalyel, and fhared in the gallant but unfortunate Sortie made under the Command of that Officer a few Days after, in which the Leader and many of his Men perifhed. The Information contained in the following Narrative is entirely from hearfay, and only brings down the Chain of Events to the 4th of July, although dated nearly a Month later. It is probable that Maj. Rogers began to write an Account of the Siege foon after his Arrival, and that this was only partly finifhed when the failing of two Veffels (mentioned on Page 59) offered a convenient Opportunity for fending it to Sir William Johnfon. At the Clofe of the Volume of Journals publifhed by Major Rogers in 1765, is an Advertifement of a fecond Volume to contain, among other Things, an Account of the

the Indian Wars in America fubfeqent to 1760. Subfcriptions were folicited and the Book was promifed within a limited Time, but from fome Caufe unknown, it was never printed. It is reafonable to infer that the following Pages were intended to form a Portion of the Book, and that this Fragment, now firft printed, may be the only Part that has been preferved. It was found among the Manufcripts of Sir William Johnfon in the New York State Library.

F. B. H.

JOURNAL
OF THE
SIEGE OF DETROIT.

A *JOURNAL of the Siege of Detroit, taken from the Officers who were then in the Fort, and wrote in their Words in the following Manner, viz:*

The 6th of May; when we were privately informed of a Conspiracy formed against us by the Indians, particularly the Tawa[1] Nation, who were to come to council with us the next Day, and massacre every Soul of us. On the Morning of that Day, being Saturday the 7th of May, fifteen of their Warriors came into the Fort and seemed very inquisitive and anxious to know where all the English Merchants' Shops were.

At 9 o'Clock the Garrison were ordered under Arms and the Savages continued coming into the Fort till 11 o'Clock, diminishing their Numbers as much as possible by dividing themselves at all the Corners of

[1] Ottawa.

the

the streets most adjacent to the Shops. Before 12 o'Clock they were three hundred Men, at least three times the Number equal to that of the Garrison; but seeing all the Troops under Arms, and the Merchants Shops shut, imagined prevented them from attempting to put their evil Scheme into execution that Day.

Observing us thus prepared, their Chiefs came in a very condemned like Manner, to Council, where they spoke a great deal of Nonsense to Major Gladwine and Capt. Campbell, protesting at the same Time the greatest Friendship imaginable to them, but expressing their Surprise at seeing all the Officers and Men under Arms. The Major then told them that he had certain Intelligence that some Indians were projecting Mischief, and on that Acc^t he was determined to have the Troops always under Arms upon such Occasions: That they being the oldest Nation, and the first that had come to Council, needed not to be astonished at that Precaution as he was resolved to do the same to all Nations.

At 2 o'Clock they had done speaking, went off seemingly very discontented and crossed the River half a League from the Fort, where they all encamped about 6 o'Clock that Afternoon. Six of their Warriors returned and brought an old Squaw Prisoner, alledging that she had given us false Information against them. The Major declared she had never given any kind of Advice. They then insisted upon naming the Author of what he had heard in regard to the Indians, which he declined to do, but told them it was one of themselves, whose Name he promised never to reveal; whereupon they went off and carried the old Woman Prisoner with them. When they arrived at their Camp, Pondiac their greatest Chief seized on the Prisoner and gave her three Strokes with a Stick on the Head, which

which laid her flat on the Ground, and the whole Nation aſſembled around her and called repeated Times kill her, kill her.

Sunday the 8th, Pondiac and ſeveral other of the principal Chiefs came into the Fort, at 5 o'Clock in the Afternoon and brought a Pipe of Peace with them of which they wanted to convince us fully of their Friendſhip and Sincerity, but the Major judging that they only wanted to caggole us would not go nigh them nor give them any Countenance, which obliged Capt. Campbell to go and ſpeake with them, and after ſmoaking with the Pipe of Peace and aſſuring him of their Fidelity, they ſaid that the next Morning all the Nation would come to Council where every thing would be ſettled to our Satisfaction, after which they would immediately diſperſe, and that that would remove all kind of Suſpicion.

Accordingly on Monday Morning the 9th, ſix of their Warriors came into the Fort at 7 o'Clock, and upon ſeeing the Garriſon under Arms went off without being obſerved. About 10 o'Clock we counted fifty-ſix Canoes, with ſeven and eight Men in each, croſſing the River from their Camp, and when they arrived nigh the Fort, the Gates were ſhut, and the Interpreter went to tell them that not above fifty or ſixty Chiefs would be admitted into the Fort, upon which Pondiac immediately deſired the Interpreter in a peremptory Manner to return directly and acquaint us that if all their People had not free Acceſs into the Fort none of them would enter it: that we might ſtay in our Fort, but he would keep the Country, adding that he would order a Party inſtantly to an Iſland where we had twenty-four Bullocks, which they immediately killed. Unluckily three Soldiers were on the Iſland and a poor Man with his Wife and four Children which

which they all murthered except two Children, as also a poor Woman and her two Sons, that lived about half a Mile from the Fort.

After having thus put all the English without the Fort to death, the ordered a Frenchman who had seen the Woman and her two Children killed and scalped, to come and inform us of it, and likewise of their having murthered Sir Robert Davers, Captain Robertson and a Boats' Crew of six Persons two Days before, being Saturday the 7th of May, near the Entrance of Lake Huron, for which Place they set out from hence on Monday the 2d Inst. in order to know if the Lakes and Rivers were Navigable for a Schooner which lay here to proceed to Michilimackinac. We were then fully persuaded that the Information given us was well founded, and a proper Disposition was made for the Defense of the Fort, although our Number was but small, not exceeding one hundred and twenty, including all the English Traders, and the Works were nigh Mile in Circumferance.

On Tuesday the 10th, very early in the Morning, the Savages began to fire on the Fort, and Vessels which lay opposite to the east and west Sides of the Fort.[2] About 8 o'Clock the Indians called a Parley and ceased firing, and half an Hour after, the Waindotes Chiefs came into the Fort, on their way to a Council where they were called by the Tawas and promised us to endeavour to soliciate and persuade the Tawas from committing further Hostilities. After drinking a Glass of Rum they went off at three o'Clock that Afternoon. Several of the Inhabitants and four Chiefs of the Tawas, Waindotes and Chippawas and Pottawattomes came and acquainted us, that most of

[2] The Channel of Detroit River opposite the Fort, ran but a few Degrees South of West, although its general Course is nearly South.

all

all the Inhabitants were affembled at a Frenchmans Houfe about a Mile from the Fort, where the Savages propofed to hold a Council, and defiring Captain Campbell and another Officer to go with them to that Council, where they hoped with their Prefence and Affiftance further Hoftilities would ceafe, affuring us at the fame Time that come what would, that Capt. Campbell and the other Officers that went with him, fhould return whenever they pleafed. This Promife was affertained by the French as well as the Indian Chief, whereupon Captain Campbell and Lieutenant McDougal went off efcorted by a Number of the Inhabitants and the four Chiefs, they firft promifed to be anfwerable for their returning y^t Night.

When they arrived at the Houfe already mentioned they found the French and Indians affembled, and after counceling a long while, the Waindotes were prevailed on to fing the War Song, and this being done, it was next refolved that Captain Campbell and Lieutenant McDougall fhould be detained Prifoners, but would be indulged to lodge in a French Houfe till a French Commandant arrived from the Ilenoes, that next Day five Indians and as many Canadians would be difpatched to acquaint the Commanding Officer of the Ilonies that Detroit was in their Poffeffion and require of him to fend an Officer to Command, to whom Captain Cample and Lieutenant McDougall fhould be delivered. As for Major Gladwin he was fummoned to give up the Fort and two Veffels, &c., the Troops to ground their Arms, and they would allow as many Battoes and as much Provifion as they judged requifite for us to go to Niagara: That if thefe Propofals were not accepted of, they were a thoufand Men, and ftorm the Fort at all events, and in that Cafe every Soul of us fhould be put to the Torture. The Major returned for Anfwer, that

that as soon as the two Officers they had detained were permitted to come into the Fort, he would after consulting them give a positive Answer to their Demand, but could do nothing without obtaining their Opinion.

On Wednesday the 11th, several Inhabitants came early in the Morning into the Fort, and advised us by way of Friendship to make our Escape aboard the Vessels, assuring us that we had no other Method by which we could preserve our Lives, as the Indians were then fifteen hundred fighting Men, and would be as many more in a few Days, and that they were fully determined to attack us in an Hours time. We told the Monf'rs that we were ready to receive them, and that every Officer and Soldier in the Fort would willingly perish in the Defense of it, rather than condescend or agree to any Terms that Savages would propose. Upon which the French went off as I suppose to communicate what we had said to their Allies, and in a little afterwards the Indians gave their usual Hoop, and five or six hundred began to attack the Fort on all Quarters. Indeed some of them behaved extremely well and advanced very boldly in an open plain exposed to our Fire, and came within sixty Yards of the Fort, but upon having three Men killed and above a dozen wounded, they retired as briskly as they advanced, and fired at three hundred Yards Distance till seven o'Clock at Night, when they sent a Frenchman into the Fort with a Letter to the Major, desiring a cessation of Arms, that Night, and proposing to let the Troops with their Arms aboard the Vessels, but insisting upon our giving up the Fort, leaving the French Auxilliary all the Merchandize and officers Effects, and had even the Insolence to demand a Negro Boy belonging to a Merchant to be delivered to Pondiack.

The

The Major's Reply to thefe extraordinary Propofitions was much the fame as to the firft.

Tuefday the 12th, five Frenchmen and as many Indians were fent off for the Ilinoes with Letters wrote by a Canadian agreable to Pondiacs Defire. On the 13th we were informed by the Inhabitants that Mr. Chapman, a Trader from Niagara, was taken Prifoner by the Waindotes, with five Battoes loaded with Goods.

The 21ft, one of the Veffels was ordered to fail for the Niagara, but to remain till the fixth of June at the Mouth of the River in order to advert the Battoes which we expected daily from Niagara.

Upon the 22d we were told that Enfign Paully who commanded at Sandufky was brought Prifoner by ten Tawas, who reported that they had prevailed after long Confultation with the Waindotes who lived at Sandufky to declare War againft us; that fome Days ago they came early of a Morning to the Block Houfe, and murthered every Soul therein, confifting of twenty feven Perfons, Traders included; that Meff[rs] Callender and Prentice, formerly Captains in the Pennfylvania Reg[t] were amongft that Number, and that they had taken one hundred Horfes loaded with Indian Goods, which with the Plunder of the Garrifon was agreed to be given the Waindotes before they condefcended to join them; that all they wanted was the Commanding Officer.

On the 29th of May, we had the Mortification to fee eight of our Battoes in the Poffeffion of the Enemy, paffing on the oppofite Shore, with feveral Soldiers Prifoners in them. When the foremoft Battoe came oppofite the Sloop, fhe fired a Gun, and the Soldiers aboard called at thofe in the Battoe, that if they paffed the Savages would kill them all, upon which they immediately

mediately seized on two Indians and threw them overboard with him and tomahawked him directly, they being near the Shore and it quite shoal. Another Soldier laid hold of an Oar, and struck that Indian upon the Head, of which Wound he is since dead. Then there remained only three Soldiers, of which two were wounded, and although fifty Indians were on the Bank not sixty Yards, firing upon them, the three Soldiers escaped aboard the Vessel, with the Battoe loaded with eight Barrels of Provisions and gives the following Account of their Misfortune, viz:

That two Nights before, about 10 o'Clock, they arrived about six Leagues from the Mouth of the River where they encamped. That two Men went a little from the Camp for Firewood to boil their Kettle, when one of the two was seized on by an Indian, killed and scalped in an Instant. The other Soldier ran directly and alarmed the Camp, upon which Lieutenant Cuyler immediately ordered to give Ammunition to the Detachment, which consisted of one Serjeant and seventeen Soldiers of the Royal Americans, three Serjeants and seventy-two Rank and File of the Queen's Independent Company of Rangers. After having delivered their Ammunition, and a Disposition made of the Men, the Enemy came close to them without being observed, behind a Bank and fired very smartly on one Flank which could not sustain the Enemys Fire and they retired precipitately and threw the Whole in Confusion. By that Means the Soldiers embarked aboard the Battoes with one, two and three Oars in each Battoe, which gave an Opportunity to the Savages of taking them all except the two Battoes that escaped with Mr. Cuyler to Niagara.

Sunday the 5th of June, we were acquainted that Fort Maimes was taken, that Ensign Holms who commanded

commanded there had been informed by two Frenchmen who arrived there the preceding Day of Detroits being attacked by the Indians, which he would hardly believe, but threatened to imprifon the French for that Report, that an Indian Woman had betrayed him out of the Fort by pretending that another Woman was very fick, and begged of him to come to her Cabin to let blood of her, and when he had gone a little Diftance from the Fort was fired on and killed. The Serjeant hearing the Report of the firing ran to fee what it was, and was immediately taken Prifoner. The Soldiers fhut the Gates and would have probably defended the Fort if one Walfh, a Trader who had been taken Prifoner a few Days before, had not advifed them to open the Gates, alledging that if they did not comply the Indians would fet Fire to the Fort and put them to death; whereas, if they opened the Gates, they fhould be well treated. Whereupon the Gates were opened, and the Soldiers grounded their Arms.

On the 10th of June we heard that Enfign Schloffer the Commanding Officer at Saint Jofephs was taken Prifoner and that all the Garrifon (except three Men) were maffacred. That the Indians came on the 25th of May with a Pretence to Council, and as foon as the Chiefs had fhaken Hands with Mr. Schloffer, they feized on him, gave a Shriek and inftantly killed ten Men.

The 12th we were told that Lieut. Jenkins and all the Garrifon of Owat'anon, confifting of a Sergeant and eighteen Men were taken Prifoners and carried to the Ilonies.

The 18th a Jefuit arrived from Michillimakenac and brought a Letter from Captain Etherinton and Lieutenant Leffley, with an Account of their being taken Prifoners. That Lieutenant Jamet and twenty-one

one Soldiers. That on the 2nd the Indians were playing Ball as usual nigh the Fort, where Captain Etherington and Lieut. Lessley happened to be looking at them, but were suddenly seized on and carried into the Woods. At the same Time the Savages had purposely thrown their Ball into the Fort, as if that had happened by Accident, and followed it directly into the Fort, where a Number of their Women had Tomahawks and Spears concealed under their Blankets, which they delivered them and put the whole Garrison to death, except thirteen Men.

The 30th we were informed that the Blockhouse at Presque Isle was burned, that Ensign Christie and all his Garrison, which consisted of twenty-nine Men were taken Prisoners except six Men, who it was believed made their escape to La Beuf.

On the Night of the 2d Instant and Lieut. McDougall were lodged at the House I have already mentioned, about two Miles from the Fort, and made a Resolution to Escape, when it was agreed on between them that McDougall should set off first, which he did and get safe into the Fort, but you know it was much more dangerous for Captain Campbell than for any other Person by Reason that he could neither run nor see, and being sensible of that failing I am sure prevented him from attempting to escape.

The 4th a Detachment was ordered to destroy some Breastworks and Entrenchments the Indians had made a Quarter of a Mile from the Fort, and about twenty Indians came to attack that Party, which they engaged but were drove off in an Instant with the Loss of one Man killed (and two wounded) which our People scalped and cut to Pieces. Half an Hour after the Savages carried the Man they had lost before Captain Campbell, striped him naked, and directly murthered him

him in a cruel Manner, which indeed gives one Pain beyond Expreſſion, and I am ſure cannot miſs but to affect ſenſibly all his Acquaintences, although he is now out of the Queſtion.

The Indians likewiſe reported that Venango and Le Beuf is taken by the Savages.

Dated at Detroit 8th Augt 1763.

To Sir William Johnſon.

GEN. BRADSTREET'S STATEMENT UPON INDIAN AFFAIRS.

INTRODUCTION.

THE following Statement upon Indian Affairs is preserved in the Hand-writing of General John Bradstreet, in a Volume belonging to the New York State Library, entitled *Bradstreet and Amherst MSS.*, beginning at Page 190. These Papers were found many Years since in the Garret of a House in Albany which Gen. Bradstreet once inhabited, and are of unquestionable authenticity.

During the Indian Wars which followed the Conquest of Canada in 1760, General B. held the Rank of Quarter-Master General, and his Opportunities for judging of the Merits or Defects of the System under which Indian Affairs were managed entitle his Opinions to Respect. The Difficulties attending this Service are clearly and forcibly stated, and the Remedies which he suggests were dictated by sound Judgment and enforced by strong Argument.

F. B. H.

GEN. BRADSTREET'S STATEMENT.

DECEMBER 17, 1764.

A BRIEF State of our interiour Situation with the Savages, the Disadvantages occasioned by the Indian Traders following them to their Hunting Country, Castles and Villages; the Benefit to all his Majesty's Subjects by confining the Trade to particular Posts and the Danger of fixing those Posts nearer the Colonys of New York and Quebec then St. Marys, Michilimicanac, La Bay, & the Detroit, &c., &c.

The Savages retain their Affection for the French Nation as much as ever, and have nothing more at Heart than their Return and Power in this Country, & are ready

ready to execute any thing in their Power to anfwer that Purpofe, and deteft the Englifh fo much, that the Traders can not quit the eftablifhed Pofts to go & Trade with them (as Canadians do, who run no rifk, but on the contrary are well receiv'd) without being murder'd and plunder'd; and Experience alfo fhews when they employ Canadians to carry on the Trade for them they are cheated and ruin'd; which muft in a fhort Time put all the Indian Trade in the Hands of the Canadians in Conjunction with the French & Spaniards from the Miffiffippi & the Settlements of the Illinois, who at this Time carry of great Part of the Trade between the Miffiffippi & the great Lakes & the Ohio. To remedy thefe Evils and recover the Trade which is much impair'd, the Savages debauch'd, become Idle and neglect their Hunting by fpirituous Liquors being conftantly carried to their Hunting Countrys and to fix the Trade with equil Advantage to all his Majeftys Subjects, it is imagin'd it fhould be limited to particular Pofts & upon no Account allow any Traders to follow the Savages to their Hunting Country, Caftles or Villages, as it moreover gives their Boat men & fome of themfelves a Taft for a wandering & independent Life, infects them with a Habit of Libertinifm & many of thefe Sort of Canadians remain amongft the Savages now; from whom they are not diftinguifhable but by their Vices & inciting them on to Acts of Cruelty againft the Englifh; and was their nothing to fear from the Entregues of foreign Enemies the nearer the Pofts were fix'd to the Colonys of New York & Quebec to more Advantage would the Trade be carry'd on, as the Savages would then become the principal Carriers themfelves, which is a very expenfive Article. But the Difadvantage of confining the Trade to Pofts nearer the Colonys then St. Marys, Michilimicanac

General Bradstreet's Statement. 143

micanac, La Bay and Detroit would be, the Savages of the northwest Side Lake Superior would find it less troublesome to Trade with the Hudsons Bay Company then to go to those Posts, and those of La Bay, the west Side Lake Superior & Lake Michigan would find it also less difficult to go to the Mississippi should the French & Spanish Traders not go to them as they actually do now and they would also soon find the way into Lake Superior with their Merchandise—and so long as those Traders come to the Savages on the Banks of the Wabash and Scioto Rivers, by the Mississippi and Ohio, our Traders at the Detroit & Fort Pitt will benefit but little from them, those of St. Josephs & Miames, which makes a considerable Number of Hunters—and to these Evils we may add a greater, namely, was the Trade confin'd to Posts as low as Niagara, the certain Consequence would be, that all the Furr Trade & Savages would fall into the Hands of the French and Spaniards & it effected soon by Means of the French Inhabitants of Detroit, Wabach, St. Joseph & Michilimicanac & those Vagabonds or Coureurs de Bois of Canada dispers'd amongst them, who when left to themselves and able to act openly & without Fear will not fail their old Masters; the dreadful Consequence of which would soon be severely felt by the Inhabitants of the Frontiers of several Colonys.

From repeated Information it can admit of no Doubt but that the French by the Mississippi are using their best Endeavours to bring all the Savages to consider the Spaniards in the same favourable light to them as the French themselves; we must therefore loose Ground every Day with the Indians if we remain idle Spectators of it; it would be of great Use in helping to prevent it as well as that of a general Confederacy of them against us when attempted were we to divide
them

them by fomenting the Quarrils generally fubfifting amongft them inftead of making them up & turn them to our own Ufe & Advantage & prevent as much as poffible the Intercourfe of the Savages of diffirent Diftricts, that is, thofe of the north weft Side Lake Superior to come down no farther than St. Mary's & Michilimicanac; thofe of La Bay, weft Side Lake Superior & Lake Michigan to the Pofts of La Bay; thofe of St. Jofephs, Miames, Wabach & Scioto Rivers to the Detroit & Fort Pitt, & the Six Nations (if poffible) to be kept from them all at the Pofts of Neagara & Ofwego, as the Meetings of different Nations of Indians have too often ended in making up their old Quarrils & ploting againft us—and to fucceed in this important Bufinefs, Men of Adrefs with a perfect Knowledge of the Polocy & Craft of the Savages fhould be employ'd.

The Number of Boats employ'd in the Indian Trade annually from this Province amounts to about 180 whofe Cargoes one with the other is in Value 300 £, at the New York Prices; which makes for the whole about 100,000 £; out of which a large Deduction is to be made from the Proffits of the Trader for Tranfportation & other Expenfes as may be conceiv'd by the Expence of one Boat to Detroit:

3 Boatmen to Detroit, - -	£60
Battoe, Oars, &c., - - -	9
Carriage over the little Falls and Fort Stanwix,	1.12
Do. Neagara, - - -	11. 8
	£82

and to Michilimicana it amounts to 112 £, about; and innormous as this Expenfe is it bears no Proportion to that of following the Savages to their Hunting Country

Country during the Winter; which the English Merchants of Canada are no Strangers to—and to this follows the Expence of Provisions, which is always very scarce & dear at the Posts. At Michilimicanac Pork sold this Summer for two Shillings and sixpence, Bread four Shillings & Butter six Shillings the Pound, and at Detroit 5 £ a hundred weight, and this scarcity of Provisions and expensive Transportation will continue so long as the Detroit remains not properly settled; the Encroachments of the French and Spaniards not prevented; the Frontiers of several Colony's not secure from the Attacks of the Savages, nor we have the full Advantage of the Fur Trade but by Detroit being made a strong Barrier to the Colonys & that Settlement encouraged or the whole of the Mississippi in our Hands; which last will bring all the Savages dependent on us for what they want; for who ever imagines the Savages of the interior Country will remain in Peace and Friendship with us whilst the French & Spaniards possess the Mississippi will find himself mistaken'd—indeed the former has not been found perminent though very expensive—and the large Sum lately given at the Congress at Fort Stanwix will operate on the Six Nations & their Friends only. From what has been said of the Expence in carrying on this Trade, it appears the Method now practis'd is better calculated to enrich the Battoe & Canoe Men than the Merchants and is one of the Causes so many fail; the regulating this, with Justice to both, seems to be absolutely necessary; but the more Vessells are employed in this Trade to more Advantage will it be carry'd on as it may be done for half the now Expence & always with Safety against the evil Designs of any Savages.

Detroit is here mentioned as being the most proper Place for an Establishment & Barrier for the Reason that

that its Situation being most proper & convenient to raise Provisions, awe and attack such Savages as are most likely to be troublesome first, to them divide and keep them so, to take up the French and Spanish Traders that may come on our Side the Mississippi, for it is to little Purpose to send Troops to attack Savages and take up People protected by them from so great Distance as the Colonys are, to return in a few Months or to depend on small Garrisons, be they ever so well posted, it being out of their Power to do more than give Protection to such as are within their Works; and it is as bad Policy to suffer the Encroachments above mention'd & the Savages to insult & murder without further Notice than giving them large Sums of Money in Presents to make Peace for a few Years, for which they have always held us in Contempt & thereby encouraged to commit frequent Depredations upon us to exact Presents from Time to Time to make it up. As the Soil of the Detroit is as good as can be & plenty of it ready for the Plow, Provisions would soon be plenty & cheap there & the Navigation of the Lakes carry'd on by the Inhabitants of that Place in Vessels at as little Expence as in this Province, which would be of great advantage to the Trade, security to the Posts as well as lessning their Expence—and without Vessels neither one nor the other can be said to be safe & secure from falling into the Hands of the Savages.

Should the Trade be limited to particular Posts it would be of advantage to establish the Prices of the Merchandise & Furrs with equal Advantage to both Sides & to prevent Impositions too frequently practiced by the Traders; and perhaps the way of doing it less exceptionable to the Traders & Savages would be by two Provincional Commissarys of Abilities and Experience from the Colony of New York & Quebec with the Indian Chiefs

Chiefs in Presence of the Officer commanding Posts and those Commissary to reside at the Posts, inspect the Trade & report from Time [to Time] every thing necessary and should it appear reasonable the Traders and Savages pay a Proportion towards the general Security of the Interior Country, the following Dutys may be laid by every Province connected in the Trade, viz:

 On Speritious Liquors 2s6d sterling a Gallon.
  Powder,   6d do a Pound.
  Strouds,   8s do a Piece.
  Blankets,   1s do each.
  Shirts,   1s do each.
  Silver Trinkets 5 p C^t on first Cost,

which may amount to six or seven thousand Pounds sterling per annum on this Province only.

 Some Court of Justice is absolutely necessary to bring Offenders to Justice, oblige People to pay their Debts and keep good Order, it being impossible those Ends can be answered by Provincial Laws so distant as the Colonys are, did their Power extend so far.

 It is submitted, if the Designs of our Ennemies to draw the Savages in general on us would not be more easily prevented & with far less Expence if undertaken before any of them commence Hostilitys against us, than it can be afterwards, and if any thing can be more effectual to answer this Purpose than the Savages seeing soon at the Detroit a respectable Force fix'd, the Posts above mentioned properly established, themselves disunited & proper Measures taking there to raise sufficient Provisions for the full Supply of the Interior Country. They know if the Posts are supplied with Provisions from the Colonys below in Boats only they have it always in their Power to cut off the Supply & even the Retreat of those Garrisons, and on it they
                chiefly

chiefly depend for Succefs in taking them and driving the Englifh out of the interior Country. How fatal a fudden & well tim'd Savage Eruption would prove to the Englifh Indian Traders & Frontier Inhabitants of feveral Colonys melancholly Experience has made it too well known to need being mentioned here, and if the interior Country is to remain in its prefent defencelefs State all Laws & Regulations for the Benefit of the Trade will be of no avail.

It would be prudent to oblige all the French & Canadian People to remove from the Wabach, St. Jofephs, Michilimicanac & otherwife difperf'd amongft the Savages to the Settlement of Detroit to put an End to the Tricks they play to our Difadvantage.

The Nations or Tribes of Savages furrounding the great Lakes that have any Knowledge of the Englifh are at this Time in a Difpofition to live well with them, refpect them and beg for Trade & Veffels in every Lake, hoping thereby that Goods will be cheaper than it can be without them. They ftill love the French to a great Degree and the French by the Miffiffippi and from the Illinois keep it up by extending Trade to all Nations they can and fending Emiffarys to propagate fuch Tales as turn moft to their Advantage & Prejudice to the Englifh. Thefe Savages are numerous, proud, delight in & practice War from a political View, knowing that fuch as neglect keeping up that Spirit muft degenerate into Effeminacy & become the Prey of fuch as do not. To infure a lafting Peace, gain their Affections & wean them from the French, ftrict Juftice, Moderation, fair Trade, with keeping them from frequent Intercourfe with each other, & a refpectable Force at Detroit is the way to obtain it, unlefs their whole dependence for the Neceffaries of Life depended upon the Englifh, which will never be the

the cafe as long as the French can come up the Miffiffippi in Safety, Land & extend their Trade on our Side with Impunity, the preventing of which will in the Execution be found difficult as the Intereft of the Savages is to fcreen & protect them, & it is faid to be carried on by the French Eaft India Company.

It is abfolutely neceffary to make Choice for the eftablifhing Pofts for the Security of Trade, of fuch Places as may be moft convenient for the Inhabitants of each Lake to carry on their Trade with eafe to themfelves, by which & their natural Lazinefs will feldom go to their Neighbors & without it they will be difcontented.

At thefe Pofts Men of Senfe, Modiration & Spirit fhould Command, & each Detachment for the fmall ones fhould not be lefs than one hundred good Men. Neagara & Detroit fhould be more refpectable, the former can not do with lefs than three Pofts upon the Communication of fifty Men each and the latter muft have as many to make good the Navigation to Lake Huron, the Straits being too difficult for Veffells, fo that Boats muft be employ'd for that Service and the Officer commanding at Detroit fhould always have it in his Power to detach from his Garrifon three hundred good Men befides Militia to chaftife any Nation or Band of Savages the Inftant they deferve it, as the taking immediate Satiffaction will make them refpect and fear us and prevent a general War, fo that Neagara can not difpenfe with lefs than one Battalion on the prefent Eftablifhment & Detroit near two Battailons.

The Pofts neceffary for Lake Ontario are already fix'd except Frontinac inftead of Fort Wm. Auguftus,[1] the latter being ufelefs, the Navigation to it dangerous

---

[1] About three Miles below the Mouth of the Ofwegatchie. See Note 57, Page 58.

and attended with great delays, and the former an excellent Harbour and from it soon into the Lake.

For Lake Erie Detroit is sufficient.

For Lake Huron Detroit and Michilimicanac.

For Lake Michigan Michilimicanac, the Bay & St. Josephs.

For Lake Superior, Falls of St. Marys with two other Posts at the most convenient Places, the Inhabitants being in that Quarter numerous, particularly in the westward of it.

These Posts of Michilimicanac, the Bay, St. Josephs, the Falls of St. Marys with the two other Posts upon the Banks of Lake Superior will take one Battailon, which makes four from Neagara westward.

All Posts upon the Banks of the Lakes from Neagara upwards to be under the control of the Officer commanding at Detroit and should Government judge it improper to establish a Civil Government there and not encourage the Colony, still some Court of Justice is necess'ry to the end Offenders, Inhabitants, Indians, Indian Traders and others might be brought to Justice & punish'd by a Law that might prevent litigious Suits & satisfy the Savages the strictest Justice is done them at all Times.

The Savages have a contemptible Opinion of all Indian Traders, it is therefore necessary the Officer commanding at the Posts should not Trade but inspect into the Trade, prevent Abuse and bring Offenders to that Justice the Law may require; by this they will be respected & belov'd by the Savages & have it in their Power to be of great Use when the Assistance of the latter may be wanted against his Majestys Enemies.

The Officers at all Posts which the Savages frequent should be enabled to treat Particulars, such as Chiefs and well affected with a little Rum, some Pipes & Tobacco

Tobacco, with Provisions in cases of Necessity; they have been accustomed to much more by the French & expect it from us, the Expence is a trifle but the Want of that may be attended with bad Consequences; for Neagara and all trading Posts above it twenty Pounds sterling except Detroit, which should be thirty Pounds annually.

The Goods to be furnished the Savages should be, if possible, as good as those they had from the French before the reduction of Canada, sold to them at the same Prices or in that Proportion if not so good, and the same Prices given for their Skins & Peltry—and to enable us to carry on this Trade to more Advantage & greater Safety than the French did, no Transportation to be suffer'd upon the Lakes but in Vessels and Government to furnish & keep up them Vessells, the Trader paying Freight for his Goods at the Rate of one half what it would cost him if transported in Boats. This would overpay the Expence of the Vessels for Trade and those necessary for the public Service and prevent drunken or evil minded Indians killing and plundering the Traders, which can not be avoided at Times, if the Transportation was carry'd on in Boats. The Number of Vessells necessary for the Trade can not be fix'd, but by Time, but the sooner there are two or three in the Lakes Huron & Michigan with two in Lake Superior the more pleasing it will be to the Savages, as they will see no Time is lost to put the Trade on an advantagious Footing for them. The Execution of this I take to be of great Importance towards fixing the Inclinations of the Savages in our Favor. The Savages should not be debar'd Spiritious Liquors; it is their darling Passion, nay they love it so much they will sacrifice their all to obtain it and will never live in Peace with us without it, but
still

ſtill the Quantity each Trader ſhould be permitted to take with him ſhould be limited in the Proportion of the Goods he takes and might extend to fifteen Pounds in Spiritious Liquors to every hundred Pounds of other Goods, paying a Duty of two Shillings ſterl. per Gallon, which they can very well bear from the enormous Prices they ſell it at.

The Savages are ſubtile & the French intreguing, it therefore becomes dangerous to ſuffer the former to hord up a large Stock of Arms and Ammunition; but this can not be prevented ſhould every Trader have it in his Power to carry with him what Quantity he may judge proper; upon theſe Conſiderations and that the Proffits ariſing from the Sail & Returns would go a great way towards defraying the public Expence for the Protection of Trade, would it not be beſt in the Hands of Government under the Care of a Commiſſary ſubject to the Control of the Commanding Officer of each Poſt with Inſtructions as to the Quantity to be diſpoſed of annually. The Honor of Government will require theſe Articles to be good and the Prices ſhould be eſtabliſhed, and

Here I muſt notice that from the Government of Pennſylvania all the Shavanes and Delaware Indians are furniſh'd with Rifle Barrel Guns of an excellent Kind and that the Upper Nations are getting into them faſt by which they will be much leſs dependent upon us on account of the great ſaving of Powder by thoſe Guns, as it certainly diminiſhes the Demand of ſuch as have them more than Half, and in their way of carrying on War by far more prejudicial to us than any other Sort of Gun; would it not be a public Benefit to ſtop the making and vending any more of them throughout the Colonys and prevent the Importation of any into the Colonies.

Should

General Bradstreet's Statement. 153

Should Government judge it necessary to take the supplying the Savages with Arms and Ammunition into their own Hands; for the upper Lakes a Public Magazine will be necessary at Detroit under proper Officers to receive & send forward to the other Posts, as likewise to receive the Remittences back; and the Commissary of the Outposts should account annually with those of Detroit, subject to the Inspection of the Governor or Officer commanding there.

Should New York be thought a proper Channel for the Conveyance up the Country, a Commissary should be there and one at Albany; but if on the contrary Canada should be thought best, Quebec & Montreal are proper Places for Offices for this Service.

Of all the Savages upon the Continent, the most knowing, the most intreguing, the less useful & the greatest Villains are those most conversant with the Europeans and deserve the Attention of Government most by way of Correction, and these are the Six Nations, Shawanes & Delawares; they are well acquainted with the defenceless State of the Inhabitants who live on the Frontiers and think they will ever have it in their Power to distress & Plunder them; and never cease raising the Jealousy of the Upper Nations against us by propagating amongst them such Stories as make them believe the English have nothing so much at Heart as the Extirpation of all Savages. The apparent Design of the Six Nations is to keep us at War with all Savages but themselves that they may be employed as Mediators between us & them at a Continuation of an Expense to the Public too often & too heavily felt, the Sweets of which they will never forget nor loose Sight of if they can possibly avoid it. That of the Shawanes & Delawares is to live on killing, captivating and plundering the People inhabiting the
Frontiers,

Frontiers, long Experience having shown them they grow richer & live better thereby than by hunting wild Beasts.

This Campaign has fully opened the Eyes of the Upper Nations of Indians; they are now sensible they are made use of as the Dupes & Tools of these detestable & diabolical Set, the Six Nations, Shawanes & Delawares, and it would require but little Address & Expence (the Posts and Trade properly fix'd) to engage them to cut them from the Face of the Earth (and they deserve it) or to keep the Six Nations in such Subjection as would put an End to our being any longer a kind of Tributary to them; and their real Interest call upon them to distroy or drive the Shawanes & Delawares out of the Country they now possess on account of Hunting; this they know and would soon put either in Execution if assured his Majesty would not suffer any other Savages to live there. Happy will it be when Savages can be punish'd by Savages, the good Effects of which the French can tell. That we can punish them is beyond Doubt whenever Wisdom, Secrecy, Dispatch & good Troops in Numbers proportionate to the Service are employ'd.

The Pass of Neagara is of great Importance & will always be an Expence to Govern^t. The principal Part of the Trade, if the Transportation is carry'd on in Vessells will pass that way & from its Proximity to the Geneseo Indians, a Part of the Six Nations & the greatest Savage Enemies we have, it will be difficult if not impracticable for some Time to come, for private Persons to keep up Boats & Carriage so well but that the Trade will meet with Delays; it would therefore be more safe & parmanent in the Hands of Government who only can make Transportation certain and by the Traders paying a reasonable Price for the Carriage

riage for their Goods, &c., there will be no ſtop and the public Service carry'd on there without Expence.

This Campaign upon the Lakes has alſo laid open the Hearts of the Six Nations and a black one it will appear for us if Gen¹ Gage has ſent the Papers reſpecting them to his Majeſtys Miniſters, to which I hope he has tack'd the immenſe Expence they have been at to Government this Year excluſive of Proviſions, which is immenſe alſo. It will alſo been ſeen by them Papers that the Upper Nations of Indians know that we are fully acquainted with the Tricks the Six Nations play us and I believe they do expect to hear that that Part of them call'd Geneſeo Indians get their deſerts ſoon.

The French accuſtom'd the Savages of the upper Lakes & Rivers to ſend Traders with Goods to Winter amongſt them for which Permit the Trader paid a certain Price each Time; I believe the Indians will expect it will be ſo again; ſhould Government think proper to grant it then the Trader can very well pay thirty Pounds ſterling for each large Canoe ſo permitted, which will make a conſiderable Sum annually; the Paſs to be given at Detroit only to prevent Fraud.

I am aſſur'd by Perſons lately from the Illinois that excluſive of the French Garriſons there, the Inhabitants are 600 fighting Men, have 1000 Negroes well accuſtom'd to the Uſe of ſmall Arms, averſe to our taking Poſſeſſion of the Country & have painted us out in ſuch Colours to the numerous Savages near them that they, the latter, will certainly endeavour to prevent the Troops getting there by the Miſſiſſippi even ſhould the Indians nearer the Sea allow them to paſs, which they think they will not, unleſs well paid for it, which will not anſwer what may perhaps be expected. They add, that it is their Opinion alſo, that

all

all Attempts to get Poffeffion of the Illinoes with lefs than 3000 good Men will fail, and that thofe Troops fhould go down the Ohio River & the Expedition carry'd on with fuch Secrecy that they may enter the Miffiffippi 90 Miles below Fort Charters before the Inhabitants can have Intelligence of it & Time to apprife all the Savages.

 I am convinced the only way to eftablifh ourfelves amongft the Savages with Refpect & Safety is to begin by coming upon them by ways unfrequented, undifcovered and with fuch Force as fhall make fuch an Impreffion as fhall be lafting, and if a Body of Troops fhould be fent to take Poffeffion of the Illinoes thofe Troops fhould vifite all the principal Nations of Indians upon the Banks of ye Miffiffippi as near the Sea as they live and endeavour to enter into an Alliance with all they can and purchafe their Aid to make War upon thofe that remain ftubborn to bring them to Reafon & open a free Paffage up the River. The fhorteft way to carry this into Execution is by Fort Pitt, provided the Troops are not to come from Canada, but if any comes from thence the beft way is by Neagara to Prefque Ifle upon Lake Erie.

 The Colony of Detroit grows faft and the Inhabitants have great Influence over the Savages; the removing them would occafion a general War with the Indians, and to leave them as they now are will take a great length of Time before they become proper Britifh Subjects; it is therefore humbly fubmitted if it would not be beft to permit & encourage Britifh Subjects to fettle there as the Increafe of the latter would be fo great in a few Years that they muft foon become one People by Marriages, &c.

 The Spirit for fettling the Kings Subjects there fhew itfelf fully by a Memorial of fixty Officers ferving in the upper Lakes in this Campaign, praying his Majefty would be gracioufly pleaf'd to permit them to fettle 639 Farms at their own Expence, with fuch Marks of the Kings Royal Favour as his Majefty may think proper.

On receiving General Gages Orders to continue the War againft the Shawanes & Delawares I demanded the Affiftance of his Majeftys new Subjects, the Ottawas, Chepewas, Hurons, Sakes & Potawatames; four Parties immediately went againft them. One returned with one Scalp which is fufficient for the whole to carry on & continue the War unleff prevented by bad Management by us.

Albany, 7th Decr 1764.

Jn Bradftreet

PAPERS

RELATING TO THE

Indian Wars of 1763 and 1764,

AND THE

CONSPIRACY OF PONTIAC.

INTRODUCTION.

THE Correspondence of Military Officers and others charged with Duties relating to Indian Affairs, during the Wars of Pontiac, necessarily embodies a large Amount of Information concerning the Causes which led to Hostilities, the Alarms which those occasioned, the Measures that were taken to suppress them, and the Opinions that were entertained as to the Changes necessary to prevent their Continuance or Recurrence. These Letters place before us in vivid Colours, the Condition of the Country, its Resources and its Wants, and narrate, without Ornament, the simple Facts which their Writers wished to communicate. A Portion of these Papers are copied from the Bradstreet and Amherst Manuscripts, and most of the Remainder from the Manuscripts of Sir William Johnson, in the State Library. In making the Selection we have avoided as much as possible including those ever before printed.

F. B. H.

PAPERS

RELATING TO THE

Indian Wars of 1763 and 1764.

Letter from Gen. Amherſt to Col. Bradſtreet.

[Bradſtreet and Amherſt MSS, p. 132.]

NEW YORK, 22ᵈ June, 1763.

SIR: Your Expreſs arrived here laſt Night and delivered me your Letter of the 19ᵗʰ with thoſe Encloſed; the Anſwers to which I now tranſmit you, that you may forward them by the firſt ſafe Opportunity that offers.

You do very right to be prepared for puſhing up Proviſions to Fort Stanwix, which I would have you do tho' I am in Hope we ſhall have ample Supplys for the Upper Poſts from Fort Wm. Auguſtus.

I ſend Orders to Captain Wineprefs to march with his Company to Fort Ontario, as I now order about forty

forty Men of the 42d & 77th Regiments, who are fit for Garrison Duty to Albany, where they will remain under the Command of a Captain of the 77th Regt who will succeed Capt. Winnepress in the Command of the Garrison. There is likewise a Subaltern of the 77th, with a Lieut: and three Serjeants of the Independents.

Major Gladwin writes me of the 14th May, that the Detroit was invested by a large Body of Indians; but that the Garrison were in high Spirits & he was in Hopes of being able to defend the Place untill he received some Succour from Niagara, & Major Wilkins acquaints me he had immediately on the Arrival of the Schooner from the Detroit, sent off a Reinforcement of fifty Men with a Lieutenant and non-commissioned Officers, which I trust will have arrived in Time to save the Place.

I well know that you are always ready, however I think it necessary to acquaint you to be ready for moving at a moments Warning, as if the Savages are not quickly reduced I believe I shall employ you on a Command, which, I am certain will be agreeable to you.

     I am, Sir,
      Your most obedient Servant,

        Jeff. *Amherst*

Col. Bradstreet,
 D. Q. M. G.
  P. S. Since I wrote the foregoing Mr. Leake has
           deliver'd

deliver'd me a Return of the Provifions, which, by the laft Returns, were at Fort Wm. Auguftus, Ofwego & Niagara, &c., of which I enclofe you a Copy, whereby you will fee, that the Quantities at thefe Pofts are very confiderable. J. A.

With Major Duncan's Letter I received one from Major Wilkins to Captain Dalyell, which miffed him by the Way, of the 3d Inftant: Nothing new then at Niagara; but one of the Men that were miffing, found, as I feared, dead & *fcalped*, near the Fort above the Falls.

Altho' none of the Letters require Anfwers at prefent, I think it beft to order the Poft to return; and I have directed Mr. Colden to order the Rider, to make more hafte than they have lately done and to be more ready to fet out from Albany, as the Service may require them, without waiting for any fixed Time.

Before I received your Letter I had apply'd to the Lt. Governor (finding that my Endeavors to accommodate Matters with the Perfons employed by the Elders & Deacons had no Effect, altho' I had fpoke particularly to the Chief Juftice for that Purpofe) to give the neceffary Directions to the Attorney-General, not only to defend your Suit, but to profecute the Corporation of Albany, for pulling down his Majeftys Fence, &c.

     I am, Sir,
      Your moft obedient Servant,
       Jeff. Amherst.

Col. Braadftreet,
 D. Q. M. G. Albany.   P. S.

P. S. I this Moment receive a Petition from one Crifp, which I enclofe that you may be fo good to give an Anfwer. I imagine that his Claim is not juft or it would have been paid.   J. A.

NEW YORK, 20th July, 1763.

SIR:

THE Poſt came in laſt Night with your Letter of the 15th Inſtant, and brought me likewiſe Letters from Major Duncan & Captain Loring, adviſing me of the latters Arrival at Fort Ontario, on the 5th, with the Sailors, and that he had fitted out the Johnſon Snow, ready to proceed to Fort Wm. Auguſtus for Proviſions. Himſelf & the reſt of the Seamen were to ſail in the Schooner to Niagara.

The Same to the Same.

[Bradſtreet and Amherſt MSS., p. 134.]

NEW YORK, 7th Auguſt, 1763.

SIR:

LAST Night I received your Letter of the 1ſt Inſtant.

You did very right to furniſh Sir William Johnſon with what Proviſions he required, for the Uſe of the Indians.

I have no Objecton to your ſending two or three Oxen, at a Time, to Fort Stanwix, for the Uſe of that Garriſon, as you ſay you can ſupply them cheaper than they can be got from New England. Lt. Colonel Campbell muſt take Care that there is a particular Account kept of what is iſſued, according to Orders, as there is no Commiſſary from the Crown at that Poſt, the Contractors Commiſſary will be only to be paid for the Flour; unleſs you ſell the Cattle to the Contractors.

The

The Daſtardly Behaviour of the Batteau Men is particularly unlucky at this Time; for I have been impatiently waiting to hear of the Arrival of the Engineers Stores at Oſwego: I hope when you ſent them back, they have proceeded with all imaginable Expedition.

    I am, Sir,
      Your moſt obedient Servant,
        JEFF. AMHERST.

Col. Bradſtreet,

The Same to the Same.

[Bradſtreet and Amherſt MSS., p. 135.]

    NEW YORK, 18th Septbr, 1763.

SIR:

I AM to own your Letter of the 12th Inſtant and I approve of your having ſupplyed Sir William Johnſon the Proviſions you mention as he expected to have a Conference at his Houſe with the Six Nation Indians.

Any Bedding that may be wanted hereafter for the Garriſons I can ſupply from hence, as there is a great Quantity now in Store, which came from *Martinique* and the *Havana*, but what you have forwarded to Oſwego, will be ſo much the nearer for being ſent to the Detroit, &c.

    I am, Sir,
      Your moſt obedient Servant,
        JEFF. AMHERST.

Col. Bradſtreet,
 D. Q. M. G.

The Same to the Same.

[Bradftreet and Amherft MSS., p. 136.]

NEW YORK, 24th September, 1763.

SIR:

I AM to own Your Letter of the 10th Inftant; I have not yet come to the Determination with regard to the fmall Pofts on the Communication to Fort George: I can keep one Man only in each of them, which I will contrive to do, to continue the Poffeffion; but you may fend a Proportion of Candles for the Garrifons of Crown Point, Ticonderoga, Fort George & Fort Edward; the three laft will have one Company in each; and there will be four Companys at Crown Point.

I enclofe you a Copy of Publick Orders, which have been given here, & which I fend now to all the Pofts, for making Stoppages to all the Provifions that may be iffued to the Troops, in purfuance of Directions I have received from the Lords of the Treafury: It has already taken place in Canada, and I have ordered the Stoppages to commence at Albany, the Dependent Pofts & the Communication to Fort George inclufively on the 1ft October, for Crown Point & Ticonderoga are to be garrifoned by Troops from Canada. The Orders are to be made publick at all the other Pofts; but I have thought proper to continue an Allowance to the Troops at Fort Stanwix & the dependent Pofts & to the feveral Garrifons above, as I think it would be hard to put them to Stoppages until the *Indian War* is entirely quelled & that they are on the fame Footing with the other Troops: This Regulation does not affect the Provincials who muft

be

be subsisted, as usual, untill the Service will permit them to be sent to their respective Homes.

I enclose you a Packett addressed to Lt. Colonel Elliott, containing Dispatches for Canada, which you will forward by one of your People, on purpose, to Crown Point; sending at the same Time the Letters to the commanding Officers at Fort Edward & Fort George. When the Companys from Canada arrive at Crown Point & Ticonderoga, Lt. Colonel Elliott, with the Men of the 55th (Leaving compleat Companys at Fort George & Fort Edward), will move down to Albany, where he will remain till further Orders.

    I am, Sir,
      Your most obedient Servant,
        JEFF. AMHERST.

Colonel Bradstreet,
 D. Q. M. G., Albany.

The Same to the Same.

NEW YORK, 28 Septb., 1763.

SIR:

A VESSEL having arrived here with the Cloathing for the several Reg^{ts} in this Country, I am sending that for the Corps above as fast as possible to Albany, that no Time may be lost in forwarding it before the Winter sets in. One Sloop is already loaded & will sail to morrow Morning: Ensign Crosthwaite, who is going to Albany, has the Care of the Cloathing in her & will deliver you the Bill of Lading; so that you will order the Cloathing to be landed & put into the Store at Albany, sending the enclosed Letter to Fort Stanwix & Crown Point, as I have directed the Commanding Officers at those Posts to send Qr. Masters

Masters & proper Partys to conduct the Cloathing to their respective Posts; the 17th, 46th & 80th to Fort Stanwix; from whence the two former will be forwarded to Oswego, for which I write to Major Duncan; and from thence to Niagara, &c., and the Cloathing for the other Corps must be sent with the Party that comes from Crown Point. Two other Sloops will take the Whole from hence; and you will pay the Hire at the usual Rate & according to what you may think just & reasonable. Swits's Sloop, which sails to-morrow, has got many other Things, I am told, on board; so that he ought to be paid accordingly; and I shall transmit you Bills of Lading of the others when they are loaded.

I am, Sir,
Your most obedient Servant,
JEFF. AMHERST.

Colonel Bradstreet,
D. Q. M. G. Albany.

Letter from Alexander Duncan to Sir Wm. Johnson.

[MSS. of Sir William Johnson, vii.]

FORT ONTARIO, 1st Octob., 1763.

SIR:

A FEW Days ago I was favored with your Letter of the 17th ultimo and yesterday that of the 26th reached my Hands.

I have forwarded your Letter to Major Moncrieff, from whom I have received a Letter dated 26th ultimo at Niagara in which he informs, that they were then preparing to set out for Detroit, but that they were obliged to carry the Provisions over the Portage on Men's Shoulders and that it would be the 5th or 6th October

October before they would be able to fed out. I have sent sixteen Oxen which are with them before now, there is likewise a Reinforcement of 260 Men that I reckon have got to Niagara this Day, these I hope will enable Major Wilkins to fed out sooner and stronger than he expected; the whole are under his Command I imagine will exceed 600 Men, they go in Battoes & carry so much Provisions as they can.

You will no doubt have heared that the Savages attacked the Schooner going up the River to Detroit on the 3d ultimo, the Master of the Vessel & one Seaman were killed & three others wounded, but the Savages were beat off; they had once got upon the Bowsprit and have hacked and cut the Vessel a great dale on the Bows & under the Stern; there was only twelve Men on board the Schooner at the beginning of the Affair, three of whom were sick. The Indians acknowledge to have left eight Men & many wounded & by some of their Canoes oversetting have lost sixty Stand of Arms.

Several Canoes have lately arrived here from Canada with Passports (to go to Detroit with Ammunition & Indian Goods) from General Gage; I have taken the Passes from the Traders & secured the Ammunition & Goods in the Fort. The People in these Canoes inform me that several Traders have got Passports to go up Grand Riviere and that one Canoe is gone to Toronto. I have informed Lt. Col. Browning of the latter, that he may send a Party & bring away the Traders from Toronto. Here follows a Copy of the Preamble to one of these Passports.

"By the Hon[ble] Genl. Gage, &c., &c. Whereas
"Messrs. Wells & Wade have represented to me, that
"it is probable that the Savages are dispersed from
"about Detroit, and therefore demand Permission to
send

"send a Canoe there under such Regulations as I shall
"think necessary to be given."

It is not easy to account for Mr. Gages Conduct on this Occasion, but I have send Copys of all the Passports that have fallen into my Hands to Sir Jeffrey Amherst, let those two Gentlemen settle that Affair. Six Canoes came here five of which were loaded, the other had put their Loading on board the Sloop at Fort William Augustus and they have no less than 75 Barrels of Gunpowder besides, &c.

Every thing continues quiet here.

I am, Sir,
    Your most obedient humble Servant,

Alex Duncan

To Sir William Johnson.

Letter from General Amherst to Colonel Bradstreet.

NEW YORK, 1st October, 1763.

SIR:

AS the last Sloop with the Cloathing is not yet failed I take the Opportunity of sending this by her (as she may reach Albany before the Post) to acknowledge your Letters of the 25th & 26th September by Captain Sowers; and to approve entirely of your Readiness in forwarding the Oxen, Carts, &c. for Niagara: Your getting the *Tyers*, &c. made at Albany has likewise my Approbation; and as they must be in want of Provender for the Cattle during the Winter, they not having had an Opportunity to make any Hay,

I

I should be glad you could forward to Niagara a Sufficiency of Corn, which you tell me you can do.

In a late Letter to Lt. Colonel Elliot I directed him to send down the Remainder of the Detachment of the 17th Regiment, immediately on the Arrival of the Companys from Montreal, which I conclude he will have done; and that Captain Morris will have proceeded to Fort Stanwix; but should Captain Morris with that Detachment be at Albany on Receipt hereof or arrive afterwards you will acquaint him that it is my Orders he proceeds, without Delay, to Fort Stanwix; as Lt. Colonel Campbell has at Present rather too thin a Garrison; especially as, from the Accounts I have received of the late Affair on the Carrying Place at Niagara, there is Reason to suspect that the Body of Savages who cut off our Convoy were mostly Senecas. I hope the other Five Nations are not privy to this Affair; altho' it is hard to say who are our Friends or Foes. The whole Race of Savages seem to be, more or less, concerned in this treacherous Insurrection.

I am, Sir,
Your most obedient Servant,
JEFF. AMHERST.

Colonel Bradstreet,
D. Q. M. G.

Letter from Capt. Daniel Claus to Sir Wm. Johnson.

MONTREAL, 1st Octob., 1763.

HON. SIR:

I HOPE mine of the 23d ultimo, by Capt. Brown, came safe to Hand, since which I had a Deputation from the Missisageys living about Toronto; their Message consisted of a large String and a Belt of about 2000

2000 Wampum, by the former they expreſſed their great Concern on acc^t of the preſent unhappy Diſturbances about Detroit, &c., and that they abhorred and deteſted it and therefore had ſince the Beginning kept out of the way in the Environs of Cataracqui, that at the ſame Time they were thereby reduced to the greateſt Diſtreſs for want of their Neceſſaries being brought among them, and therefore requeſted & implored the General to let ye Trader La Farge alias Tawaniawe the Swegachie interpreter, who uſed to ſupply them heretofore with Neceſſaries come to their Village this Seaſon that they might not be prevented from this Winters Hunt for want of Ammunition, &c. ——— the Belt.

Genl. Gage without Heſitation replied them that as to their Profeſſions he could or would not ſo far doubt them, tho' he was ſure of ſome Canoes having been purſued by Miſſiſagey Ind^s and when overtaken & found they were French were told that they took to be Engliſh whom they lay in wait for. However be that as it would he ſhould not give them an Anſwer upon their Meſſage, that if they wanted to exculpate themſelves they muſt addreſs themſelves to you as the principal Perſon of their Affairs who only had the Power from the King to hear & ſettle ſuch Matters & as to ſending a Perſon to trade among them he would never agree to it, neither was it in his Power, and ſo ſent them away. They were 3 in Number and had with them a Pany who deſerted from hence when this Place was taken and being found out by his Maſter was taken from them by him upon the Gen^{ls} Order and put into the Provoſts. A Frenchman that came from Niagara this Sumer informed the General that he was purſued by ſ^d Pany and coming up to him with his Knife in his Hand told him that if he was an Engliſhman would looſe his Life.

I

I afterward examin'd the Frenchman, whether any of these Ind^s were in Company with the Pany but he was sure they were not.

I then spoke to them in my Room, and made them as much sensible as I could of the heinous Behaviour of those Nations that occasioned the present Disturbances, and that they must attribute every Inconveniency they now labored under to them only, and endure it till such a Time as proper Satiffaction was given for their vile & inconsiderate Actions, etc.

I had their Arms mended for them and gave them a little Ammunition, Tobacco & Rum and dismissed them, tho' they expected some Cloathing, being in a Manner naked; I also gave them a Passport to go your way in case their Nation would send them.

I impatiently wait for the Return of the Caghnawageys as well on account of knowing the Determination of the 6 Nations who I hear had a numerous Congress at your House, as my Destination for the ensuing Winter.

This goes by Maj^r Abercrombie who I hear is to be one Genl. Amherst's Family.

I am, with the greatest Respect and Compliments to the Family,
    Hon. Sir,
     Your most dutyfull
      and obedient Serv.

To the Honble Sir William Johnson, Bart.
I beg leave to trouble you with the enclosure.
            Letter

Letter from Maj. Robert Rogers to Sir Wm. Johnson.

DETROIT, October 7th, 1763.

SIR:

MAJOR Gladwin has told me that he will enclose you all the Proceedings at this Place since the Date of my last Letter, as also every particular Account concerning the Indian War, the first beginning, &c.

For these Reasons and as I think it would come more correct from him than from me, I defer mentioning any other Particulars relative to our Condition at this Place.

McCormick will deliver you this Letter, he has a Bill on Col. Croghan. I should be obliged to you if you would gett him the Money, for it would serve me greatly to make my Payments speedily.

Aaron the Mohawk Indian came into the Fort this Day, Daniel and Jacob is also in this Garrison but I have not any Intelligence from them but what Major Gladwin will communicate, tho' I soon shall & some that they tell me & no man shall at this Place know but myself, but you shall have it in full from me, and one of the Indians you sent up will convey the said Account, the other four is now in Sandusky where there is a grand Council, but will return in a day or two; the Schooner sails directly, therefore I can not send to you their private Information, but surely will do it by themselves the first Opportunity.

There is about one thousand Indians in this Settlement at present waiting for some Troops that is coming up; I wish they may not get a Flogging.

I beg you'll be so kind as to inform Mrs. Rogers if there is any likelyhood of my coming down this Fall,

for

for my Part I know nothing of the Difpofition for this Place at prefent, neither does Major Gladwin.
I am Sir, Your moſt obedt
Humble Servant.

To Sir William Johnſon,

The Same to the Same.

DETROIT, Octob. 7th, 1763.

SIR:

SINCE I wrote my Letter, Aaron the Mohawk has come in and tells me that he was in the Council yeſterday and that all the Nations here he ſays the Indian War begun through the Five Nations and that ſince the Belt came here that Aaron ſays he told you was brought by one Indian laſt Fall, that a ſecond Belt came laſt March and told the Indians to begin, and with that a Tomahawk was delivered and the Indians that brought this Belt from the Five Nations told and aſſur'd the Indians that they would begin at the Time the Corn was planted. The five Nations was to ſtrike from Niagara to Schenectady and the Taways and other Nations to take the upper Poſts on the Lakes, that the Senecas and Cahugees were the People that ſent this Meſſage and further told them that they would meet them at the Windotes town early this Spring.

Aaron

Aaron tells me that the Hurons were obliged to ſtrike the Engliſh as they were threatened by the Toways and other Nations and that the Toways now tells the Hurons if they attempt to make Peace without their Conſent or Advice they will directly deſtroy them, and that if they attempt to come to the Fort they will be conſidered by them as Engliſhmen.

Aaron ſays that they have ſeen our Troops that are coming from Niagara at the Long Point on the north Shore, and that all the Savages here are determined to attack them at Point a Plee.

Aaron ſays he will lett you know further ſoon and what he has told you now you may depend upon is true, that the Hurons deſire that you may know that the Taways and other Nations on the Lake are now their Maſters, their Numbers being ſo ſmall they can't help themſelves, they are going to the Huron River about thirty Miles from this Fort, where they intend to winter, and the Taways are reſolv'd to winter at Miame River, the other four Indians that came up with Aaron are gone to Sanduſky.

    I am, Sir,
      Your moſt humble Servant,
          ROBERT ROGERS.

Endorſed. Wrote to Jn Glen, Eſqr. for 15 Barrels Pork & Flour in Proportion, 5 to be ſent to Cherry Valley, 5 to Conradt Franks, 5 to Caghnawagey.

Memorandum. 10 Pr Strouds, 6 do. Aurora, 6 do. Blankets, 540 Shirts; 12 ps Stocking Stuff, 108 lb. Vermillion, 719 lb. Verdigreaſe, 100 Pipe watches, 8 Groce of Knives, 20 Yds Ribbon, 6 ps Silk handkerchiefs, 11 groce Rings, 10 lbs Beeds.

Letter from Sir William Johnson to Colonel Eyre.

JOHNSON HALL, Octbr 13th, 1763.

DEAR SIR:

I AM to thank you for your Favor of the 3d Inst., altho' the Want of the *Packet*, as you obferved, muft prevent your having any material News. I moft heartily wifh whenever it arrives it may bring the News of their being perfectly acquainted in England with the Commencement of our Indian War, as without that they will be unable to take any proper Meafures & the firft News which was fent Home in June poffibly did not appear very interefting.

About 2 Days ago I had an Account that a confiderable Body of Indians are affembling at the Sufquehana with Defign to deftroy this Country from Schenectady upwards, or elfe to fall upon Efopus or Shamokin, &c. Both the former I look upon to be in their Power & therefore believe it is probable they will put one of them in Execution; for my part I can not fee what will prevent their Succefs, as you know the Nature of the Country People fufficiently to fuppofe they can not be kept in a Body for any Time, but muft follow their feveral Occupations, fo that I have only to rely on the Hopes of fome previous Intelligence & on the prefent favorable Difpofition of all the Nations (except Senecas) many of whom are ready and defirous to join our Troops, but how long they may continue in this Difpofition is uncertain, as the great Succefs of our Enemys & the fmall Oppofition they have hitherto met with renders our Friends very apprehenfive of their Refentment from their daily Threats and may occafion their Defect^n, efpecially as we are not able to give any neceffary Succour which might

might enable them to withstand our Enemins. I have from several Hands the Particulars of our unlucky Affair at Niagara by which it appears that our Troops were attacked in such a disadvantagious Situation that they were hurried down the steep Cliffs near La Platon unable to make any Resistance & most of them perished, many of them were found sticking in the Forks of Trees; the Senecas of Cheneseo (who were the Principals in this Affair) have not brought in any Scalps, with only one Man wounded on their Side. This is particularly unlucky at this Time and I fear will be followed by more such blows if the greatest Care be not taken.

I shall expect when any thing occurs that you will let me have the Pleasure of hearing from you, as
 I am,
  with Sincerity, &c.
Col. Eyre.

Letter from Sir Wm. Johnson to Lieut. Gov. Colden.

JOHNSON HALL, October 13th, 1763.
 DEAR SIR:

I HAVE just received an Account, that a considerable Body of Indians from towards the Ohio & the Seneca Country are assembling on the Susquehanna and that they are destined to fall either on Shamokin, Esopus, or to destroy the Mohawk River Settlements from Schenectady upwards, the first of these Places is capable of making a Defence, but I can see little to prevent their Success against the two latter, particularly in these Parts from the sad State of the Militia and the great Want of Ammunition, &c.

I have acquainted Col. Hardenbergh of the Danger
of

Indian Wars of 1763 and 1764.

of the Settlement of Esopus and as I have no doubt that one of these Designs will be put in immediate Execution, must beg the Favour of hearing from you thereon as also of your Answer to mine of the 10th of Aug. last concerning the Vacancies & Additions necessary for this Regiment.

In the mean Time I shall take every effectual Measure for the obtaining the necessary Intelligence on which the Safety of this important Frontier must chiefly depend, and on Warning of the Enemy's Approach shall make the best Disposition the Nature of the Country will admit of.

The many Successes of our Enemies, together with their large Number, may prove of dangerous Consequence by influencing our Friends to joyn them thro' fear of their Power, Vicinity & Resentment, especially as we are not able to afford them the Assistance which Allies should require, but I shall continue to use all my Endeavors to prevent a Defection, which as Matters now stand must prove the Destruction of this Country as well as to cut off so essential a Communication to the Lakes.

I hope to have the Pleasure of your Answer and
    I am with great sincerity
             & Esteem, &c.
Lt. Governor Colden.

Letter from Gen. Amherst to Lieut. Gov. Colden.

NEW YORK, 15th October, 1763.

SIR:

IN a Letter I have this Moment received from Sir William Johnson of the 6th Instant, among other Intelligence concerning the bad Intentions of the Indians

dians, he says he has learnt, "that the Senecas & De-
"lawares were now daily marching to *Kaghraandote* on
"the Susquehana, a Place appointed for their Ren-
"dezvous; that when all were assembled their Leader,
"*Quaghquoandax*, would then agree to fall on one of
"the following Places, namely, Shamokin, Esopus or
"Cherry Valley; and the Mohawk River from Sche-
"nectady upwards."   I therefore think it highly necessary to give you this Notice, that you may take
proper Steps for putting the Militia on their Guard as
it is absolutely impossible for me to spare one Man from
the Posts above; for I have pushed on every Man I
could spare to Niagara & the Detroit; and you know
I have none below. Sir William Johnson, I doubt
not, will take every Precaution in his Power for pro-
tecting the Settlements on the Mohawk River. But
the Inhabitants everywhere on the Frontiers can not
be too much on their Guard & indeed the only thing
they have to do is to be unanimous in repelling by
Force any Attemps that may be made by the Savages.
    I am with great Regard,
        Sir, Your most obedient,
            Humble Servant,
                JEFF. AMHERST.
Hon[bl] Lt. Governor Colden.

Letter from David Vanderheyden to Sir Wm. Johnson.

SIR:

I AM this Moment inform'd by Robert Lansingh,
who came last Night from the *Groote Imbogt*[1] that
one *Dirk Ehl* at that Place had rec'd a Letter from a

---

[1] The *Groote Imbogt* (or Great Bend) was on the Hudson River, just below the Mouth of the Catskill Creek, on the west Side,

Kinsman

Kinsman, living somewhere on Delaware River, informing him that about 60 Families were destroy'd thereabout.

I fear that the Indians that have now been to N. York with Saml Pruyn are Spy's, tho' they behaved very complisant & civil to me & my House: my Negro Wench tells me this Morning, that the youngest of them, who talks the best English, had told her Husband, Capt. Steph^n Schuyler's Negro, that the Indians were all join'd, & that they did not fear the great Guns but enjon'd him to keep it Secret as the Negros would be in no Danger. And by some Traders I am inform'd that he is the same that caused a Disturbance at Oswego & Niagara last Spring a Year.

I communicate these out of Zeal for the Service and am with unfeign'd Regard,
  Sir, your Honor's
    most obedient humble Servant.

David van Der Heyden

Albany, the 19th October, 1763, a 8 A. M.
To the Honble Sir William Johnson, Bt.
 at Johnson Hall.

Letter from F. Decouagne to Sir William Johnson.

     Niagara, Octob. 22d, 1763.
 Honorable Sir:

IN your last you desired to know whether Daniel & the rest of the Indians was gone to Detroit, the former has been up with two Parties & has the Character of a good Man from every one, but most People
           give

give an indifferent Acc^t of Aron. There has been no Indians here; the Traders at this Poſt are all Suttlers. Major Wilkins is gone with the laſt Partie & has taken with him all the Belts and Bands Wampham to the Wapagamat Indians. I dont learn by any Accounts that the ſ'd Indians have done any Miſchief at preſent. I have no more to relate at this Juncture than have ſent encloſed Mr. Stedmans Acc^t of what happen'd the 19th & 20th Inſt., the ſ'd Perſon being preſent at the whole Affair.

I have an Intention to go as I think wou'd be proper amongſt ſome of the Wapagamats to get Intelligence but believe it will be very dangerous, therefore beg your Inſtructions by the firſt Opportunity.

I am, Sir,
Your moſt Obed^t Hum^l Servt

De Couagne

SIR:
I have further to inform you that all the Canadians who have Paſſes from General Gage to Trade are ſtopp'd at the different Poſts.

To the Hon. Sir William Johnſon, Bt.,
 at Johnſon Hall.

Indian Wars of 1763 and 1764.

Letter from General Amherſt to Colonel Bradſtreet.

[Bradſtreet and Amherſt MSS., p. 141.]

NEW YORK, 29th October, 1763.

SIR:

I ARRIVED here on Thurſday Morning and gave immediate Orders for getting ready the Iron Work for the Schooners that are intended to be built for the Service of Lake Erie, &c. A ſufficiency for one of 60 Tons, with the Rigging will be ſent on Saturday next, & Preparation ſhall be made for two more & ſent up as faſt as poſſible. I need not deſire you to forward the whole in the beſt Manner you can.

This will be delivered to you by *Bogardus* in whoſe Sloop Mr. Napier has ſhipt the Bedding as per the encloſed Invoice & Receipt, and you will pleaſe to receive the Whole and order them to be ſafely ſtored to be ready for ſupplying any of the Poſts above : Tho' ſome of them have been uſed, Mr. Napier aſſures me they are as clean, ſweet and good as if they had not been uſed. As Mr. Napier is accomptable for this Bedding, it will be neceſſary that you ſend him a proper Receipt for them.

Lt. Colonel Campbell writes me, that the Bridges on the Communication between Fort Stanwix & the Flatts[1] were broke down by the Oxen that were lately ſent up; and that if they are not repaired before the Winter, the Roads will be impaſſable for Sledges : I have wrote to Sir William Johnſon on this Head & requeſted him to endeavor to get the Inhabitants to effect this uſefull Service ; but if you can anyways lend a helping Hand it will be ſo much the better, for I

[1] German Flats.

fear we can not depend much on what the Country People will do, without they are preſſed to do it.

   I am, Sir,
     Your moſt obedient Servant.
           JEFF. AMHERST.

Colonel Bradſtreet,
 D. Q. M. G.

The Same to the Same.

     NEW YORK, 30th October, 1763.

 SIR:

IN all Probability the Sloop with the Beding will be at Albany before the Poſt reaches you. I however encloſe you a Duplicate of my Letter that went by her & I likewiſe tranſmit you a Liſt of the Ironworks that are getting ready for the Schooner, and which with the Rigging, will, I hope be embarked from hence on Saturday next.

 I encloſe a Packett addreſſed to Governor Burton at Montreal, which you will pleaſe to forward by the firſt ſafe Opportunity; and likewiſe a Letter for Major General Gage which you will keep until he arrives at Albany, where you will ſoon ſee him, as I imagine he is on the Route by this Time & it might miſs him, were you to ſend it on.

 On my Arrival here, I applyed to the Lt. Governor regarding the ruinous Condition of the Fort at Albany & repreſented to him how neceſſary it was to have it repaired in Time, as 'tis Shamefull to ſee it: he has promiſed to make Application to his Aſſembly for that Purpoſe; but as the Fort is going in the mean Time to Ruin & that we may always want to keep a few Men there, I would have you order the Maſonry or
               the

the Parapets to be repaired, if it can be done at a small Expence, as it will be too late before the Assembly will determine. The Coping them with wood, as the north Curtain is & the Work in the Inside of the Fort, may be done later in the Season, & I hope will be done at the Expence of the Province.
   I am, Sir,
     Your most obedient Servant,
        JEFF. AMHERST.
Col. Bradstreet,
 D. Q. M. G.

The Same to the Same.

NEW YORK, 1st November, 1763.

SIR:

THIS will be delivered to you by Lieut. Godwin, whom I send to Albany, with a non-commissioned Officer & three Men of the Royal Artillery, which are all that I can spare from hence, & I think they may be usefull in forwarding any Artillery Stores that may be sent to the upper Posts, or giving their Assistance to other Services at Albany, and I write to Lt. Colonel Elliot accordingly.

To avoid any Disputes about Quarters, I would have you provide Lieut. Goodwin with a Room in the Hospital.

I have this Moment received your Letter of the 26th October, and with it I have one from Major Gladwin of the 7th October. Every thing as well as we could expect at the Detroit: Moncrieffe, with the Reinforcements, just setting off on Lake Erie the 14th and I hope they will arrive in Time to give the Bar-
             barians

barians a Check before the Winter fets in, tho' it is too late to expect much.

I have applyed to the Provinces of New York & Jerfey, for two thoufand Men, to be raifed early in the Spring, 1400 from New York & 600 from the Jerfeys. Five Companys of the former, of 60 Men each, to be raifed immediately for the Protection of the Communication between Albany & Ofwego. How far my Requeft will be granted I know not; but I fhall acquaint you, as foon as I receive the Governors Anfwer. In the meantime I would have you make the neceffary Preparations for the new Boats, fhould the one you are building anfwer, of which you will be the beft Judge, and you muft be fure of your Succefs.

I may now acquaint you that His Majefty having been gracioufly pleafed to give me Permiffion to return to England, Major General Gages, with whom I am to leave the Command of the Troops & who will foon be at Albany on his way hither, will have full Directions concerning the future Operations; and you may confult with him regarding the new Boats, as well as the Preparations for the other Matters; for by the Time he arrives here I fhall be able to judge of what Affiftance may be expected from the Provinces and we muft prepare accordingly. I have ordered two light Six Pounders to Albany.

   I am, Sir,
    Your moft obedient Servant,
        JEFF. AMHERST.

Colonel Bradftreet,
 D. Q. M. G., Albany.

             Extract

Extract of a Letter from William Edgar at Detroit to Sir William Johnson.

Novb. 1st, 1763.

I HAVE lately received a Letter from Hombach which came by an Officer from Illenois, who brought a Belt & Letter to the Savages, with the Account of the Peace, between England and France, which neither the Savages nor the French *here* believed till now. In Consequence of which, our most implacable Enemys, the Ottawas (who were the only Nation here disposed for continuing the War, all the rest having begged forgiveness for what they have done, of our worthy Commandant) are now, with the others, suing for Peace, in the most abject Manner. Mr. Prentice is very well at Sandusky, as is Mr. Winston, at St. Josephs, and from the present Disposition of the Savages, I apprehend they will soon bring them in.

Letter from Sir William Johnson to the Authorities at German Flats.

Novbr 3d, 1763.

GENTLEMN:

AS I understand that some Chenopsco[1] Indians (who are now our Enemies) make a Practice of coming to the German Flatts to purchase Powder & other Things w^h you know is not allowed, besides, when there, they have an Opportunity of making their Remarks & seeing our Strength, you should in order

---

[1] Genesee.

to prevent yᵉ like for the Future, take up all such as you find of that Nation & send them Prisoners to Albany under a good Guard, first being certain that they are our Enemies—not doubting but that yʳ own Prudence will lead you both to do every thing of that Kind with Propriety & Discretion. I need add no more.

Letter to Justices Frank & Harkemer to apprehend any Chenupscos who may come to the Flatts.

Letter from Volkert P. Douw to Sir Wm. Johnson.

ALBANY, Novemb. 3d, 1763.

SIR:

I THOUGHT it not improper at this Time to acquaint you as being Commissioner of Indian Affairs that last Night arrived here three Tennesie Indians directly from there Castle as they say; they also say they waited on you as they passed in there way to Albany of which I doubt much; they have a small Quantity of Beaver with them but no Person chuses to Trade with them without Liberty. I am at a loss how to act with regard to those Indians and should be glad of your Direction therein by the Return of the Bearer.

I am, Sir,
Your most Humˡ Servant,

Volkert P. Douw

To Sir William Jonson, Barnit.

Orders

Indian Wars of 1763 and 1764.

Orders iſſued by Captain Guy Johnſon to the Garriſon at Schenectady.

ORDERS.

AS the Safety and Protection of Schenectady depends in a great Meaſure on the keep of a good Guard in the Town, it is Sir Wm. Johnſons Orders that the Commanding Officer of the ſecond Bataillon of Militia for the County of Albany do immediately appoint a Guard conſiſting of a Subaltern, Serj't, Corporal and twenty Men to mount at the Block Houſe in the Albany Street and to be regularly relieved every 24 Hours till further Orders, which Guard is to poſt Centinels at ſuch Places as the Commanding Officer of the Battaillon ſhall judge beſt, the Centinels to be regularly relieved by the Corporal of the Guard every two Hours and the Officer to let no more than two Men be at any Time abſent from the Guard. Every Evening at Sunſet the Officer of the Guard is to have his Men under Arms, the Roll called & Mens Arms, &c. examined & ſee that they are furniſhed with 12 Rounds of Powder & Ball, no Perſon is to be abſent on pain of Puniſhment and the Town Major is at the Time he thinks neceſſary to viſit the Guards & Centinels & make a Report thereof to the Commanding Officer. The Serjeant of the Guard to viſit the Centinels frequently during the Night and the Officer on being relieved to make a Report of the Guard in Writing to the Commanding Officer who is to ſee theſe Orders ſtrictly complied with.

In caſe of an Alarm the Militia are to aſſemble at the Dutch Church and there to follow ſuch Orders as they ſhall receive from the Commanding Officer for the Protection of the Town, the Guard turning out & continuing

continuing under Arms until they shall receive the Commanding Officers Orders.

And the Commanding Officer is to transmit in writing to Sir Wm. Johnson a Return of the state of the Blockhouse and other Fortifications about the Town, as also of the Number, State & Quality of the Cannon & Ammunition, &c., immediately.

Johnson Hall, Nov'r 3d, 1763.

*G. Johnson Capt & Adjutant
of the Regt of Albs militia*

Col. Vanflyke, &c.

Letter from Gavin Cochrane to Sir Wm. Johnson.

DEAR SIR:

I CAME here yesterday & had the Pleasure to find all your Friends here well—the Battoe is in a Hurry to go down which prevents my having the Pleasure of waiting on you. Capt. Daniel, at parting, pressed me much to give an Account of his Behaviour whilst with me when I was guarding the Wreck; I was there above a Fortnight & in all that Time he was but once drunk, always at my Elbow, & very Industrious to do every thing to ingratiate himself with me, and so was Jacob, who was with him. We were fired at for near two Hours by 25 or 30 Indians, as they guessed from the Tracks afterwards & Daniel kept close by me & showed great Zeal—we lost 3 Men; the Enemy came very near but we could not get one Shot at them—the Behaviour of Aaron, &c. occasioned me to be sollicited not to send Daniel up with the Schooner, but I sent him;

him ; nor will I believe the Mohawks in general dishoneſt.

Fatigue & Cold gave me an Illneſs which tho' I have not yet quite recovered I am pretty well, only in a very bad Weather I am pretty ſure ſtill of an Ague Fit. I am ſo far on my Way to New York.

The Troops for Detroit, about 600 Men under Major Wilkins got out from the Head of the Rapids at the Entrance into Lake Erie the 20th of October. Two Boats were fired upon at embarking there & all in them except a Serj^t killed or wounded ; five were killed & one died of his Wounds, as did alſo Lt. Johnſon; there were a good Body of Men ſtill aſhore who purſued & engaged in the Woods for ſome Time & than returned in good Order to the Boats. This is the Serjeants Account who remained unhurt, who ſaid he ſaw this at a Diſtance but knows no other Particulars.

I don't know whether it is worth mentioning to you that whilſt I was at Fort Stanwix I was told a Squaw of the Oneidas that had juſt come ſaid there was a Report amongſt them that 20 of their Young Men had been killed by our People in the Cheroquee Country & that the Oneydas were holding a Council about it. I am, with great Sincerity,
  Dear Sir,
    Your moſt obedient & very humble Servt.

     Gavin Cochrane

Fort Johnſon, Novb. 5th, 1763.
The Number in the two Boats that were fired upon were 14 excluſive of the Officers.

Letter from General Amherst to Colonel Bradstreet.

NEW YORK, 6th November, 1763.

SIR:

I HAD last Night your Letter of the 31st October: The Account given by *Silverheels*, I believe, is too true and I am not surprised the Inhabitants on the Mohawk River are alarmed: They can not be too much on their guard, until they can get an additional Assistance, which I hope the Province will furnish, when the Assembly meets.

I have mentioned to the Lt. Governor how necessary it will be to get a Law passed for impressing Carriages, as well as billeting the Troops on this Occasion. But whether he can bring it to bear, or not, I know not.[1]

I am very glad to find you have such Hopes of the Boat answering; but am sorry to hear you have such bad Reports of the Stuff fit for building Boats at Oswego; however I am apt to think the Batteaus from Canada may answer; General Gage will know that.

---

[1] This Law was not passed. The only Acts passed by the General Assembly of New York with reference to the Wars of Pontiac were the following:

"An Act providing for three hundred effective Men, exclusive of Officers, to be employed against the Enemy Indians, and for one hundred and seventy-three Men, Officers included, to garrison the several Forts on the Frontiers of this Colony, in such Manner as the Commander-in-Chief of all his Majesty's Forces in North America shall think proper, and also for three hundred effective Men, exclusive of Officers, to guard the western Frontiers of the Colony under the Direction of the Governor or Commander-in-Chief thereof.

Passed Dec. 13, 1763."

"An Act providing for one hundred and eighty Men, exclusive of Officers, to be employed against the Enemy Indians and other Purposes therein mentioned."

Passed April 21, 1764.

General

General Gage, in all Probability will be with you before this reaches Albany, and as he has no Family with him, I hope he will have found all the Affiftance he could require on the Route.

The Sloop with the Iron work, &c., as mentioned in my laft, failed on the 4th. I enclofe you a Lift of the Whole, but the Mafter went off without figning the Invoice of the Sails, Cables & Anchors: you have his Receipt therewith for the Iron work, and you will pleafe to take care that he delivers the Whole, agreeable to the enclofed Lift. I need not defire you to forward them in the beft Manner you can.

As Captain Loring, I imagine, will be down foon, I would chufe to wait for his Opinion of the Size of the other Veffel, before I fent the Materials; but fhould he not come foon, I fhall order Iron work, &c. to be forwarded for the fame Kind of Schooner as the one for which the Materials are now fent.

    I am, Sir,
      Your moft obedt. Servant,
        JEFF. AMHERST.

Colonel Bradftreet,
 D. Q. M. G. Albany.

Message of Lieutenant Governor Colden to the General Assembly of New York.[1]

[Gaine's Journal of General Assembly, ii, 720.]

Gentlemen of the Council and General Assembly.

THE great and defireable Work of Peace, being by the Wifdom and Magnanimity of our gracious Sovereign, happily accomplifhed fince your Recefs; I cordially congratulate you on this joyful Event, fo highly glorious to his Majefty, and extenfively Beneficial to his People. His American Subjects, who will derive from it a Security, unknown fince the firft Eftablifhment of thefe Colonies, muft receive this Mark of the royal Attention to their Intereft and Safety, with the warmeft Sentiments of Loyalty, Gratitude and Affection.

The Enjoyment of folid Tranquility is however unhappily fufpended by the daring and unprovoked Attacks of fome of the Weftern Tribes of Indians, who under the fpecious Appearance of Friendfhip, have treacheroufly furprized fome of our remote Pofts, and are in open War, renewing with relentlefs Cruelty, that Horror and Defolation among the defencelefs Inhabitants, from which they were fo recently delivered.

To fupprefs this dangerous Defection, pregnant with the moft fatal Evils, before it becomes more extenfive and formidable, is our indifpenfable Duty.

The Prefervation of our own Frontier, fhould be our firft and immediate Care, every Motive of Policy,

---

[1] The General Affembly of New York met on the 8th of November, 1763, and on the Day following the Lieutenant Governor addreffed to them the preceding Meffage relating to the Indian War.

Juftice

Juſtice and Humanity, unitedly demanding the Protection of our fellow Subjects, whoſe diſtant and diſperſed Situation muſt otherwiſe leave them an eaſy Prey to mercileſs Savages.

But barely to defend ourſelves would be giving the Enemy every Advantage, and expoſe us to perpetual diſquietude. It is neceſſary a Force ſhould be raiſed, ſufficient to chaſtiſe theſe faithleſs People, that feeling the Weight of our Reſentment, they may be awed for future by the Fear of Puniſhment; experience evincing, that deſtitute of every juſt and humane Principle, nothing elſe can ſecure us againſt their continual Ravages and Depredations.

Since then, not only the Proſperity of the Colony, but the very Exiſtence of a great Part of it, depend on the moſt active and ſpirited Meaſures, no Arguments can be wanting to animate you to a vigorous Exertion of your Strength in the Accompliſhment of this eſſential Object.

I ſhall therefore content myſelf with laying before you a Letter I received from his Excellency Sir Jeffrey Amherſt, Commander in Chief of his Majeſty's Forces, preſſing this Government to furniſh a Proportion of Men, to proceed early in the Spring in conjunction with the regular Troops, on this important Service. Did the Subject require it, his ſuperior Abilities, would render it unneceſſary for me to enforce, what he ſo wiſely urges for ſubduing that reſtleſs, fierce and cruel Spirit of the Savages, the Source of the moſt dreadful Calamities.

Gentlemen of the General Aſſembly,

I flattered myſelf the ordinary Support of his Majeſty's Government, would have been the only Aid required of you at this Time. But the unexpected Revolt

Revolt of the Indians, renders a much greater Expence unavoidable. Besides providing for the Company now posted at Fort Ontario, Niagara and Detroit, which General Monckton, by the Advice of his Majesty's Council, a few Days before his Departure, directed to be continued on that Service, I earnestly recommend you will grant the necessary Supplies for raising, cloathing and paying, a Body of Forces, sufficient with the other Troops, to avert the Dangers we fear; avenge the Injuries we have received; and convince the Savages of our Ability to compel them to Submission.

Gentlemen of the Council and General Assembly,

The Enemy have already infested the Border of Orange and Ulster, and though I am confident of the Spirit and Activity of the Militia, yet as this Duty will soon be too severely felt, I assure myself, you will enable me to ease them; and by the most vigorous Resolutions in this important Conjuncture, secure to yourselves the great Advantages of a Peace, peculiarly calculated for the Happiness of America.

CADWALLADER COLDEN.

Fort George, New York, Nov. 9, 1763.

And then the Letter mentioned in his Honour's Speech from Sir Jeffrey Amherst, was read, in the Words following, that is to say,

NEW YORK, October 30, 1763.

SIR:

ON a due Consideration of the most probable Measures for crushing the present Insurrection of the Indians, and punishing the Guilty as they deserve, I find it absolutely necessary to make Application to the Provinces most nearly concerned, that a respectable Body of Men may be raised, so as to proceed

early

Indian Wars of 1763 and 1764.

in the Spring, in Conjunction with such regular Troops as can be collected, to put in Execution such offensive Operations as may be judged most effectual for reducing the Savages, and securing Peace and Quiet to the Settlements hereafter.

I am in great Hopes that the Provinces to the Southward will chearfully raise such Quotas, as may be required of them, for reducing the Delawares, Shawanese, and other Tribes on that Side; and as I intend to assemble a respectable Body of Men early in the Spring at Niagara, for the Punishment of the Senecas and other Savages on Lake Erie, &c. who have so treacherously commenced and are now carrying on Hostilities against us, I think it but reasonable that the Provinces of New York and Jersey, should contribute their Shares towards a Service of so much Consequence to the future Security of their respective Inhabitants; and therefore I am now to lay before you, a Requisition, which I am persuaded will not only meet with a proper Reception from you, but that you will enforce the same to your Council and Assembly, backed with such Arguments (if any Arguments can be necessary on such an Occasion) as will at once remove every Obstacle that could be started to a Compliance therewith.

The Proportion I must demand from your Province is fourteen hundred Men, exclusive of commissioned Officers, twelve hundred to be divided in four Corps of five Companys each, commanded by a Field Officer, who may have the Rank of Major; and each Company to consist of a Captain, and two Subalterns and sixty Men, including three Serjeants and three Corporals; the other two hundred to have a Field Officer, and to consist of four Companies of fifty Men each, with the commissioned and non-commissioned Officers as above; for the Service on which they will be employed requires that there should be a good many Officers; the Men to be cloathed, but in a light Manner; a cloth Jacket, flannel Waistcoat, Leggins, &c. will be full sufficient; and it will be necessary that the whole are raised and ready to proceed to Albany by the first of March next.

But as the Settlements on the Mohawk River, are open to the Enemy, and that it is not in my Power at present to spare Regulars for their Protection, so much as I wish to do, I must recommend it to you, to use your Influence with the Assembly to raise five Companies of the above mentioned Quota with the utmost Expedition, that they may be posted during the Winter, on the Communication between Albany and Oswego, and be ready for any Service they may be called for, which may be a great Means of preventing any Incursions that might be attempted by the Savages, and give that Confidence to the Inhabitants, which is so necessary to enable them to repel, by Force in Case of an Attack.

Particular Care should be taken that in recruiting the Men, none should be raised but such as are able bodied; neither too young nor too old, but fit for the most active and alert Service.

Although by an Order from Home, the regular Troops are subject to a Stoppage for the Provisions issued to them, belonging to the Crown, yet upon this Occasion I will take upon me to order Provisions to the Provincial Troops, that shall be raised and take the Field; and they shall likewise be provided with Arms, unless any of them chuse to bring their own Arms, for which they shall have the same allowance as was made in former Campaigns, should any of them be
lost

Indian Wars of 1763 and 1764.

loft, or damaged in actual Service. Tents will alfo be furnifhed to them as formerly.

The Time of Service may be limited to the firft of November, although it is much to be hoped, every Thing will be finifhed long before that Period, in which Cafe the Men will be fent back to the Province.

I am, with great Regard Sir,
    Your moft obedient humble Servant,
        JEFFREY AMHERST.
A true Copy, examined by G. Banyer, D. Sec.

Letter from Captain Gerret A. Lanfingh to Sir William Johnfon.

[MSS. of Sir William Johnfon, vii.]

SIR:

AGREABLE to your Orders I have been round the Town to revue the Condition and State of the Fort, Blockhoufes, Cannon, Amanition, &c., likewife the Stockagadefs; as for the Fort is but in a verry confetreable Condition, whants a good Teal of preparing and the Blockhoufe at the Widow Van Eps at the North Side of the Town is unfit for Service, no Shimble in nor Flowr, at the Blockhoufe at Daniel De Graff at the fouthweft End of the town is entirely unfit for Service is ready to fall down. The Blockhoufe at Mr. Ryner Mynders whants lettle repairing. As to the Block Houfe on the South End of Albany Street is fit to keep a Wacht in, and the Block Houfe which formley ufe to ftand at Mr. Thomas Nixfon Door is intirely takeing away and no more of, and as for Stoagadeges about the Town there is about feventy of them moftly rotton; as for Cannon in the Fort that belongs to it there is none fit for Service, there is no Cannon in the Block Houſes not a ſingle one, and there is a few Cannon lying up the Albany Hill unfit for Service which has been takeing out of the Fort and Blockhouſe and have been tryed by Soldier & Conductors of the Royall Artellery and is found to be condemned; as for Powder there is two Caſk of about 50 Wieght each which belongs to the Townſhip of Schenectady likewiſe 30 Wieght grave Schot and about ſeventy or eighty ſmall Hand Granades.

I am Sir
Your moſt obe^d hum^{bl} Servt

Gerret a Lanſing Capt

To Sir Wm. Johnſon, Bar^t.

[*Endorſement on Back of Letter.*]

Capt. Lanſinghs Return of y^e State of y^e Blockhouſes, &c. at Schenectady.

A Return of Condition & State of the Fortification of the Townſhip of Schenectady. Novbr. 11th, 1763.

Letter from T. De Couagne to Sir William Johnſon.

[MSS. of Sir William Johnſon, viii.]

NIAGARA, 27th of Novbr, 1763.

S$_R$:

I HAVE rec'd your Letter dated Novbr y^e 3d, 1763, wherein you write me word to be more particular or circumſtantial than hitherto. You may depend I do everything to y$_e$ utmoſt of my Power for my Employer

ployer, likewife for his Majeftys Service, yᵉ Troops is come back thath was going to Ditroit with yᵉ Lofs of one hundred Men, yᵉ got within lefs than one hundred Miles was caft away and loft there Ammunition was forft to return for Want; yᵉ had to I am inform'd, but eight Rounds a Man thath yᵉ could not proceed & have fpoke to yᵉ Officer Commanding, Major Browning, about yᵉ Indians coming in, he has give out an Order thath yᵉ muft not fire upon any fmall Party of Indians upon no Account & thath on their march in fight of yᵉ Garrifon he fays if yᵉ fhould fall in with Fort Slhoffer he cant be accountable what happens as they are daily killing our People. In yr Letter you fay you do not underftand what I mean by yᵉ Voifeagamigate, Sr he is yᵉ chief Man North & Weft upon Lake Ontario and fo far upon Lake Erie as yᵉ big River, which is fixty Miles from Little Niagara, yᵉ Troops goes fifhing every Day and no body hurt. I can't promife the do no mifchief in there own Country but what they do otherwife I can not tell.

Sr, I have wrote you word before of Major Wilkins taken fome Belts of Wampum from heare, he is come back, I have fpoke to Colonel Browning for to gett them. In yᵉ next Letter I fhall fend Word if Collonel has rec'd.

DE COUAGNE.

Sir yᵉ Indians is arrived this Day from Detroit which you will yᵉ News more particular from them are yᵉ Veffel fails emediately.

Letter from Aaron the Mohawk to Sir Wm. Johnson.

[MSS. of Sir William Johnson, viii.]

FORT PITT, 1ſt Decemr, 1763.

SIR:

HAVING been ſent Expreſs by Major Gladwin from De Troite to this Place, on arriving at Sanduſky meeting with about 300 Shany and Delaware Indians, who ware at the ſame Time holding a great Counfill and by which I underſtood and was told by them the breaking out of this Warr was occaſioned by the Seneca Indians who went about with a bloody Belt and Tomahawk to all the Nations engag'd in this Troubles. The Taways alſo expreſſly told me that the Senecas were the Beginners of this Warr, they alſo defired me (the old Men of the Delawar's & Shanees) to acquaint you that if you deſire, that they would come down to you, and ſwear before you that this Warr was begun by the Senecas. The old Men of the Wiandots Nation want very much to ſee you, and if you deſire they will come immediately, you being pleaſ'd to let them know. I had the Misfortune to be rob'd of 4000 of Wampom, a Tamihok and all the Powder and Ball I had by the Delawar's, Shanees & the Five Nations.

Sir, Remain with great Reſpect,
    Your Obedient Humble Servant.

AARON.

Letter from John Stuart[1] to Sir William Johnson.

[MSS. of Sir William Johnson, viii.]

CHARLES TOWN, 10th December, 1763.[2]

SIR:

I AM now to acknowledge the receipt of both your Favors of 24th July and 2d September, which my being at the Congrefs with the Indians in this Diftrict prevented my receiving and anfwering fooner. I have a grateful Senfe of your polite and friendly Expreffions, and fhall cheerfully embrace every Opportunity of cultivating a Correfpondence with, and rendering you any agreeable Service. I am fincerely forry for the Rupture with the Indians in your Department, which is attended with fo much Bloodfhed and Defolation and neceffarily with fo much Trouble to you.

Immediately after the Receipt of your laft Letter, I wrote to the Cherokee Nation, to know if they would fend fome Parties againft the Northern Indians according to their Propofal to me at the Congrefs. As foon as I receive an Anfwer I fhall communicate it to you. Some Officers of the Independent Companies in this Province, who are on the Point of being reduced, have offered to accompany fuch *Cherokees* as can be prevailed upon to go and act jointly with his Majefty's Forces againft the Northern Tribes. It would be a delicate Point to propofe any thing of this Nature to the *Creeks* at this Juncture, when they are apt to conftrue every Propofal as containing fome hidden Defign; the Impreffions left on their Minds by the French, and their Jealoufy on account of the late

---

[1] Mr. Stuart was Superintendent of Indian Affairs in the Southern Department,
[2] Received Feb. 15, 1764.

Ceffion

Ceſſion of Florida and Louiſiana, not being as yet totally effaced.

The *Chactaws* have but newly entered into the Covenant of Friendſhip with us. Their Country is a vaſt Diſtance, I ſhall endeavor as ſoon as poſſible to inform myſelf of their Diſpoſition and the Practicability of engaging them to ſend Parties as you propoſe.

The *Chickaſaws* are perpetually at War with the Northern Indians, but then they only act defenſively, being reduced to 450 Men at moſt, and ſurrounded by great Nations with whom they never are upon Terms of ſincere Friendſhip, for which Reaſon they dare not weaken themſelves by ſending out ſtrong Parties, ſo far as they are able their Friendſhip and Attachment to us may be depended upon.

The *Catawbas* are willing and brave, but reduced by War and Sickneſs to 60 or 70 Gunmen. The Northern Indians infeſted them all laſt Summer, killed and carried off ſeveral of them.

This may be depended on that I ſhall take every Meaſure to induce Parties from the Northern Nations within my Department to go and act jointly with his Majeſty's Troops employed againſt the Nations at War with us, and ſhall be extreamly glad to hear from you and receive the General's Inſtructions relative to my Conduct in this Matter.

Our Conferences at the late Congreſs ended with the moſt friendly Appearance. The Indians of every Nation went away well ſatiſfied, and made the ſtrongeſt Profeſſions of Attachment to the Britiſh Intereſt. They are all appraiſed of the War between the Northern Indians and us, but know nothing of the particular Events.

A minute Journal of the Proceedings at the Congreſs

Indian Wars of 1763 and 1764.

grefs is now in the Prefs. As foon I can be furnifhed with a Copy for you I fhall fend it.

The *Tafcaroras* inhabit a Tract of 10,000 Acres of Land laid out for them in North Carolina. I have wrote to Governor Dobbs for a particular Account of them and of their Situation with refpect to Debts or whatever elfe may hinder or retard their going to join their People. Governor Dobbs told me when at the Congrefs, that they confifted of about one hundred Men able to bear Arms, Women and Children in Proportion.

I am now to inform you, that on my return from Augufta, I received a Letter from the Right Hon[ble] the Lords of Trade declaratory of His Majefty's Orders, that the Agents for Indian Affairs fhould correfpond with their Lordfhips in all Matters regarding their Departments, and fhould tranfmit them all fuch Information as they fhould require. In Confequence they have required from me a regular and conftant Correfpondence upon thofe Points. Their Lordfhips have likewife directed me to tranfmit to them as foon as poffible, a full and particular Report of the State of Indian Affairs within this Department, and an accurate Defcription of the feveral Nations of Indians, their different Interefts, Claims and Difpofitions and what will in my Judgment be a proper Plan for the future Management and Direction of thefe important Interefts.

The Tafk impofed upon us I confider as arduous and what requires very mature Confideration, on which I have not as yet been able to turn my Thoughts, having a multiplicity of Affairs to fettle in confequence of the late Congrefs, it will give me the greateft Pleafure to coincide with you in Opinion, but to form *a general Plan* by which a Trade to the Indian Countries may

may be at the fame Time *well regulated* and *free* to all his Majefty's Subjects, is not very eafy. It will give me great Pleafure to hear from you foon, being with moft fincere Regard,
  Sir,
    Your moft obedient humble Servant,

John Stuart

Letter from T. De Couagne to Sir William Johnfon.

[MSS. of Sir William Johnfon, viii.]

TRANSLATION.

NIAGARA, 15th X^{ber} 1763.

SIR:

SINCE my laft which I had the Honor of writing to you, by which I have mentioned the Accident which happened to Major Wilkin's Party which has retreated, Major Rogers arrived with his Corps and two Mohawks, Daniel and Jacob, two Days after.

The Commandant has fent the Man named Jacob with a Ranger to Detroit, and Daniel has decided to join the Party returning with Major Rogers, to rejoin you, and who can relate to you all that has happened in thefe Parts, as well as what has become of the other Mohawk. He has told me that the Man named Ouapacamigatte a Miffiffague had a Paffport from the
           Commandant

Commandant at Detroit to come hither with a Message, and I believe it would be apropos if the Commandant would consent that I should send him with one or two others to speak with you upon this Business. I believe that there is not here this Winter any Indian whom I could send for some Time. And I remember nothing further of which to appraise you. There are Parties crossing every Day to the other Side of the River upon the Lands of the Mississagaes but they have not returned with any Scalps.

The Man named Rossin .... a Seneca of whom you speak in your Letter has not arrived. I have spoken to his two Sisters about him in a way that has flattered them much.

I have the honor to be with profound Resp^{ct}
Sir, Your very humble and much
obliged Servant,
DE COUAGNE.

It it impossible at this Moment to write to you in English, as every body is engaged, and I can not find a Secretary.

Letter from Colonel Bradstreet to General Gage.

[Bradstreet and Amherst MSS., p. 169.]

ALBANY, 20th Decr, 1767.

SIR:

I RETURN your Excellency, enclos'd, the Papers you sent me relating to small Arms taken by my Order at Oswego for the Indians in 1764—with my Certificate of the Number. Those Gentlemens Accounts & Affidavits you will please to observe fix the Time of my ordering those small Arms to be taken in

1763—near twelve Months before my Arrival at Ofwego.
                I am,
                            Jno. Bradstreet.
His Ex. Genl. Gage, &c. &c. &c.

Letter from Sir Wm. Johnson to Major Gen. Gage.

[MSS. of Sir William Johnson, viii.]

Johnson Hall, Decr 23, 1763.

 Dear Sir:

YOUR Excellency's Favors of the 30th ult. & 1ft of this inft. were accompanied with two Letters from the Lords of Trade, the one of Septr and the other of October laft, enclofing me one of the King's Proclamations, and expreffing Approbation of His Majefty & his Minifter and that of their Lordfhips on my late reprefentations, as alfo his Majefty's reliance on my Endeavors to bring Matters to a happy Iffue, and his Orders that I fhould caufe the Proclamation therewith tranfmitted to be made publick and ftrictly complied with throughout my Jurifdiction.

 I am hopeful that on receipt of my laft Letter, their Lordfhips will be able ftill further to contribute towards the falutary Points in view relative to Indians as I apprehend fome Additions may be added to the Royal Proclamation, which at prefent does not contain more with regard to them than has been already communicated to them by virtue of former Orders, &c. tranfmitted to America. This Proclamation does not relieve their prefent Grievances which are many, being calculated only to prevent the like hereafter, altho' there are numberlefs Inftances of Tracts which have
indeed

indeed been purchased but in the most illegal and fraudulent Manner, all of which demand Redress.

I have made at this Meeting the best use in my Power of his Majesty's Proclamation for the convincing the Indians here of his gracious and favorable Disposition to do them Justice, and shall communicate the same to all the rest.

The Indians have been here for several Days to the Amount of 230, are now mostly departed for their respective Nations, for which Purpose I have dismissed them with a Present. They are accompanied by several of the yet friendly Senecas from *Kanadasego*[1] as also by three Deputies sent from *Chenassio*, to desire to be informed of our present Resolution, and to know whether the Offer of Peace which they have now made will be accepted of, in which they are seconded by all the rest who earnestly desire the same might be taken into Consideration and after representing the Manner in which the Senecas of Chenassio had been led into the War, intimated that should we now receive them into our Friendship the Generosity of the Indians would cheerfully join us in any Operations against the rest, particularly against the *Shawanese* and *Delawares*, whom they represented as the principal Authors of all the late Troubles, to which after giving them ye most severe Reprimand in ye Presence of all ye rest, I answered them, that I could do nothing therein, but would lay the same before you. I must therefore request your Direction and Sentiments thereon.

This was the chief Purport of the late Conference, the rest of their Speeches consisting of a Repetition of their Promises and Assurances of their unvariable Attachment to his Majesty.

---

[1] Near Geneva, Ontario County, N Y.

On this Subject I must beg leave to offer my Opinion that the 5 friendly Nations must naturally be very uneasy at any Attempt against the Senecas, as they are a Part of their Confederacy, however justly they may deserve our Resentment, but I am confident that the whole would readily joyn against their perfidious Dependents, the *Shawanese* and *Delawares*, as well as any others who have acted as Principals in the War. The Hurons of Detroit from the concurring Accounts of all Persons were with the utmost Difficulty and by severe Threats, persuaded to engage in the War by the Ottawas under Pondiac, who with the before mentioned *Shawanese* and *Delawares* have sufficiently shown themselves as Principals in the War.

I imagine that any Hostilities committed in or about Pennsylvania and Jersey must be done by the Delawares.[1] All those of that Nation who have lately become our Enemies, have lately removed from the Susquehanna to the Ohio amongst the Shawanese, and those who remain on or about the Susquehanna, particularly from its Source down to *Owegy* are our friends, and here I cannot help remarking that the absurdity of most of the Acc'ts received from the Provinces is apt to give a very unjust Idea of Indⁿ Affairs. For instance, in one of the late New York papers you must have observed it is insinuated that a Party who defeated Capt. *Westbrook* on the Borders of *Pensilvania* consisted of Mohocks, which they pretended to know from their Caps, and Manner of cutting their Hair. The Fidelity of the Mohocks deserves a better Return, and the Folly of such Representations should certainly be removed, least it come to the Knowledge of our

---

[1] The following Sentence is here interlined in the original Draft without apparent Connection with the Text: "*Wyaloosin* is an Indian Town a confiderable Distance from any Settlement."

friendly

friendly Tribes who might entertain much Rancor from such a Falsity. The Mohocks do not wear Caps, nor any Nation of the Confederacy except the Senecas and some Cayugas, the former learned that Practice from their vicinity to *Niagara,* where such were usually worn during the Winter, neither are the Authors of that Paragraph or any other Persons capable of distinguishing one of these Caps from another or knowing to what Nation it belonged any more than they are of discerning one Blanket from another.

The House of Assembly have been very moderate in their Resolves. I have received from the Lieutenant Governor in consequence thereof some blank Commissions for raising two Companies of 50 Men each to be stationed at *Schohare* and *Cherry Valley* which I shall give to such Persons as I shall judge best qualified to answer their Intention.

I am informed by Letter from Niagara that Wabbicommicot, Chief of the numerous Nation of the Chipeweighs who accompanied me to the Detroit in 1761, and has since behaved very well on his Part and prevented Numbers of his People from joyning against us, proposes to visit me shortly on public Business, which if he does, or that I am attended by any other dist^t or Enemy Indians, indeed I shall be glad to have your Sentiments concerning my Behavior on that Occasion and in what Manner you think it most necessary to treat them.

I am, &c.

Letter from Sir Wm. Johnson to Lieut. Gov. Colden.

[MSS. of Sir William Johnson, viii.]

JOHNSON HALL, Decr 24th, 1763.

DEAR SIR:

I AM juſt favored with your Letter of the 7th Inſt. encloſing me two Captain's Warrants & 2 Commiſſions as alſo three Lieutenants Warrants & 4 Commiſſions, from which I conclude that 'twas a Lieuts Warrant which was given to Mr. *Ten Eyke.* The reſt of the Warrants ſhall be given to ſuch Perſons as I judge will anſwer the public Expectations in the moſt expeditious and moſt effectual Manner. The Companies when raiſed ſhall be muſtered agreable to your Directions, but the ſmall pay of the Officers in a Country where People are accuſtomed to high Wages and where Men are now raiſing by Col. Bradſtreet at much higher Rates, will I fear greatly retard their completing, and I am a good deal ſurpriſed how your Letter and encloſures could have been ſo long by the Way.

The Indians who had been with me from all the 6 Nats for ſeveral Days are juſt departing for their reſpective Habitations. They numbered 230, and were accompanied by ſeveral of the yet friendly Senecas from *Kanadaſego* as alſo by three Deputies ſent from the *Chenuſſio* requeſting to be informed of our preſent Reſolutions and to know whether Offers of Peace will be accepted of or not. In this they were ſeconded by the reſt of the Nations who after repreſenting the Manner in which the *Enemy Senecas* had been drawn into the War, intimated that ſhould they now be received into our Friendſhip the whole of the Six Nations

tions would heartily joyn us againft the reft of our Enemies particularly againft the Shawanefe and Delawares whom they reprefented as the principal Authors of all the late Troubles, and I know the Difpofition of thefe People fo well as to forefee that any Attempt againft the Senecas muft naturally create uneafinefs amongft the reft of the Confederacy, particularly the Cayugas and Onondagas who are more connected with them than any of ye reft.

I have juft received two Letters from the Lords of Trade (one dated in Septr the other in October laft) enclofing me the King's Proclamation and expreffing the Approbation of his Majefty and his Minifters and that of their Lordfhips on my late Reprefentations as alfo his Majefty's Reliance on my Endeavors to bring Matters to a happy Iffue, and his royal Orders that I fhould caufe the Proclamation therewith tranfmitted to publifhed and ftrictly complied with throughout my Jurifdiction, and I am hopeful that within a fmall Period of Time things may be fettled on a ftill more fatiffactory Plan.

I am a Stranger to what Caufe the Affembly attribute the unhappy Rupture, which is not a general Defection of the Six Nations as is infifted, nor indeed of any others except ye Shawnefe, fome of the Ottawaes and Chippawaies, alfo Delawares. I fhall not take upon me to point out the original Parfimony, &c. to which the firft Defection of the Indians can with Juftice and Certainty be attributed but only obferve as I did in a former Letter that the Indians (whofe Friendfhip was never cultivated by the Englifh with that Attention, Expenfe and Affiduity with which the French obtained their Favors) were for many Years jealous of our growing Power, were repeatedly affured by the French (who were at the Pains of having many

proper

proper Emissaries among them) that so soon as we became Masters of this Country we should immediately treat them with Neglect, hem them in with Posts and Forts, encroach upon their Lands and finally destroy them, all which after the Reduction of Canada seemed to appear too clearly to the Indians who thereby lost the great Advantages resulting from the Possession which the French formerly had of Posts and Trade in their Country, neither of which they could have ever enjoyed but for the Notice they took of the Indians and the Presents they bestowed so bountifully upon them, which however expensive they wisely foresaw was infinitely cheaper and much more effectual than the keeping of a large Body of regular Troops in their severall Countries which however considerable could not protect Trade or cover Settlements, but must remain cooped up in their Garrisons or else be exposed to the Ambuscades & Surprises of an Enemy over whom from the Nature and Situation of their Country no important Advantage can be gained.

From a Sense of these Truths the French chose the most reasonable and most promising Plan, a Plan which has endeared their Memory to most of the Indian Nations who would I fear generally go over to them in Case they ever got Footing again in this Country, and who were repeatedly exhorted and encouraged by the French (from Motives of Interest and Dislike which they will always possess) to fall upon us by representing that their Liberties and Country were in ye utmost Danger and that a Fleet and Army, was arrived at Quebec, and an Army coming by way of the Mississippi to their Assistance, all which the Indians were persuaded to credit until their Messengers sent to the Ilinois returned and contradicted the Report so industriously propagated by the French, which imediately struck at our Trade,

gave

Indian Wars of 1763 and 1764.

gave them some distant Hopes of a reëstablishment by embroiling our Affairs and drew down the valuable Fur Trade by the way of the Ilyones & Mississipi and the Ind^s once embarked in the Quarrel were easily induced by their Success and Advantages of Plunder to continue their Ravages. In the midst of which however I have the Satisfaction to find that my unwearied Labors hath hitherto preserved the whole Confederacy (Chenusseos excepted) with many other Nations and thereby secured this very important Communication to the Lakes, also that by the River St. Lawrence, together with these Western Frontiers from the Fate which hath attended the neighboring Colonies, to effect these important Ends, as I have sacrificed all my Tranquility and domestic Concerns so I have the Pleasure to find myself rewarded in the favorable Sentiments with which his Majesty and the Ministry have been lately pleased to express themselves concerning my Labors for the public Welfare.

The present unhappy Rupture was long foreseen and frequently represented by me, but I had the Mortification to find that it did not meet with sufficient Credit, which Neglect at length brought on the Calamities in which we are involved and from which I apprehend we can never be free unless we remove the Jealousies which the Ind^s entertain of us, and purchase their Friendship with Favors and Notice, which Friendship once obtained and established will enable us to withdraw our Expenses by imperceptible Degrees.

These are my Sentiments on the present State of Indian Affairs and the Causes to which the Hostilities are certainly to be attributed and I hope they may tend to the further Information of any who may be desirous to enquire into the Subject.

The Petition which you sent me I was informed of

some Time ago and that Geo: Klock a Person of an infamous Character at Conajoharie had made it his Business to procure it signed by sev¹ Persons (the greater Part of whom I know to be his Relations and Retainers, and his own Name is erased at the Head of them) whom he persuaded thereto on Promise of Rewards and of procuring them Commissions, which the ignorant People readily believed, I have however sent for the Officers complained of and shall transmit you my further Inquiries therein.

I am Sir, &c.

Letter from the Rev. Samuel Dunlop[1] to Sir William Johnson.

[MSS. of Sir William Johnson, viii.]

CHERRY VALLEY, Decem^r 25th, 1763.

HONOURED S^r:

NOT Reflecting upon you, because perhaps the Matter does not lye alltogether within the compass of your Power, we the Inhabitants of Cherry Valley, think we are deserted, we hope not of God, but we think in a great Measure of Man, and exposed to the mercyless Insults of our Enemies without Covert or Relief.

---

[1] In 1738, John Lindesay and others procured a Patent of 8000 Acres in what is now Cherry Valley, and soon after Mr. L. met in New York the Rev. Samuel Dunlop and prevailed on him to visit the Tract, offering him several hundred Acres upon Condition of his using his Influence with his Friends to settle upon the Land. The Proposition was accepted and Mr. Dunlop visited Londonderry in New Hampshire, where several of his Acqaintances resided, and induced Numbers to emigrate to the new Tract. Mr. D. was a Native of the North of Ireland, and had traveled quite extensively in the Colo-

You

You know General Amherst was condemned for not making some Provision for the Safety of the Inhabitants by covering the Frontiers, and it was expected when he resigned that General Gadge and your Honour, or the Persons to whom the Care and Management of these Things were committed (you know best who they were) wou'd have made an alteration before now. But Things seem to remain in statu quo, with the poor and unhappy Fronteers and the Council of the Heathen held some Time agoe seems to have had its accomplishment against all the Places they intended, us only in this Quarter escaped. Matters appear darker and darker with us, and the Time now seems to be at Hand to fetch us the intended Blow, and Schoharry's being warned off we take to be a bad Omen of our aproaching Ruin.

And if Man neither can nor will help us, may Allmighty God, either ward off the Blow or endow us with that Firmness of Spirit that may make us bear the Thoughts of Death without Amazement, and bring our Minds to an equal Poize between the strong Inclinations of Nature to live, and the Dictates of Reason and Religion that should make us willing to die when he pleases.

Death and a destroying Enemy may curtail a few Years of this mortal Life, from those of us that are old,

nies, particularly in the South. He left Ireland under an Engagement of Marriage which he returned and fulfilled. He opened a School for the Instruction of Boys, at Cherry Valley, and has the Honor of beginning the first Grammar School West of Albany within this State.

In the memorable Massacre of November 11, 1778, Mr. Dunlop's Wife was killed, but himself and Daughter were spared by Little Aaron, a Mohawk of the Aquago Branch. He was released soon after, but the combined Effects of Age, Fear, and Cold, led to a Decline, which terminated in Death about a Year after.—*Campbell's History of Tryon Co.*

but

but thanks be to God can never deſtroy our immortal Life. But it's a Pity the young and riſing Generation ſhould be cutt off, and the Hand of the Heathen embrewed in their Blood, who if ſpared, might make ſome Figure in the World and be uſefull to Generations to come, and therefore, if you can mediate any Timous Relief I beg you may.

For it is but a poor Redreſs to come to our Aſſiſtance when dead, and to bury our ma[n]gled Corps when we are gone, which is but too often the ſenſeleſs Cuſtom of the Country where we live, tho tis the beſt Redreſs the Caſe will then admit of. But the Matter is to ſecure againſt the Blow beforehand and therefore once more I would beg of you Honourable S^r that you would mediate ſome Relief for us, or ſome way to ſecure us if in your Power before it be too late. And if we fall, as Chriſt prayed for his Enemies, Father forgive them for they know not what they do, ſo I pray God our Blood may never be laid to their Charge who had it in their Power to help us and did it not. Pleaſe to give my kind Compliments to Capt. Guy Johnſon & all your good Family. I add no more, but remain Sr your

     Humble Supplicant,

       Samˡ Dunlop

Letter from Sir William Johnſon to Lieutenant Governor Colden.

[MSS. of Sir William Johnſon, viii.]

JOHNSON HALL, Decr 30, 1763.

DEAR SIR:

YESTERDAY I was favored with your Letter of the 19th Inſt. in anſwer to mine of the 5th. I have received particular Information of all the late Tranſactions at the *Detroit*, as well from the Officers as from one of the Mohocks (whom with others I ſent there to be of any Service in their Power), who is juſt returned from thence charged with ſeveral Belts, &c. to me.

As the chief Cauſe of the Hoſtilities committed by the Indians was intended to procure themſelves Redreſs of ſome Wrongs, and to obtain a better treatment, together with occaſional Gifts and Rewards, for the admitting Poſts in their Country, I am of Opinion their Offers of Peace ariſe principally from an Expectation that they will for the Future obtain theſe deſired Ends which they could not get by any other Means than by having recourſe to Arms, having found all amicable Proceedings ineffectual.

For this Reaſon I conclude they have made their late Offers, and I likewiſe believe they would abide by their Promiſes if we for the Future gratify their Expectations, but I am fully convinced they will never preſerve Peace on any other Terms.

They know their own Strength and Situation too well to be as yet apprehenſive of our Reſentment, and they will never want Ammunition whilſt the French can ſupply them by the Variety of Communications open

open to the western Indians and beyond our Power to shut.

The Five Nations have had no Occasion to alter their Behavior, which as it has saved this Communication and the Frontiers of this Part of ye Province, justly entitled them to all necessary Supplies for themselves; more they did not require, nor are they so well affected to these Nations who have made War upon us as to give them any Ammunition even tho' they had plenty. Indeed the Indians are very chary of Powder, and although they often waste it when they have plenty (yet that has not been since the Surrender of Canada) yet they are not so weak as to part with it to others, besides they have never had more than a bare sufficiency, often expended before their hunting Season was near over.

If therefore they should be denied Ammunition it would immediately confirm them in the Sentiments which greatly contributed to produce the Defection of the rest, and would counteract all my Endeavors to remove that too general Opinion for the suspecting their Sincerity w^d make them dangerous Enemies, and of this I have had repeated Experience.

I wrote you pretty fully in mine of 24th by which you will see the Difficulties which may arise in punishing the *Chenassios* and the Advantages which will attend our turning our Arms against the rest of our Enemies, which will equally answer the important Purpose of giving them a just Idea of our Abilities and Resentment.

As I am well acquainted with the Inclinations of the friendly Indians I know the lengths they are to be trusted on the Article of Ammunition, of which I am certain they will make no bad Use. It is an Article so hard to be procured here, that I have not had it in

my

my Power to give them what they stood in ye greatest need of, and the Trade being now over they can have little if any from that Quarter, altho' I must confess the Danger they have run from the Attachment to which we have hitherto own the Safety of these Parts sufficiently merits such a Return from us as will shew them that they are not losers by their Fidelity.

From what I have heard from the Senecas, as well as from the good Disposition of the rest, I should be induced to hope that that these Frontiers might enjoy a State of Tranquility, at least for a Time, but as this must be very uncertain (especially if the Peace offered by the Senecas is not accepted of), I apprehend the two Companies for these Frontiers may not be amiss but I fear they cannot be easily raised at this Time, as I have offered the Warrants to sev^l who declined accepting of them, by Reason of the lowness of the Officer's Pay, and the Bounty now offered in Albany, &c. for raising Men for other Service. Be assured I shall give you imediate Notice in case there appears a Prospect for compleating them, at well as give you any further Intelligence which may come to my Knowledge worthy your Information, and I have a particular Pleasure in assuring you how much I am,

Dr Sir, &c.

Memorial of Indian Traders.

[MSS. of Sir William Johnson, viii.]

[Copy.]

To his Excellency Thomas Gage, Commander-in-Chief of His Majesty's Forces in America, &c. &c.

May it please your Excellency as we conceive some Hopes from the Accounts we have from D'troit of having a Peace with the Indians in the Spring, and as your Excellency has the ordering of every thing on the Continent, knowing your Inclination of serving every Person to the utmost of your Power, and your Excellency's Desire strictly to adhere to the good of his Majesty's Subjects, we humbly beg leave to Petition your Excellency and represent to you the Misfortunes we have labored under from the Plunder that was made by the Indians at the Time that the Forts were surprised, and to hint to you what we think may be to our private Advantage without any Detriment to the Nation and wherein our Losses may be in some Measure repaid without any Retardment to the publick Peace. According to the Custom of Trading several Indian Nations having taken up Goods upon Credit to a very considerable amount, and are all of them capable of making Payment for the same, some of them having heard nothing of the Indian Warr had brought their Peltrys to Discharge their Debts, but on seeing the Distress we were in their good Intentions were laid aside and they took a Part with our Enemies. These are the Indians who have been most distressed during the Time the Warr has continued, and we hear are most desirous of bringing Things to an End. The Ottawas, the Chipaways, the Miamis, the Pouteoutamis,

Saguinaw, Iroquis, &c. with all the Indians who trade on Lake Superior. If your Excellency thinks proper, when they propofe Terms of Peace, to mention to them to pay their Debts, if your Excellency thinks it will be no Detriment to the Publick Good it will make us fome Retalliation for the exceffive Loffes we have fuftained, will put us again on a good Footing for Trade and will relieve from great Diftrefs your Excellency's Petitioners, and moft dutiful & obed^t Serv^{ts}.   Signed,

Ja's Howard,	Hen'y Bostwick,
Jno. Chinn,	Forrest Outres,
Edwd Chinn,	Gorsen Levy,
James Stanly Goddard,	Holmes & Memsen.

Dated 30th Decr 1763.

Letter from T. De Couagne to Sir William Johnfon.

[MSS. of Sir William Johnfon, viii.]

Sir:

I HAVE the Honor to acquaint you on the 20th of Novr I got hear from the Seneke Caftles the Chiefs promifed me that they would fend the Horfes here. The Seneke Indians comes in evry Day, brings in Bevers and Vennifon and behaves very well, as alfo the Miffafagoes. I have no more to add, but if any thing happen fhall inform you, fo conclude.

Y^r moft hum^l Servt to command.

De Couagne.

Niagara, Jan'ry 4th, 1764.

Letter from Sir Wm. Johnson to Lieut. Gov. Colden.

[MSS. of Sir William Johnson, viii.]

JOHNSON HALL, Jan'y 12th, 1764.

DEAR SIR:

A GREAT Indispofition under which I have labored for several Days, and from which I am not yet recovered, prevented my anfwering your Favor of the 28th ult° fooner.

In my Letter of the 30th ult° I gave you my Sentiments on the Reafons which induced the Indians to propofe an Accommodation, as alfo concerning the Article of Ammunition, reprefenting that none received any but thofe on whofe Confidence I might perfectly rely and to whom a Refufal might prove of dangerous Confequence, and that even the trifle of Ammunition which they received was too little and too much valued by them to part with. In my Letter of the 24th ult° I acquainted you with the Occafion of my having been vifited by the 5 Nations accompanied by fome Seneca Deputies.

Laft Week arrived here feveral of the Senecas on the fame Errand as before, whom I acquainted that I was not as yet authorized to treat with them on Terms of Peace, they were followed by the 5 Nations amounting to near 300, who came to repeat their Offers of taking fuch fteps againft our Enemies as I fhould direct, to which I have affured them in the beft Manner I could. But thefe Senecas having come contrary to my Defire and not being defirous to give any Satiffaction farther than a Promife of affifting us againft the reft, I have accordingly difmiffed them until I hear from General Gage. I however apprehended a white Man now amongft them, and who was formerly delivered

livered up but went back to the Indians and has had as I am informed the Treachery to act againſt us in the late Operations of our Enemies particularly at Niagara Carrying Place, I ſhall therefore commit him to Jail.

The Generality of the People have certainly great Reaſon to be irritated againſt the Indians, and I am glad to find ſuch a Spirit of Alertneſs as you expreſs amongſt them, tho' I fear they will not find it an eaſy Matter to puniſh thoſe who really deſerve it, and the falling upon thoſe yet our Friends and who are conſequently not aware of any ſuch Deſign, would I apprehend be very imprudent as well as diſagreeable to you ſince it muſt inevitibly involve us in a general Quarrel.

The general Thirſt for Revenge ſo juſtly raiſed amongſt our People may without proper Inſtructions direct itſelf to a wrong Quarter as was lately the caſe in *Penſilvania*, to prevent which, as well as to promote the Succeſs of all the hearty Volunteers I muſt obſerve that the greateſt Part of our Enemies are removed a great way up the Cayuga or Tohicon [?] Branch of *Suſquehanna*. Thoſe of *Wawilooſin* (our Friends) are gone chiefly to Philadelphia and the reſt are removed to *Chughnot* on the *Suſquehanna*, ſo that our Enemies chiefly reſide from Diaoga[1] up that Branch, vizt *Singſink, Pepiquaghquey,* &c. The meeting of theſe our Enemies is very uncertain, as they have not made any long Reſidence at any Place ſince the Commencement of Hoſtilities, but the Indians of Caneſtio, a Village between Chenuſſio & Fort Auguſta, who are chiefly Renegadoes of proflicate Fellows from ſev^l Nations, & who murdered the two Traders in Novr 1762,[2] are

---

[1] Tioga.
[2] Upon learning of theſe Murders Sir William Johnſon ſent up Lieut. Johnſon to attend a Meeting very

very proper Subjects of our Resentment and have been Principals in carrying on Hostilities.

I heartily wish that whatever Party goes out, may be able to strike such a Blow as will give the Indians in general a good Opinion of our Abilities, but to give any Hopes of Success in my Opinion it will be necessary that they should at least consist of 400 Men, and those expert and well qualified for the Service, acquainted with the Woods and furnished with Snow Shoes and all other necessary Articles. The distressing and annoying the Enemy in Winter if well conducted must prove very useful. I am now preparing some Parties of trusty Indians for that Purpose of which I hope the General will approve.

As the Trade by Reason of the War hath been at an end for some Time I apprehend it will not be thought advisable to grant any Passes till Matters are better settled, whenever that may happen I am humbly of Opinion that you will judge it necessary the Traders should give Security for their fair Dealings, and also be permitted to trade at the principal Posts only, as *Fort Stanwix, Ontario, Niagara,* &c. At these Posts they will be in the most security and their Conduct can be best enquired into, which if justly blameable and so represented by the com^{dg} Officer they may forfeit their Recognizance, for the indulging them in a liberty of trading in the Indian's Country or at their Castles, will always produce Complaints from the latter, of Frauds and Extortion, as well as render the Traders liable to be murdered, and their Effects seized on any future Quarrel which may happen.

called at Onondaga to insist on the immediate Apprehension of the guilty Parties, but the upper Nations did not attend and the rest of the Indians could do nothing but promise that if the Senecas did not apprehend the Murderers they would themselves go in quest of them— *Letters of Sir William Johnson to Lieut. Colonel Wm. Eyre and Gov. Monckton.*

With

With some Difficulty I have got Persons to accept of the Warr^ts for raising the 2 Companies for the Security of this Frontier, and I am just now informed they are almost compleated with good Men. I shall accordingly have them mustered and report to you thereon.

As Lt. Johnson, who by his Majesty's Proclamation is entitled to a Grant of Land, is desirous to know the Limits within which you consider the same may be granted, I must request the Favour of your informing me on that Head, also your Directions concerning the Steps he is to take therein and whether he is entitled to his Share as Captain of the Provincials in 1758, or is to abide by his Title as Lieut. of the Independent Companies.

I am with very perfect esteem, &c.

P. S. I have great Reason to apprehend that many mercenary Persons inhabiting along the River sell Ammunition and other Articles to the Senecas, I could heartily wish you could interpose your Authority to prevent the like for the Future.

Letter from Sir William Johnson to the Commanding Officers of the New York Provincials at German Flats.

[MSS. of Sir William Johnson, viii.]

JOHNSON HALL, Jan'y 19th, 1764.

SIR:

AS some Deputies from the Senecas, our Enemies, who have been here with a Message from their Nation to me, are now returning Home and being probably not so well disposed as they pretend, may be induced

duced to do some Mischief at or about the German Flatts, these are therefore to desire you will be sufficiently on your guard to prevent them, and in Case they should attempt Injury the Persons or Properties of the Inhabitants or the Troops under your Command, you will immediately seize upon them (taking Care that none escape) and send them down Prisoners to Albany, under a strong Guard, sufficient to prevent them from getting off.

In Case you find it necessary to take this Step it will require the utmost Precaution to be taken to prevent the greater Part of them from escaping, which will in a great Measure defeat the Design proposed by making them Prisoners.

I am Sir your most humble Servt.

P. S. The Inhabitants will enable you to distinguish the Senecas, who are upwards of 20, but it will not be prudent to mention my Name as the Occasion of their being apprehended at this Juncture. Should any of the Inhabitants sell them any Ammunition, Clothing or other Necessaries, you will immediately give me Notice thereof, and also prevent them for the Future from trading with any Indians who have been in Arms against the English.

Letter from John Stuart to Sir William Johnson.

[MSS. of Sir William Johnson, viii.]

CHARLES TOWN, 16th January, 1764.

SIR:

SINCE my last of 10th December I have not had the Pleasure of hearing from you.

I have not as yet received any Information about the

the Tuscarora Indians, as soon as I do, you may depend on its being communicated to you.

On the 24th ultimo 14 of our back Settlers upon Long Cane River were murdered, and we have since found out by seven Creeks, who for some Years past resided in the Cherokee Nation. The Creeks have sent me a Talk upon the Occasion and disclaim the Murder and the Murderers, who say they, the Cherokees ought to kill to show their Innocence. I have sent off Talks to all the Nations within my District, but I must acquaint you that in this Department every Governor acts as if he were sole Agent, they will hardly be directed by each other and do not consult me, so that it is odds but we counteract each other; this requires some Regulation.

By next Opportunity I will write you fully, it being my Intention to keep you regularly informed of the Occurrences within the Department.

I am with great Respect,
Sir, your most obedient
Humble Servant,
JOHN STUART.

Letter from Sir Wm. Johnson to Lieut. Gov. Penn.

[MSS. of Sir William Johnson, viii.]

JOHNSON HALL, Jany 20th, 1764.

SIR:

I HAD the Favor of your Letter of the 31st ult. and fifth of this inst., together with the Enclosures, and I heartily congratulate you on your Arrival to your Government, wishing that your Appointment may prove to your entire Satisfaction.

The

The Steps you have taken to discover those rash Offenders were certainly very judicious as well as highly necessary and I am hopefull they may be attended with Success for bringing them to Justice.

I apprehend that after their first Offence in murdering the 6 Indians at Conestoga their mistaken Resentment would have ended, and that first Act was sufficient to create much uneasiness amongst all the Indians, but their last public Insult to the Laws and the Government itself certainly demands the most strict Enquiry as well as the severest Punishment.

You may be assured I shall use every Argument with the Six Nations, for removing the unfavorable Ideas which they must certainly entertain of such a Proceeding, as well as to satisfy them that your Government highly disapproves of it and will severely punish the Offenders, but I am aware of their Sentiments on the Subject and [am] greatly apprehensive it will stagger the Affections of the 5 hitherto well affected Nations, who consider the Indians of your Government as connected with them and under their Protection, and as the murdered have been all along peaceably inclined, the friendly Indians in these Parts may be induced to doubt our Faith and Sincerity toward themselves from the unhappy Fate of our late Friends in Pennsilvania, which will cause them to expect the same Treatment whenever it is in our Power to destroy them. This I fear may greatly check the Ardor they have lately expressed to me of assisting us against our Enemies and even spirit up many to obtain Revenge within your Government.

The Threats which the riotous Parties have since thrown out, that they would destroy the Indians in the Neighborhood and under the Protection of Philadelphia, favors so much of Madness that I cannot acc't for

for them. Your gratifying the Indians Requeſt thereon of coming to me muſt therefore appear pleaſing to them, but I have juſt received a Letter from Lieut. Gov. *Colden* informing me that the Council "have adviſed him not to admit them into this Province." This will probably prevent me from ſeeing them, and I heartily wiſh their return back may not expoſe them to freſh Inſults, which would certainly occaſion a general Defection.

Several Deputies from the Enemy Senecas have been lately with me here, making ſome friendly Offers of Peace, but I am convinced that nothing but a good Treatment accompanied with occaſional Favors will ever enſure a laſting Peace from the jealous Sentiments which our Enemies entertain of the Engliſh and the Preſents the French have accuſtomed them to, for the Toleration the Indians afforded them in their Country inſomuch that any future Neglect on our Parts will immediately produce a diſcontent and apprehenſion of our Deſigns which will inevitably occaſion a renewal of Hoſtilities, ſo that a Peace made with theſe People without proper ſubſequent Steps to remove theſe Jealouſies and eſtabliſh a good Opinion with the Indians is always liable to be violated to the great Detriment of Trade and the certain Deſtruction of the Frontier Inhabitants wth their Dwellings, and the Expence in which the Crown muſt be involved to ſuppreſs ſuch Devaſtations will certainly am[t] to a much greater Sum (indep[t] of the Loſs the Provinces muſt ſuſtain) than would conciliate the Affections of the Ind[s] and enable us to extend our Settlements and Trade with the utmoſt Security.

I heartily wiſh that the Law you have propoſed may be agreed to by the *Aſſembly*, as it appears to me highly neceſſary

necessary and essential as well to the Credit as the Safety of the Province.

I am with great Esteem
Sir, Your most obed^t humble Servt

Letter from Sir Wm. Johnson to Lieut. Col. Eyre.

[MSS. of Sir William Johnson, viii.]

JOHNSON HALL, Jany 29th, 1764.

DEAR SIR:

I THANK you for your interesting Letter of the 7th Inst. which I would have sooner answered but for the Business in wch I have been engaged for this Fortnight past with a large Number of the 5 Nations and some Seneca Deputies.

It would have given me much Pleasure to have seen you on your Return from *Niagara.* I dispatched a Letter in answer to yours, with Directions that it might be left at *Ontario* till you came back, which I hope you received altho' I understand you did not return by that Post.

I cannot but coincide in Opinion with you on the greatest Part of what you have mentioned on Ind^n Affairs, and I could wish for the good of the Public that every Person had been of the same way of thinking, which might have proved a Means of preventing the many Losses we have lately felt.

The Causes to which the Defection of the Indians may be attributed are: First. Their Jealousy of our growing Power, and occupancy of the Outposts where they neither met with the same Treatment nor reaped any of the Advantages which they enjoyed in the Time of the French. Secondly. The Reports industriously propogated

propogated by many of the French, tending to set our Designs in the most odious Light and to represent the Indians as being on the Brink of being enslaved.

It will not appear extraordinary that the French who had purchased the Ind⁸ Favour at a high Price should obtain Credit from such a Representation, especially when there were but too many concurring Circumstances to strengthen the Belief of a People naturally credulous and jealous of their Liberties. The Indians began with Remonstrances, represented many Grievances and demanded Redress. Their Complaints I communicated from Time to Time with my Sentiments and Apprehensions thereon, but the inconsiderable Opinion too universally entertained, of their small Power and Abilities occasioned it to be treated with Neglect. To particularize all their Complaints would exceed the Bounds of a Letter; it will be sufficient to observe that I declared it as my Opinion that the Indians would not be totally neglected, but that (after redress of their Grievances) we should cultivate to the utmost of our Power a good Understanding with them, at least until we became more formidable and our Frontiers better established, and this I thought we could effect at an Expense infinitely less than any other Method, and on Principles the best adapted for securing Peace, promoting Trade and encreasing our Frontiers.

The Expence, Difficulty and Dangers attending other Expedients, the stagnation of Trade, destruction of our Posts and Frontiers, and the small Advantages to be gained by a War with us, are now obvious to most People, and are so well represented in your Letter that they need not to be enlarged upon.

The Difficulty and even Impossibility of securing our Communications or maintaining our Outposts

contrary

contrary to the Indians Inclinations is very clear to me, but I am pretty certain we can purchafe all thefe Advantages and fecure their Inclinations by a proper Treatment which will gain us a fufficient Credit with them, and awe of this Country, as it will remove all their Prejudices and which no other Steps can effect. The inland fmall Pofts don't appear to me very neceffary, they are too great a Temptation to the Ind^s whenever they are induced to quarrel, and from their Diftance and difficulty of obtaining Succours muft always fall into their Hands. The fame Reafons induce me to think, that the Perfons and Property of Traders would be fafe amongft them, for whilft there are any French there, they will certainly thro' Jealoufy promote a Quarrel, and even were there none there the Expence of tranfporting Goods is fo great, that they muft fell at a Price which would not be agreable to the Indians as well as be guilty of many Frauds not in the Power of an Officer to difcover or prevent. Whereas the Indians (who think little of going a great way to purchafe Neceffaries) would find them cheaper at our large Pofts, and the Traders would be lefs expofed to Rifque.

Wherever we can have a good Communication by Water, we might tolerably well maintain Pofts, and if fome fmall Veffels are kept up on *Lake Erie*, *Detroit* or even *Michilimackinac* might be kept up, the latter being well fituated for drawing down the northern Furs. After all that can be faid, we fhall be liable to many Broils, till the French Inhabitants and Jefuits are removed, the latter (being no longer a Society in France) we might very well appropriate their Lands to his Majefty's Ufe. I dare fay they would be fufficient to endow a *Bifhoprick* in Canada, and for good Miffionaries, and I imagine an Epifcopal Foundation in that Country

Country would greatly contribute to bring over the French, and make good Subjects of them in Time.

The late Offers of Peace made by some of the Nations has been greatly promoted by the Attachment the 5 *Nations, Indians of Canada,* &c. have manifested during the Course of the War, which makes our Enemies dread they will accompany our Troops against them in the Spring, for they have much more Reason to fear Indians than the best Troops in the World.

Indeed the beforement[d] Nations have made me so many Offers of Service that I have no doubt of their Sincerity, and I am now sending out a considerable Party of *Oneidas* and *Tuscaroras* who I hope will greatly distress our Enemies, as well as convince them that we are not without *Allies* of their own sort. This will likewise contribute to disunite them, a Circumstance too important to be neglected.

Whenever the present unhappy Trouble shall be ended by an Accomodation, I trust such Measures will be taken at Home as may ensure a lasting Peace to the Northern Colonies, on which Subject I have lately received some Letters from the *Lords of Trade* expressing his Majesty's favourable Sentiments and those of their Lordships concerning my late Representations.

I am heartily sorry to hear that the Animosities in England have not subsided, as such Party Differences must greatly prejudice public Affairs and tend to divert the Attention of the Ministry from many important Objects of public Concern.

Letter

Letter from John R. Hansen to Sir Wm. Johnson.

[MSS. of Sir William Johnson, viii.]

SCHOHARIE, Capt. Thos. Eckkers, }
Feby 1st, 1764. }

HONOURED SIR:

AFTER Lt. Coll. Van Derhyden's muftering my Men, I immediately march'd for this Place where I arrived with my Men 28th of January, and have proceeded perfuant to your Order in getting the Men quartered in the moft convenient Manner with the Advice of the Juftices and Capts of Militia.

I have fince fent one of my Lts to the uppermoft Part of *Scohare* with a Command of 16 Men, which was judged moft neceffary, whom I have order'd to be ftation'd in the beft Manner the Situation of that Part would permitt off.

The remainder 34 Men I have with Advice quartered within a Mile hereabout, if there fhou'd be any Occation to fend out Scouting Parties there's no Poffibility of getting any Snow Shoes, at this Place, if they fhou'd be wanted.

I am, Honoured Sir,
Yours at Command,

JOHN R. HANSEN.

To the Honble Sir Wm. Johnfon, Bart.

Extract

*Extract from a Letter from Ferrall Wade to Sir
William Johnson.*

[MSS. of Sir William Johnson, viii.]

PHILAD^a Feby 6th, 1764.

SIR:

YOUR Fav^r of the 5th Jany was handed me a few Days ago, which I should have answered before now but being in continual Alarms on account of a Numb^r of People comeing from the Frontiers in Arms with an Intent to murder all the Indians in this City and under the Protection of this Government, but the Oposition they met with by most Part of the Inhabitants being in a Posture of Defence obliged them to return as they came, excepting two, which was apointed to lay some Grievances before the Government.

* * * *

Letter from Sir William Johnson to Gen. Burton.

[MSS. of Sir William Johnson, viii.]

JOHNSON HALL, Feby 11th, 1764.

SIR:

CAPT. Claus, my Deputy for Canada will deliver you this, as I would not send him to this Duty without doing myself the Pleasure of writing you, as well as giving you some Account of the present State of Affairs in this Quarter.

The Indians of five out of the six Nations who from the Commencement of the present Indian War have shewn great Zeal and Attachment towards the English have thereby preserved these Frontiers and the important

ant Communication to Ontario, both of which muſt have inevitably fallen but for their Fidelity. As I am now impowered to comply with their Requeſt of going upon Service, I have accordingly equipped a party of near 200 Indians accompanied by fev¹ Indian Officers, &c. who marched two Days ago (nothwithſtanding the Snow is here 3 Feet deep) againſt the Delawares, Shawaneſe and others our Enemies in that Quarter, and I have great Hopes that their Operations will be attended with Succeſs, as it muſt appear evident that they are the beſt calculated to go in queſt of one another, and that the engaging them as Party's in the War, will effectually create a Diviſion among them w'ch will prove a great Check to their Power hereafter.

As the Indians of Canada have likewiſe acted a very good Part and made me Offers of Service when here laſt Year, I ſhall likewiſe put their Zeal to a Trial, nothing doubting but it muſt ſtrike a great Damp on the Spirits of our (hitherto elated) Enemies, when they ſee the Strength of our Alliances and that they are liable to be attacked on all Sides even by their own Sort, which will greatly contribute to the Succeſs of the approaching Campaign, and make our Enemies very cautious how they violate a Peace hereafter with a People who can employ one Nation againſt another.

Capt. Claus will give you any further Particulars neceſſary for your Information on the preſent Poſture of Affairs in the Indian Department.

I ſincerely wiſh you an eaſy and agreable Government and remain with much eſteem,

     Sir, &c.

Letter

Letter from Thomas McKee to Sir William Johnson.

[MSS. of Sir William Johnson, viii.]

Hon. Sir:

MY Son returned Home the 1st Inst, when I was honoured with your Warrant, Instructions and Favour of the 3d January. I was extremely sorry to hear of your Indisposition & sincerely hope you had a speedy Recovery.

I make no doubt but my Son at that Time informed you of the Conduct of the Frontier Inhabitants of this Province[1] who murdered six Connistogo Indians at

---

[1] The Disorders here alluded to have been known in History as the Paxton Riots, from having originated in the little Town of Paxton on the East Bank of the Susquehanna, a Place which had been burned, and many of its Inhabitants butchered in 1755. A Band of Rangers had been formed here under the Auspices of the Rev. John Elder, under the Command of Matthew Smith. The irritation of Feeling towards the domesticated Indians on the Susquehanna, in Consequence of some Murders by unknown Parties, led the Government to gather the Moravian Indian Converts of Nain, and Wecquetank near the Lehigh, and of Wyalusing near Wyoming, numbering about 140 Persons, to Philadelphia for Protection. It required all its Strength to protect the defenceless and peaceful Indians from the ferocious Abuse of the excited Frontiermen, and as they passed on their way to the Asylum provided they were everywhere threatened, and at Germantown came nigh being murdered by the Mob that followed them. They were marched to the Barracks but the Soldiers refused to receive them and boldly set the Governor's Orders at defiance. After standing several Hours before the Barracks surrounded by the insulting Mob, they were marched down the Street and conducted to Providence Island below the City, where Buildings were hastily prepared for them by the Quakers.

About the Middle of December, 1763, it was reported to Smith, Leader of the Paxton Rangers, that an Indian who had committed some Depredations, had been traced to Canestoga, a small Iroquois Settlement near the Susquehanna, and not far from Lancaster. Without waiting for a Confirmation of the Story or its Circumstances, a Resolution was at once formed, with the Con-

their Town near Lancaster, being all that were at Home at that Time except two Boys who made their Escape from them. The remaining Part fourteen in Number, Women and Children, being dispers'd through the Country were seized by the Sheriff and Magistrates of the County and confined in the Work house of Lancaster, in order to guard them, but upon the back Inhabitants receiving Information of this, they again

sequences detailed in the above Letter. Mr. Elder used all his Influence to divert his Neighbours from their barbarous Purpose, as they were about to set out for Lancaster, but with the Fury of Demons they rushed forward on their Errand of Blood. Breaking into the Jail on the 27th of December, they murdered fourteen Men, Women and Children. Before the Magistrates and Citizens could be rallied the white Savages were gone, and nothing remained to be done but to give decent Burial to the mangled and mutilated Remains of these friendly Natives. The News of this Outrage quickly spread through the Country and aroused the Quakers in particular to loud and bitter Denunciations of the Act. The Memory of Indian Murders, still fresh throughout the frontier Counties, led many to sympathize with the Rioters, to which they were rather instigated than deterred by the indiscriminate and sweeping Abuse of the Quakers, which included not only the Rioters themselves, but the whole Presbyterian Sect. Emboldened by this Sentiment, the guilty Parties openly proclaimed their Achievement as in the highest Degree meritorious, defended it by Reason and Scripture, and defied the civil Authorities in any Attempt at Punishment.

They even went further, and reeking with the Blood of the passive Victims of their Fury, resolved to complete the Work of Death upon the Moravian Indians gathered at Philadelphia. An armed Mob marched towards that City at about the last of December, with the avowed Purpose of Murder, if not of overturning the Government and expelling the Quakers, whose Sympathies with the Indians were bitterly denounced and whose Motives were unscrupulously impugned. At Midnight on the 4th of January, the Authorities, hearing of the Approach of this Party, hastily marched the Indians through the Streets, and having been supplied by their Friends with a few Necessaries, they were escorted to Trenton, and from thence to Amboy, with the View of sending them to the Protection of Sir William Johnson; but before notifying either him or the Government of New York of this Intention or asking Permission.

At Amboy they were met by a positive Order from the Governor

assembled

Indian Wars of 1763 and 1764. 243

assembled themselves in a Body and came down armed to Lancaster, broke open the Work house and in a most inhuman Manner butchered the whole, sparing neither Women or Children, an Action I look upon not inferior to any of the Cruelties committed by the Savages since the Commencement of the late or present War. As to my Knowledge these Indians have lived all their Lives within eight Miles of Lancaster, of New York, forbidding their Entrance into that Province, and soon after from the Governor of New Jersey, requiring them to leave the Territory of that Province. They were marched back to Philadelphia under a Guard of Regulars, and quartered in the Barracks where the Soldiers, conquered by the meek Endurance and patient Suffering of the Indians, received them. The Paxton Boys hearing of the Return of their Victims, rallied in great Numbers, the City was thrown into Uproar, and for several Days it was the Scene of intense Excitement, and active Preparation for Defense. The Advance of the Insurgents was checked by this Show of Resistance, and the Affair finally ended in Negotiation.

The humane and sagacious Sir William Johnson, perceiving the Perils that would attend the March of these Indians through the Interior, upon application immediately devised a Plan for their removal from Amboy to Albany, and their Support among his friendly Indians until the Tumult was over. The Victims of these Riots, shut up in their Barracks, suffered dreadfully from the Small Pox, which destroyed a third of their Number. In about a Year after their Arrival, quiet having been restored in the back Settlements, and Peace with all the Northern Tribes, these Converts were allowed to return with their Missionaries to their wasted Fields, and the Sites of their burned Cabins, on the Banks of the Susquehanna.

The Government was too sensible of the exasperated Feeling which prevailed in the Interior to attempt any Arrests until nearly eight Years after, when Lazarus Stewart was apprehended on a Charge of murdering the Indians at Conestoga.

Learning that his Trial was to come off in Philadelphia, where Conviction would have been certain, he broke Jail, called a Number of old Associates around him, and setting the Provincial Government of Pennsylvania at Defiance, withdrew to Wyoming and joined the Connecticut Settlers in that Valley. It is not improbable that the Desolation of that Settlement by the Indians and their Tory Companions in the Revolution, a few Years after, may have had some Connection with their Knowledge of the Retreat of the former Butchers of their Kindred. *(Parkman's Pontiac; Loskiel; Hazard's Pa. Register; Rupp's York and Lancaster; Sparks's Franklin.)*

in

in Peace and Quietness with their Neighbours, and I do not believe were ever concerned against us.

 The Government made some faint Efforts to find the Heads of these People, which only encourage their Impudence, as I am informed a few Days agoe, to the Number of three hundred assembled themselves in Arms and came down to Philad[a] in order to cut off some Indians the Government have here, but upon some Promises being made them by the Government, they have dissuaded them from murdering those in Philad[a] and they are return'd Home again, and they now carry Things to great Length as to threaten the Lives of sundry private People who have not agreed with them in Opinions but condemned this as a most detestable Murder, and not only contrary to the Laws of Government but Christianity, and every thing that ought to distinguish us from Savages, as this leaves us no Room to find Fault with their killing our innocent People in cold Blood, as they may now say we are satiated in the same Manner on them. I should be far from espousing their Cause did I not think they were innocent, as no Person has suffered more by the Savages than I have done, and I should have thought the People who have thus behaved more excusable if they had cut off in Philad[a] maintain'd at the Public Expence, as there is some Reason to believe that some of these have acted against us. But the others in a Manner were become white People, and expected the same Protection from us. I thought proper to acquaint your Ho[r] with this Affair, as you might perhaps want to acquaint the Indians with the true Circumstances relating to it.

 My Son presents his Compliments to your Honour and begs if you have not sent a Warant for his Acc[t] that you would be kind enough to forward one as soon as it may be convenient to you & if it likewise suits
your

your Conveniency I should be glad your Hon[r] would accompany it with one to me for some Money, as I am really at present in Necessity.

I have nothing further to add, but that I am with greatest Respect, your Honour's

most obedient and very humble Servant,

Thomas M.½

Part of a Letter from Colonel Bradstreet to General Amherst.

[Bradstreet and Amherst MSS., p. 146.]

ALBANY, 20th Feb. 1764.

DEAR SIR:

YOUR Excellency's Favor of the 13th Instant was delivered me yesterday. The Boats for 2000 Men only have long since been built and I directly stopt building any more untill your farther Directions.

To fix the Number of Carriages [at] the Carrying Place at Niagara, it will be necessary to know whether you would have all the Provisions, Stores, &c. transported acrofs before the Troops proceed to any other Service, and what Number of Days you would have taken up on that Service only. Gen[l] Amherst talk'd to me of leaving 600 Men at the Post to the westward of Neagara with 18 Month Provisions; if that is still to be the Case, and our whole Numbers amount to no more than 2000, it will require about 6000 Barrels (for your Ex. knows we should not count by Ounces

but

but give a proper Allowance for the Kind of Service) which will take 50 Ox Carts 15 Days to carry it a crofs at a full Load of 8 Barrels each Trip, exclufive of every thing for the Veffels & Pofts to be eftablifhed; but if Accidents, which we certainly muft expect from the Diftance the Cattle have to go & the badnefs of great Part of the Road, of which Major Moncrief can inform you, the Time required would be much longer.

As for the Boats I fhall begin to provide as many Horfes & Carriages as fhall be fufficient to carrying them over with the Baggage of Troops in Proportion to the Ox Carts. By this your Excellency fees it is moft probable the Tranfportation at Neagara will laft three Weeks at leaft; a long Time indeed, but it would be impertinent in me to urge to one fo well inform'd as you are of their Treachery and good Senfe of the Savages the abfolute Neceffity of entering this inland Country with a Difpatch hitherto thought by them impracticable in us, and more particularly fo fhould our Strength fall fo prodigioufly fhort of the Threats denounced againft them & the Pains taken to let them know it and therefore doubt not you will think it neceffary to direct me to augment the Number of Carriages to do the Work in the Number of Days you fhall judge we ought to remain on that Carrying Place.

I take it for granted I muft provide Teamfters & Waggons, but in this I fhall not act untill I receive your Exl^s Directions upon it.

I hope Gov. Murray[1] will not difappoint you, and I alfo hope the Eaftern Affemblys will think no Credit ought to be given to an Indian Peace but what comes

---

[1] JAMES MURRAY had been appointed Governor of Canada on the 21ft of November previous. He remained in Office until June, 1766.

to their .... directly from you, which I am perfuaded they need not expect this Spring.

Letter from Henry Monture, Wm. Hare and John Johnston to Sir William Johnson.

[MSS. of Sir William Johnfon, viii.]

KAUNAWAU KOHARE, Feb. 21, 1764.

SIR WILLIAM:

SIR: The Bearer hereof pleafe to deliver eight Dollars for which we war forc'd to do for the good of the Service, for a Hog for the Warriours to make a Feaft as we could not do any otherwafe as'tha faid it was a cuftomary Thing and they hope Sir William would not make any Differance now, and pleafe to fend Paper and Sealing Wax up to their Prieft as I have ufed fome of his Paper and Wax. A Quire and Stick of Sealing Wax. Pleafe to fend no more, but we remain

Your humble Servta

HENRY MONTURE,
WILLIAM HARE,
JOHN JOHNSTON.

The Same to the Same.

[MSS. of Sir William Johnfon, vii.]

KUANA WAHOHARE, Feb. 21, 1764.

SIR WILLIAM:

AFTER our Refpects to you we muft inform you of the Reafon of our detainment here, at this Place, we being in great Confufion here ever fince our Arrival for Reafon why, becaufe one Conokuiafi and one big Nichols

Nichols of Oneida haft sent two Belts through the Six Nations to the Sinackefs to tell them of all our Designs and force this Castle to likewise comply with their evil Purposes, and one young Warrior called Wyyautaukeen from old Oneida has said he would very soon scalp some white People and then immediately fly to the Six Nations, and there is one of the Head Warriors call[d] Cut the Pumpkin has sent Word he will meet us at Teurogoa to try what we are, and he wishes to see Jacob the Mikouder[1] of Stockbridge as he is so long a coming when he could have the Impudence to pretend to withstand him. Last Evening we received yours dated the 12th Instant wherein we acquainted the Indians your giving your Love to theire Warriors and Chiefs and then your Desire of their exciting themselves in this Affair, depending which should never be forgot, and would redound unto their Credit hereafter, and your Desire of our pushing on and not delaying our Time in Things of no Consequence or Moment, and likewise the hearty Wishes of all the Governors and Chiefs of the Country and Prayer of all good People.

The Answer of the Indians to your Letter:

Friend and loving Brother Wawaukaugee, we return you Thanks for your good Will and Complement to us and likewise the Complement of the Governors and Chiefs. We should have been set out before had it not been for them Belts sent by Conokgoraffe and Nichols as we had Reasons to think what would be the Consequences that might likely attend us and this Body of our Enemy coming down against us, for which Reasons Brother, we must acquaint you that yesterday our Chief Warrior Cowaha set out for Onandaug in order to see if the upper Nations would come down at the re-

[1] Mohegan.

quest

quest of them Belts and he to try his best to alter there Minds and send them back, and at his Return they imagen the whole Party will joyn us. However tomorrow Morning early we set [out] from this on our March for Auqquage and what Warriors have a Mind to joyn us to proceed and the rest to follow us as soon as Gowaha returns. These Indians desire you would send for these Fellows to know the Meaning of their sending this Belt and let some of these Indians come down also along with them that he may hear what they have to say for themselves. The aforesaid Cut the Pumpkin sent Word by Capt. Monture to come along as he would be very glad to see him, and we hope Sir William will hurry all of them that is behind to push up to Auqquage to joyn us so as in Case of a Retreat that we will be able to push on them again and indeavour to rout them. The Indians of this Castle request of Sir William that you would be so good as to supply their Women with Provisions if required at Fort Stanwix in a reasonable Manner and that what few Men there is left accordingly you will supply them with Fire Arms and Ammunition, and such Things as they will be short of in case of an Attack.

No more at present, but our Advice to you, to be on your guard in and on every Part of the Mohawk River, Schohary, Stone Rauby and Cherry Vally. We remain your sincear and ever devoted hum^l Serv^{ts} till Death.

HENRY MONTURE,
WILLIAM HARE,
JOHN JOHNSTON.

Letter from Robert McKeen[1] to Sir Wm. Johnson.

[MSS. of Sir William Johnson, viii.]

CHERRY VALLEY, February 25th, 1764.

SIR:

I HAVE thought proper to acquaint you with the present State of my Company and have the Pleasure to acquaint you that they are all in a good State and in high Spirits.

I have kept a regular Guard at Capt. Wells[1] ever since I arrived at this Settlement, and reviews my Men every Week and has them stationed in the best Manner I could for the Protection of this Settlement.

I should be glad if your Honour wou'd let me know if it is necessary to send a monthly Return to the Lt. Governor.

I am Sir your most Humble Servt

Robert McKeen

---

[1] Captain McKEAN resided at Cherry Valley and early in 1776 raised a Company of Rangers for the Protection of that Place. He was an enterprising and fearless Partizan, and was mortally wounded in the Summer of 1781 in an Expedition against a Tory Band in the Border of Schoharie Co.—*Campbell's Tryon Co.*

[2] Mr. ROBERT WELLS and his Family perished in the Massacre of Cherry Valley, Nov. 11, 1778. The Family consisted of himself, his Mother and Wife, and four Children, his Brother and Sister and three Domesticks, not one of them escaped excepting John, one of the Children, who happened to be absent at School at Schenectady. A Tory boasted that he killed Mr. Wells while at Prayer.—*Campbell's Tryon Co.*

P. S.

P. S. In Cafe of an Alarm my Men is always in readinefs to affemble at the Place appointed for an alarm Poft.

A monthly Return of Captain Robert McKeans Company of Provincials now lying at Cherry Valley, Febuary 25th, 1764.

Prefent for Duty.
Captain, - - - - - 1
Lieutenants, - - - - 2
Rank and File, - - - 50
Total, - - - 53
ROBERT MCKEEN, Capt.

Letter from Sir Wm. Johnfon to Gov. John Penn.

[MSS. of Sir William Johnfon, viii.]

JOHNSON HALL, Feby 27th, 1764.

SIR:

THE Exprefs delivered me your Favor of the 7th laft Night concerning the perfecuted Indians now in Philadelphia. The Rancours with which they have been purfued by the Rioters is as extraordinary as it may be dangerous to the Public, and leaft their Defigns might be put in Execution I cannot but approve of your Propofal of fending them hither, for fhould they fall a Sacrifice to unjuft Refentment it muft certainly occafion a Breach with all the Friend Indians.

The fending them thro' the back Parts of the Country at this Time might fubject them to the Infults of the Rioters, neither would it be practicable. I think the fafeft and beft Way would be, what you propofe of fending them by Water from Amboy to Albany, after which I fhall difpofe of them (altho' it will bring
fome

some Expense on the Crown) amongst the Friend Indians whilst the present Ferment continues. I shall accordingly write immediately to Governor Colden, and represent the Necessity of removing these Indians for a Time, as highly essential to our Interests and the public Safety, and I shall request the Governor in case ehe Government has no Objection to their coming to give you Notice that no Time may be lost.

I am Sir your most obed^t & most Humble Servt

To the Hon'ble Govr Penn.

Letter from Sir Wm. Johnson to Lieut. Gov. Colden.

[MSS. of Sir William Johnson, viii.]

JOHNSON HALL, Feb'y 28th, 1764.

DEAR SIR:

I HAVE just received your Favour of the 17th Inst. as also a Letter pr Express from Govr Penn representing the late audacious Attempts of the Rioters to murder the Indians under the Protection of Philadelphia, as also his Apprehensions concerning their future Safety there, on which acc't he proposes sending them by Land thro' his Government or else by Water from Amboy to Albany. The former may subject them to too many Insults and Hazards, and as I am well satisfied that should these Indians or any of them fall a Sacrifice after what has already happened, it will prove highly prejudicial to our Affairs as well as dangerous to the public Security, I cannot avoid recommending the Proposal of transporting them by Water to Albany, after which I shall dispose of them amongst the Indians here till matters are accommodated. If it is judged advisable

Indian Wars of 1763 and 1764.   253

advisable a Line from you to Gov' Penn will enable him to take the necessary Steps without loss of Time.

Whenever any thing farther transpires relative to Mr. Lydius,[1] I shall let you know it. I am told that one of his Sons has been lately thro' the Country in Company of a Justice of the Peace to obtain Affidavits for what Purpose I know not, but probably in support of his Claims.

Isle la Motte[2] is supposed to be to the southward of the 45th Degree of Latitude, but perhaps on future Observations it may appear in the *Quebec* Government. The Lands above the Great Falls on Otter Creek may be good tho' a good deal out of the way for small a Tract.[3] There is a small Piece of Land within about

---

[1] Among the extravagant Grants of Land made by Governor Fletcher which have rendered his Name a Synonym for Corruption, and occasioned among other Things his Recall and Disgrace, was that of a Tract covering eight hundred and forty square Miles in the present County of Washington, N. Y. and the southern Part of Vermont. This Tract was granted Sept. 3, 1696, to the Rev. Godfredius Dellius, Minister at Albany, for the annual Rent of one Raccoon Skin, payable annually, on the Feast Day of the Annunciation, at the City of New York. The Grant was annulled by the General Assembly of the Colony, May 12, 1699, but Dellius denied the Authority of that Body, and continued to regard the Claim as valid. He soon after sold his Claim in Holland to the Rev. John Lydius, his Successor in the Pastoral relation at Albany. His Son, Col. Lydius, to give additional Claim to this Title, made a Settlement on the Hudson at Fort Edward and engaged in Trade with the Indians. In 1744 this House was captured and burned by the Indians, and a Son was carried Prisoner to Canada. The Writer refers in the Text to Efforts made by this Family to substantiate their Title to this Tract. *(Transactions of N. Y. State Ag. Soc., vol. viii.)*

[2] Now in Vermont, forming a Part of Grand Isle County. It lies in Lat. 44° 57m. and Long. 3° 41m. E. from Washington. It is 28 Miles N. W. from Burlington, 13 West from St. Albans, and contains 4,620 Acres. It was first settled about 1785, and is celebrated for its extensive Limestone Quarries, which afford a black Marble.

[3] It will be remembered that at

3 Miles of Lake George, on the Road leading from Fort Edward. Please to inform me whether it can be granted, but I find at the back of my Patent here and at 10 or 12 Miles from the River, a small Piece which is an Intervale and I should be greatly obliged to you if you would grant it, on the Indians consenting thereto. Lieut. Johnson[1] will have a Certificate shortly from Gen. Gage as you desire.

There are now several Partys marched against the Enemy,[2] one of these amounts to about 200 Indians, many more are collecting to follow them and my whole Time is occupied in Conferences, in fitting out Parties, &c. The Indians will not be discouraged by the Rigors of the Season. The Posts I have sent them to are the Forks and Branches of Ohio and Susquehanna, where many of our Enemies reside, and the Alacrity which our Friend Indians manifest gives me great Reason to hope I shall shortly have the Pleasure of acquainting you that they have in a great Measure destroyed and removed these dangerous Enemies who have infested the neighboring Frontiers.

I am, &c.

P. S. One Mr. Tice of Schenectady has been mentioned to me as a very proper Person for a Provincial Comp.y I must beg leave to recommend him to your Notice, sho.d such be raised, as he has served as an Officer for some Years.

---

this Period the Colony of New York claimed Jurisdiction over the Territory embraced in the present State of Vermont, and were granting Lands in lavish Profusion, in Quantities of a whole Township at a Time. Sir William Johnson was peculiarly favored in these Allotments of the King's Domain.

[1] Referring to Sir John Johnson's Son.

[2] The Success of one of these Parties is related in a succeeding Letter, dated March 2, 1764.

Letter

Letter from Henry Monture, Wm. Hare and John Johnston to Sir William Johnson.

[MSS. of Sir William Johnson, viii.]

AUQOUGE,[1] Feb. 28, 1764.

SIR WILLIAM:

WE have the Pleasure to inform you of some Part of our Success, which if failed of some Parts of the Mohawk River must unavoidably suffer, as we suspect Cherry Vally or Schoharey.

The Prisoners we send to you as a Token of our prosicuting your Instructions as far as we are able; the Commander Sir William will singal out and several of them as principal Murderers during the War and reward them according to their Desert. The Woman bringing down we adjudge as Scheme that they might not be suspected they are Murderers that has been and they have come some of them from Kanisteo. So we leave Sir William to act as he pleases.

We remain your ever Devoted and hum^l Ser^{ts}

HENRY MONTURE,
JOHN JOHNSTON,
WILLIAM HARE.

Please to excuse the Pen and Haste, one of the Prisoners a young Man had the Impudence to bring some English Prisoners through this Place.

---

[1] Endorsed Oghquago, and variously written as Onohoghwage, Auqoage, Oueqoago, Oghquaga, &c. It was situated on the East Branch of the Susquehanna in the present Town of Windsor, Broome Co., N. Y. The Hills here slope gently towards the River on both Sides, forming a beautiful Vale of three or four Miles in Length, and from a Mile to a Mile and a half in Width, where the Indians resided in great Numbers prior to and during the Revolutionary War,

The

The Same to the Same.

[MSS. of Sir William Johnson, viii.]

AUQOAUGE, Feb. 28, 1764.

SIR WILLIAM:

THIS Day with Pleafure we can acquaint you of our Proceedings and Succefs, after our Arrival, which we fhall deliver to you in the following Maner from the Indians:

After our Love and Refpect to you as Governor & Chief, and then to the Commander of the feveral different Places in America. Firft three Days after our Arrival at this our Settlement we were informed that a Body of our Enemies were arrived here and going down under fome Pretence to the River, but on the contrary we fufpect to do Damage as they formerly have done to kill, burn and deftroy, being noted for murdering, notorious Villains. Laft Night we feized feven of there chief Warriors here in our Caftle and the famous Captain Bull of their Party, after fome little Refiftance, bound them Hand and Feet. This Morning we all fet out for their Encampment, and unbeknowing to them about Day, feized eleven Men of there Warrors and eight Women and three Children, which make twenty-nine in Number.

And now Brother you fee our Fidelity in opening the Door and we hope you will confider our Care, and that we lay expofed to Cenfure and ill Will of all Nations that are not found in the Caufe. We hope you will look into our Cafe and liften to us as well as we liften to you, as we think we are equally bound to each other. Confider Brother that this our Settlement and Chininga and Chuknut are our Bounderies of Friendfhip

Friendſhip ſo as we expect you will liſten to our Requeſt, that is to ſend a Party of Men to Conawa Rohare[1] at Oneida and another Party to this our Settlement at Auqqoage of a Safeguard for our Women and Children, and to hurry all Partys of Warriors to come to our Aſſiſtance immediately as we are very weak at preſent and make no delay. So after our Arrival we found all our Warriors as redy to execute and deſign as we were ready to propoſe, but we are ſorry to think that the Oneidas differ ſo much in their way of thinking and that is one of the Reaſons we requeſt a ſafe Guard, and when we heard the Sound of our Brother Warriors coming from you and from Conawa Rohare it revived our Spirits and was like a pleaſing Toy to a Child or like a Phyſick that refreſh a ſick or weak Bodye, ſo as tho we are delay'd from proceding untill we get more Aſſiſtance.

You uſed to ſay that your Body was light and it was only the Word for you to ſay March, and every one muſt comply and you was never ſhort of Proviſion.

Tomorrow we ſend the Priſoners by the way of Onida, for the Reaſon that perhaps that ſome of the Friends of the Priſoners may meet each other and breed a Quarrel. No more, but we remain

Your truſty Brother Indians.

Atteſted by us,
    HENRY MONTURE,
    WILLIAM HARE,
    JOHN JOHNSTON.

---

[1] Stated in a ſubſequent Letter, dated March 2, 1764, to be within twelve Miles of Oneida Lake. See p. 262.

Letter from Sir Wm. Johnson to Maj. General Gage.

[MSS. of Sir William Johnson, viii.]

JOHNSON HALL, March 1st, 1764.

DEAR SIR:

I HAVE had the Pleasure of your Letters of the 13th and 20th ult° and embrace the first Opportunity which Time has permitted of answering them.

The exact Number of Indians who may accompany the Army must be uncertain, nor is it possible to know how many they will consist of. The present Spirit amongst them gives me great Hopes of a powerful Assistance and I shall use every Endeavour in my Power to keep it up for this Purpose. I apprehend however that I may rely with Confidence on the Attendance of 4 or 500, perhaps they may be twice that Number, but it will greatly depend on Circumstances and the Time I shall have given me to collect them with the help of several proper Indian Officers who must necessarily be appointed for that Purpose. The Friend Indians in general will readily joyn either against the western Nations or the Shawanese and Delawares, and if Affairs are not speedily settled between us and the Senecas, I have no doubt but they will march also against them.

I apprehend the Shawanese and Delawares will suffer greatly from the Partys I have already sent out, and shall continue to send against them, which will make easy Work for the Troops on the Campaign. These two Nations appear the most determined but their Party decreases, many of them have already fallen off on hearing the determination of our Friends and I am hopeful they will (as Affairs are now circumstanced) be

unable

unable to perfuade the weftern Nations to renew Hoftilities, efpecially as the latter will fhortly difcover that fuch a Proceeding muft involve them in a War with the Friend Indians, which they would by no means relifh. The like Reafons will (I hope) have the fame Effect on the Senecas which will prove of great Service to us, as the Indians in general would certainly proceed with greater Alacrity againft the reft.

Many Steps have already been taken by the Friend Indians to bring over the Senecas, to which their Inactivity for fome Time paft muft be chiefly attributed, and I truft that the Belts and Meffages lately fent to them will be productive of an Accommodation of which I expect to have Notice in a very fhort Time, as the upper Nations will fhortly be down. I mean to treat with them outwardly as a mifguided People whom we are defirous to compaffionate and forgive on certain Terms rather than to give them any Confidence in their Abilities by expreffing a Defire to promote a Peace with them, and I truft this Conduct will have a good Effect.

I have fent out sev[l] Partys fince the firft and fhall continue to do fo, as I have the Pleafure to find that our Enemies are already greatly alarmed at the Refolutions of the reft.

Letter

Letter from Henry Monture, William Hare and John Johnston to Sir William Johnson.

[MSS. of Sir William Johnson, viii.]

OUCQOAGO. March 21, 1764.

SIR WILLIAM:

THIS Day the Prisoners set out for your House by the way of Oneida, and all the Oneidas that came with us likewise return with them, as they said they had fulfilled your Pleasure by taken of so many Prisoners and chief Warriors. Yestarday we rec^d your two Letters by an Onida, the one dated the 21 of Feb'y and the other the 23d of Feb'y, wherein we acquainted them of your Concern for their Wellfare and your Desire of our proceeding. They were very glad and made Answer that they had done according to your Will, which would be a welcome Sight for you to see so many of your sworn Enemies, as they had but one Belt they thought they could return with Honour. They pres^d very hard for us to come along with them in Company, but we consider of our Errand refused, knowing at least Sir that we was short as yet for the good Work now in Hand before us. We then remain here untill such Times as the Arrival of other Forces to joyn that we may strick the Blow to Purpose, which Sir you will not neglect sending us a Reinforcement as soon and as quick as possible, if you should think proper to send us a Body of two hundred Whites to joyn the Body of Indians you are about to send us, we think with Gods help we may destroy a great Part of their Settlements along the Dioago[1] River, the Ouqoagos are very harty and only wait for any thing of a party to joyn

[1] Tioga.

that

that they may ſtrick the Blow as they ſay their Work is as yet before them. There is here in Store ſix Barrells of Flour and about a hundred Weight of Sugar belonging to Mr. Wells of Cherry Vally, which Sugar would be very uſefull for any Body of Men to make Ouquickare and the Flour likewiſe in Caſe required. We ſend you one Capt Bull, the famous Head Warrior belonging to the Sqoaſhcutter, a great Villain, and the reſt of his Crew of Warriors. We hope Sir William will not take any Excuſes from them but puniſh them with Severity as they deſerve. Two Brothers, Fidlers, excepted, being by all Accounts not Party concerned, as Capt. Monture knows them very well. As to our ſpeedy Return it is uncertain, as Sir William muſt judge by Circumſtances, but you may depend on our preſſing it on as far and as faſt as poſſible we can, and with Gods help we hope is ſhort of give you pleaſant Detail of our Succeſs. We remain your ever devoted and

Hum^l Serv^{ts} till Death.

HENRY MONTURE,
WILLIAM HARE,
JOHN JOHNSTON.

P. S. Be ſo good as to forward the Party. The Prieſt of the Pariſh here gives his Complim^{ts} to you and all his Family.

Letter

Letter from Sir William Johnson to Col. Bradstreet.

[From the Original in the Possession of M. M. Jones, Esq. of Utica.]

JOHNSON HALL, March 2, 1764,
At Night.

DEAR SIR:

IT gives me great Pleasure that I now inform you of the Success of the first Party I lately sent out against our Enemy, an Express being just arrived with Letters acquainting me that on the 26th ult° in the Evening, near the main Branch of Susqehanna, as they were pursuing their Rout, they received Advice that a large Party of our Enemys the Delawares, were encamped at a small Distance on their way against some of the Settlements hereabouts, upon which Intelligence they made an expeditious March to their Encampment, which they surrounded at Daybreak, then rushing upon the Delawares (who were surprised and unable to make a Defence) they made them all Prisoners to the Number of 41, including their Chief, *Capt. Bull*, Son of Teedyuscung, and one who has discovered great Inveteracy against the English, and led several Partys against them during the present Indian War. They are all fast bound and may be expected here under an Escort in a few Days.

The Indians of Onoghquagey and Canawaroghere, the latter within twelve Miles of Oneida Lake, are very uneasy least our Enemys should take Advantage of the Absence of their Men, and destroy their Familys, on which Account they are very solicitous for a Guard till their Men return, & I apprehend if their Request is complied with, it will give new Spirits to the Partys and encourage more to go on Service.

I

I have therefore mentioned it to the General, and am of Opinion it may be eafily done by Partys from the Provincials at German Flatts.

I am of Opinion it will be beft to fend the Prifoners to New York as the beft Place of Security, there to remain till fomething be done with them.

I am with great Refpect,
Sir, your moft obedient
humble Servant,
WM. JOHNSON.

Letter from Capt. John R. Hanfen to Sir William Johnfon.

[MSS. of Sir William Johnfon, viii.]

Capt. Eckerfon's, WISERSDORP,[1] March 12, 1764.

HONOURED SIR:

RECEIVED yours of the 3d Inft. and have fince proceeded according to your Directions, in difpatching a Serg^t with 10 Men of my Comp^y and 6 of the Militia in Company with 6 Indians for Ouaghquago laft Saturday. Yeftarday five of the Indians, all Mohawks, returned here to me, with two Indians which they fay are their Prifoners, and told me for what Reafon they had taken them, they at firft refufed to tell me, and infifted that I fhould take them and fend them down to your Honour, and if I would not that they would immediately kill them. I then requefted of the Head of them, one Jofeph a Sachem, that he would fend one or two of his Men along with

---

[1] Weifer's Dorp was on the Site of the prefent Village of Middleburgh, Schoharie Co. It was named from Conrad Weifer, a prominent early German Settler,

the

the Prisoners to your Honour. He told me he could not do that for he was afraid if he did not go off with his Warriors and our Men to Onoghquago that his Brethren there would suffer.

He then cautioned me in particular about the Prisoners and in particular against one of these named *George O'Moke* and said that the said *O'Moke* had threatened one of their old Indians and a Squaw and say'd as soon as the young Men their Warriors was gone against their Brethren the *Delawares*, that they then would kill their Wifes and Children here. This Morning two of the Mohawks again returned to me, who having heard that I should have ordered the Prisoners to be unty'd and say'd if I order'd any such Thing and the Prisoners should escape, that they would be afraid to go to Onoghquago for fear of the severall Threats made by the Prisoners.

The Serg^t who I have gave the Command of those Men assigned for Onoghquago I have gave particular Instructions agreable to my own Instructions received from your Honour; the Serg^t is pretty well acquainted with the Indian Tongue. His Instructions are, that he shall act no farther than what is agreeable to Heads of that Tribe or as your Honour may further direct him.

The remaining Part of my Comp^y are all fitt for Duty. I have placed so the best Advantage in Case of an Attack with our Arms in the best Manner. The Company having never received any Pay yet since they have been raised causes an infinite Trouble, notwithstanding all I can do to the contrary to prevent it.

   I am Honoured Sir,
    your most obedient Servt to Command.
          JOHN R. HANSEN.

To the Honour^{ble} Sir Wm. Johnson, Bart.

              Extract

Extract of a Letter from Sir William Johnson to Lieutenant Governor Colden.

[MSS. of Sir William Johnfon, viii.]

JOHNSON HALL, March 16th, 1764.

DEAR SIR:

I HAVE had the Pleafure of your very kind Favor of the 19th Inft. and in Addition to the Succefs of my firft Party, I have the Pleafure to acquaint you that another Party of only ten headed by Thos. King, which I had lately fent out, met with a Party of nine Delawares, who were finging their War Song againft the Englifh, on which they imediately killed and fcalped one and took three Prifoners, who are now on their way here. This is a fmall Affair, but as 'tis the firft who has been killed by our Indians, it will prove of fome Confequence, and I have Reafon to expect good News daily from the other Partys.

The firft Prifoners taken arrived here yeftarday, and this Morning I fent down 14 Men of them to the Care of Coll. Elliot at Albany. One of the ftouteft remains wounded at Aughquago, and I was obliged to give them People 5 Prifoners for their good Behavior, others to the Oneidas, Tufcaroras, Onondagas and Mohawks, and to detain 4 myfelf which I diftributed amongft the moft deferving to replace Perfons deceafed, for which Purpofe the reft were given according to the Indian Cuftom.

The Confternation our Enemies are in on acc't of our employing Indians againft them is very great, and will I hope foon be the Means of bringing the difaffected to our Terms. Near 400 Senecas, &c. are coming here to make fome Propofals, as the Onoghquago's quago's are very Apprehenfive that their Familys may fuffer by the Enemy in the Abfence of their Warriors, I thought it very neceffary at this Time to comply with their Requeft of a Guard, and accordingly fent them an Officer and 30 Men from the Cherry Valley and Schohare Garrifons with 6 Militia, and the General having given me the Direction of the future Security. Thefe Deputies with Numb^{rs} from the Five Friendly Nations now here, amount to about 500. From the latter I fhall fend out feveral Partys amongft the Shawanees and Delawares, who are the only Nations at prefent that have not made any Offers of Accomodation.

I received feveral Letters in Autumn and the begining of Winter from the Lords of Trade, one of which contained Orders of a like Nature with thofe you mention, which I anfwered fome Time ago as well as I could under fo much Hurry and Bufinefs. As I underftand the Board have the Regulation of Trade, &c. under prefent Confideration, I apprehend it may be too late to lay Matters of that Nature before them fo as to anf^r the Defign. All that I thought neceffary on that Head was, that the Indian Trade fhould be free to all his Majefty's Subjects and carried on at only the principal Outpofts, where the Traders fhould be under tha Protection of the Garrifon and thereby avoid the Rifque they often run of being robbed and murdered, their Goods being a great Temptation to Indians if they are in the Indian Villages, and fuch Robbery or Murder might prove the Foundation of a future War, as the Indians feldom ftop at the firft Crimes, neither is it eafy to perfuade them to make any Reftitution. Another Matter of Confideration is, that the Traders at the principal Garrifons by being under the Eye of the Comd^{rs} Officer would not be fo ready to overreach them,

them, fearing a Difcovery, whereas in their Villages they are often impofed upon and apt to redrefs themfelves. The Commanding Officer could alfo banifh the Trader on Proof of Extortion. The reft I obferved to their Lordfhips regarded the State of the Department, the Interefts, Difpofitions and Numbers of the Indians.

I am much obliged to you for the Particulars you communicated concerning the Nations to the fouthward, as alfo about the Tufcaroras, and fhould be glad to hear further from you on that Head.

It gave me Concern to hear of the Hoftilities committed by the fouthern Ind^s & I heartily wifh a fpeedy Stop may be put to them as well as that the fev^l Governors may act fuch a Part as may enable you to bring them to Reafon, for whilft People act upon different Plans it is impoffible for a Superintendant to difcharge his Truft as he would wifh. The French are probably at the Bottom of the Affair, as they have been to the northward, for it gives them fenfible Pleafure to foment Differences between the Ind^s and us, from which they are apt to flatter themfelves with reaping an Advantage.

I fhall not omit acquainting you in a little Time, with any material Tranfactions in this Quarter, and am,
&c.

Letter

Letter from Sir William Johnson to John Stuart.

[MSS. of Sir William Johnson, viii.]

JOHNSON HALL, March 18, 1764.

SIR:

I HAVE had the favour of your Letters of the 10th Dec^r & 16th January laſt, which I ſhould ſooner have anſ^d but for the extraordinary Hurry and Buſineſs I have been engaged in, the great Reſort of Indians and the Variety of their Affairs occupying my whole Time, nor eſpecially at this Seaſon can they be neglected with Prudence.

Since the Command of the Army devolved upon General Gage I have been impowered to make uſe of the Services of the friendly Nations ag^{ſt} our Enemys, and have ſent out in different Partys above 300 of them. The firſt of theſe Partys ſurpriſed at the North Branch of Suſquehanna 41 Delawares with their Chief. I deliver'd over ſev^l of them amongſt thoſe who attached to our Intereſt to replace their deceaſed Relations, and ſent 14 of them with their Chief to Albany under a Guard, from whence they will be forwarded to New York. A ſmall Party of 10 has ſince fallen in with a ſcalping Party of 9 Enemys (who ſeemed deſtined againſt ſome of the Frontiers of Penſilvania), of theſe they killed one and made three Priſoners, whom I daily expect. The killing of this Indian by a Party of their own Sort will greatly promote the Cauſe and intereſt our Friends more heartily in our Behalf.

Theſe Partys have already ſhown their Importance, the Enemy are greatly alarmed, Numbers have retired towards the Twightwees, and the reſt knowing that Indians are beſt calculated to deſtroy them, have for-
ſaken

Indian Wars of 1763 *and* 1764.

faken their Caftles and will fhortly be reduced to great extremity if not totally fubdued.

The Chenuffios and other Enemy Senecas have fent me feveral Deputys from each of their Towns with Propofals of Peace, which will not be granted them but on Terms moft adventageous to our Provincials at the German Flatts. I have ordered Aughquago to be reinforced by a Detachment of a Capt. 2 Sub^s and 60 Men, and fent the like Number to Canowwaroghere, a Village of Oneidas, whofe Men are all going out againft the Enemy. Thefe Garrifons for the Indians will not be required for above 4 or 5 Weeks and will greatly forward the Service by the Encouragement it will give the Indians.

I cannot but agree in Opinion with the Council, that the Wyaloofins, &c. might give bad Impreffions to the reft, but I was determined and prepared to guard againft that and hoped to be able to remove any unjuft Sufpicion they might conceive having (without vanity I may fay it) a greater Influence now over the many Nations in our Alliance than ever. However as General Gage informs me that he has propofed an Afylum for them in Burlington Barracks, I think it will anfwer very well for the prefent.

Capt. Duncan[1] of Schenectady has requefted I would reprefent to you his Requeft, whether he may have his Proportion of Land, he fold out of the 44th Regiment, but thinks he may claim fome Title on account of the Service he performed laft Year, as will appear from Lt. Campbells Certificate.

---

[1] JOHN DUNCAN, a Merchant of the City of Schenectady. He died at Albany, on the 5th May, 1791, aged 69 Years.

Extract

Extract of a Letter from His Excellency the Honble Major General Gage to Major Gladwin, Commanding at the Detroit, dated New York, 23d March, 1764.

[MSS. of Sir William Johnson, viii.]

YOU will there be informed, I accepted of the Proposals of Peace, which the Indians of Detroit had made you, and I am now to defire, if you find the Savages amicably difpofed, and fincerely inclined to conclude a Peace with us in earneft, that you would give them Notice in a proper Manner to repair to Niagara by the End of June, at which Time Sir William Johnfon will be there to meet them. You will beft know what is moft proper to do, on fuch an Occafion, fhall therefore add, that it may be neceffary to acquaint them that the Reprefentatives they fend to this Bufinefs need not be apprehenfive of receiving any Infults from the Troops which they will probably meet in their way, as when we find they are fincere in their Overtures the Troops will have Orders not to moleft them, and they fhould likewife have Notice to collect all the Prifoners and Deferters which they may have amongft them, who fhould all be delivered up to us on this Occafion. If you think of any Propofals proper for Sir William Johnfon to make on this Occafion of Peace, you will write to Sir William on that Head.

Letter

Letter from John Campbell to Sir William Johnson.

[MSS. of Sir William Johnson, viii.]

FORT STANWIX, MARCH, 31, 1764.

SIR:

I AM favoured with your Letter of the 17th March, concerning the Women of the Oneida Village, called Canowoarohere, being in great Diftrefs for the Want of Provifion on account of the Abfence of their Men. I have therefore agreable to your Letter this Day fupplyed the Women of faid Village with a Quantity of Provifions fuppofed to ferve them till the Return of their Men, which I dare fay will meet with the Generals Approbation, it being fo very neceffary and prudent to treat them with Civility at this prefent Juncture, which is the moft effectual Method of gaining their Affection and of cours to promote the good of the Service.

I had the Satiffaction of feeing Capt. Bull when the Prifoners paffed here, whom I think the beft looking Indian I ever faw. He is quite the fine Gentleman.

The Succefs that attends the Partys that you have fent out gives me infinite Pleafure, as it muft to every Perfon that has the good of the Service at Heart, and heartily wifh that the like good Fortune may conftantly accompany your unwearied Attention to his Majeftys Service.

I hope Mr. Johnfon has remembered to apologize my going away fo abruptly from your Houfe the Morning I left it without my paying my Refpects to you, which I beg you will excufe as I was afraid ot difturbing you fo early in the Morning.

I am with the greateft Efteem Sir, your moft obedient, humble Servant.   JOHN CAMPBELL.

P. S.

P. S. I have received Orders from the Gen[ll] to be in Readiness to take the Field with the 17th Regiment next Campaign.

Letter from Whitham Marsh to Sir William Johnson.

[MSS. of Sir William Johnson, viii.]

BAYARD HALL, Ap[l] 2d, 1764.
$\frac{3}{4}$ p. Merid.

SIR:

ALTHO I had not the Happiness of receiving some more agreeable News by Capt. Post, yet I cannot help acquainting you that last Monday I visited Capt. Bull in Jail. He confesses the Shawaneze are Rascals, and that the Chenussaes sent for him and other Delawares. This was confirmed in the Morning of this Day in presence Mr. Nic's Bayard, Sen[r] at the Jail by *Joe Newtimas*, who may remember at Easton. When I asked whether any *white Men* of Pennsylvania (you well know who I mean) had desired them (y[e] Delawares) to strike us, Joe answered, *he did not understand the Question*. Bull owned there were 22 Ind[s] who made Inroads into the Jerseys, by whom poor Westbroke (at whose House we lay'd) was killed. I much want to get at the Bottom of the Delaware Scheme, I am sure some *quaking Devils* originated the Business. Excuse me Sir, for saying no more now, as the Post Rider waits in the Entry. I am with all due Deference and Respects to yo[r] Families y[r]

Most obed[t] & humble Serv[t]
WITHAM MARSH.

P. S. Darlington sends by me when I embark a great Curiosity of Shellwork. It is a Grotto.

Letter from Colonel Bradſtreet to General Amherſt.

ALBANY, 6th April, 1764.

DEAR SIR:

I HAVE received your Excellencys Packett of the 1ſt Inſtant and ſhall obay your Commands in every thing in my Power. I have already inform'd your Excellency that Major Hogan could not enliſt but ſixty Men to ſerve to the firſt of May, & that they were not fit for Service; and I may now add, that they cant get any more this way, nor have they try'd for ſome Time paſt.

That I may know the exact Number of Boats to take from Schenectady, I beg to know if there is any more Troops to go beſides the following, viz:

17th Regiment,	314 including the Draughts.
Yorkers,	300
Connecticut,	250
Jerſeys,	240
Canada,	300
	1404

I ſet the 17th Regiment at 314, as I am aſſur'd they can not at this Time make out but 140 Men fit to go on Service, but they have ſome which may do in Garriſon.

What Exploits may be expected of 1400 Men, one half of them new raiſed Provincials, and the half of the other half but lately the Subjects of the French King, acting in the Center of the Savages ſurrounding the great Lakes, known to be our inveterate Enemies, I know not, but ſure I am, if the whole were of the beſt Troops his Majeſty has, the Number is far from being equal to Service;

Service; however it is my Duty to obay and to doe the best I can for the Service. After the 55th has given 174 Men to the 17th, they will have about 230 good Men left. If I could be allowed two Detachments of 50 each out of them, to be replaced from the Provincials, it would be of great service, but your Excellency is the best Judge and I hope will excuse this Liberty.

I mentioned your Excellency there was but 50 Barr^s of Powder here, including what was sent from New York, since which Sir Wm. Johnson has had ten Barrells. I beg to be allow'd sufficient for the Service and Practice.

There is no muskets arriv'd from New York yet & but 300 in Store here.

Permit me to ask your Excellency if there is to be no kind of Staff allowed us.

Letter from Colonel Bradstreet to Major Duncan.

ALBANY, 30th April, 1764.

DEAR SIR:

SEVEN Days after the Letters from Neagara got here I received a Letter from Col. Browning, by which I find it absolutely necessary to send the Grenadiers & another Company of the 55th Regiment from hence to Neagara, they are compleat to 45 Rank & File with two Subalterns to each, and I must beg of you to add to them as many Officers & non-commissioned Officers as you possibly can from your Garrison, and to make them in every respect, as respectable as possible. I suppose Capt. Daly will join his Company as soon as possible after knowing it has gone on Service.

Some

Some York Provincials are also on their way to you, but in order to get up the Boats I am obliged to send them half man'd; then you'l please also to send on to Neagara and you will be the best Judge what Provisions to put in each Boat, of the whole, as they leave you.

If the Canadian Battoe Men should have made their second Trip from Swegache[1] before I get up and any Provisions remains there pray send them back for it, or at least as many of them as will be sufficient to bring it away, and let the others push on to Neagara, not only to land their Provisions at the Landing but to be employ'd in carrying the Provisions at the Fort to Landing, &c. and if any make the third Trip they must do the same if you think it necessary and safe.

Pray endeavour to get an exact State of all the Provisions from Swegache to Neagara as soon as you can, that we may provide in Time if more is wanted.

By Mistake Lieut. Grant has taken a new Mainsail belonging to the Schooner on the Onida Lake; be so good to write for it by the first Conveyance and send it her.

Pray caution all the Detachments that leave you for Neagara to be watchful, for it may possibly happen if the Savages find they can't do much to the People employ'd at the Vessells or on the Carrying Place they will endeavor to surprise our People on some Place on the Banks of Lake Ontario.

Please to let me know if the Canadian Battoe Men have Arms, if they have not and that you can supply

---

[1] Ofwegatchie, now Ogdensburgh, St. Lawrence Co., N. Y. A flourishing Indian Mission at this Place, formed in 1749 by Francis Picquet, a Sulpitian Priest, was mostly broken up by the Conquest of 1760. There was a strongly fortified Island in the River three Miles below, and as it lay at the Foot of Navigation from the Lake this Station possessed great Importance.

them

them that go to Neagara with the Provisions, pray do it.

 Sir Wm. Johnson tells me he has sent some Friend Indians to assist at Neagara which will prevent your being troubled with so many as was first intended. I make no doubt but the Draughts & Yorkers are near leaving Oswego for Neagara and that you gave the Arms with the Draughts. I will settle it with the Artillery Officer and Col. Campbell will give the proper Receipt for them when he gets to Oswego.

 Major Duncan.

Letter from Colonel Bradstreet to General Amherst.

NEAGARA, 4th August, 1764.

DEAR SIR:

THE Indians of the Bay, those of Arbrecroche, some Cheppawas & Mississages now here have so settled Matters with Sir William Johnson, that he acquainted me he thought it absolutely necessary to send those People Home well satisfied, and that it could not be done without allowing them to trade for every thing, except Arms & Ammunition, which has been allowed them as you will see by the enclosed Order & Regulations. The Prices were fix'd by three Indian Traders & inspected by Sir William. For the greater Security of the Troops to be posted at Michilimicanac, I thought advisable to desire Sir William to tell the above Savages they need not expect Trade to extend so far as this Country without Posts & Garrisons to Protect the Traders and see that Justice is done them; on which they desired Michilimicanac should be reëstablished and that they would endeavor to protect it.

As

As to the Genesea Indians a Message arrived at Oswego from them before we left it to Sir William Johnson, desiring four Boats with Provisions should be sent them to Irondequoit in which Part of them would proceed with all the English Prisoners they had to this Place. The Boats & Provisions by Sir Williams desire I ordered thither directly, but they were so far from keeping their Words, that they were not there to receive them, but on being sent to, sent Men & Horses for the Provisions. For some Time after this, the Accounts we had from them were, that they seem'd more inclinable not to keep the Peace they made last Winter but continue the War; but at length they finding the Troops remaining here & suspecting it was on their Account and having no Time to hunt for Provisions & thereby starving, they took the Resolution to set out for this Place in different Parties, and the 18th Instant we were informed of their being on the way, but that they were bringing but four of our People instead of thirty which they had Prisoners amongst them with many other Circumstances showing plainly Necessity only makes them submit more than Inclination; whereupon Sir William & myself were of Opinion, that suffering any longer such Insults might or would be attended with bad Consequences, at this Time in particular, as the Eyes of the upper Nations was upon us and would judge of our Strength & Spirit from what pass'd upon this Occasion, and that it was for his Majestys Service we should send them Word that unless they would punctually fulfill every Article they promis'd at the making the Peace last Winter, they had no Business and that we did not desire to see them; and determin'd also, if they return'd, it was absolutely necessary to march against them and treat them as they deserve. It appears to me, the true Cause or Reason
for

for this Conduct of the Senecas proceeds from their utter Abhorrence to us, that they do not think the other Part of the Six Nations in general will hurt them, that we live a great Distance from them & that the Shawanes, Delawares & their Friends can do them great Damage, and consequently it is their Interest to be well with the latter. But to return to their Conduct; on the 21st July they sent in two Men here to tell us, that upon receiving the Message we sent them, they had sent off Runners to bring in all the Prisoners and that the principal Part of their Men, Women and Children would be here the 23d, and on that Day came in about 60 Men with about 150 Women & Children, and said the Remainder would immediately follow and do every thing that could be desired of them; but they did not arrive untill the 1st Instant with nine Prisoners only; nor would they have been here then had they not fear'd we should march against them, which they were several times given to understand. The 2d Sir William Johnson called them together, they acknowledged their Faults and insist on it that they will be very good for the Time to come, and that they will deliver up the King and War Chief of the Delawares and Shawanes & be amenable for the future Conduct of the Rest which they took under their Protection this Spring, provided we grant them Peace also, which is agreed to. I expect to see this Place clear of Savages in a Day or two so as to be able to proceed with Troops to the westward; and I think it prudent to take with me as many Indian Warriors as will go, it being certain the Savages round Detroit, &c. will take it much amiss in them, which if properly managed will be of infinite Service to the Nation whenever either those to the westward or five Nations break out again; their additional Expence in going on will only
be

be Provifions, and altho' one half or more may be
fufpected of loving their own Color better than us,
ftill I think it my Duty to rifk it for the Advantages
which may attend it hereafter. It will be impoffible
to know the Numbers of them until they are in the
Boats.

Letter from Colonel Bradftreet to General Amherft.

NIAGARA, 5th Auguft, 1764.

DEAR SIR:

I HAVE received your Excellency's Letter of the
2d Inftant and I will fend to the Savages of the
Illinois as foon as I get to Detroit and fhall not fail to
do all I can for Pontiac. You will fee by the inclofed
Letter from Major Gladwin, the Sandufky Savages
have lately offer'd to make Peace; had I not been
ftopt here, I fhould not have received that Letter &
perhaps might have had the good Fortune to have cut
up that Band, which I think would have been more
for the Public good than making Peace with them.

From very good Information I find it impoffible to
get to the Siotio River by Water, but from Prifq Ifle
Shataquau and fo round by Fort Pitt, which would
take up fo much Time; even was there Water at this
Seafon, which there is not for many Miles at firft fet-
ting off, that I do not think we fhall have time to undertake it, and I have great Reafon to think Major
Gladwin has been mifinformed, when told that the
Shawanes & Delawares Indians were but two Days
march from Sandufky, as the fame Savages who gave
him the Information now tell me that they are ftill at
their old Caftle near the Ohio, except a few, and this
is confirmed by others. But you may depend upon
my

my marching to them by Land if it is possible for us to undertake it, which perhaps may be about the Time Col. Bouquett on the move this way.

I am not without Hopes of falling on Mr. Pondiac's Friends and shall push first for that. The Putewatamas have also offeerd Peace, which I am sorry for, as I think I could not well fail of making them repent of what they have done as well as those of Sandusky, if not prevented by being so late.

Untill I came here no Place of Security for the Vessels of this and of Lake Erie was found and they were under the Necessity of coming to anchor in the open Lake & exposed to every Storm & to be lost; add to this they had more than twenty Miles to send for their Loading; but on examining the north Shore a proper Place has been found to secure the Vessells by the help of a Wharf just above the Rapids; a Post is now building there & all that can be done towards finishing under our Circumstances this Season will be done; and to avoid giving Offence to the Senecas Savages to whom the Land belongs, I have desired S. Wm. Johnson to ask it of them and they have granted it.

I enclose your Ex^l Returns of the Troops with a Plan & Report of what we have done for the Security of the Carrying Place & Vessells from hence to the Rapids on Lake Erie.

P. S. I can not discarge the Teamster & Waggoner altho' that Business is done, being obliged to employ them at clearing the Wood of each Side the Road over the Carrying Place, Battoeing Provisions to Fort Erie, making Hay, &c. and have employ which is absolutely necessary for many more than I had then.

This Instant I have received the enclosed from Major Gladwin, saying the Outawas ask Peace & have brought

brought in three Prisoners. Fear has brought all these Civilities about, but how long they will last when the Danger is over Time must tell. The enclosed Staff of the Baker here will appear strong to your Exl. and believe you will approve of my ordering the Man to be paid no more than what he receives from the Troops & direct Mr. Lake to pay it being a great Saving to the Crown.

Col B. to the General, Niagara.

Letter from Colonel Bradstreet to General Gage.

PRESQUE ISLE, 14 Aug. 1764.

DEAR SIR:

AGREEABLE to your Instructions to grant Peace & His Majestys Protection to such Savages who shall lay down their Arms & beg for Peace, I enclose you what has pass'd between me & the Deputys of all the Nations of Indians, who inhabit the Lands of Sandusky, Scioto Plains, Muskinhem, the Ohio, Presque Isle, &c. and your Excellency may depend upon my marching to the Plains of Scioto if I find they intend to play me the least foul Trick. Surrounded as I shall soon be by Numbers of Savages who ask Peace from Fear only, makes it impossible for me to fix any other Plan than acting as Circumstances occasion, so that I can now only say that I shall do every thing in my Power for the Honor of His Majestys Arms & the Benefit of the Nation. I am, &c.

J. BRADSTREET.

P. S. I send this by the way of Fort Pitt; out of 574 Indians which was said at Niagara I should have with me, we have 255, 100 of whom belong to Canada.

His Excell. Gen. Gage,

Letter from Colonel Bradſtreet to Gov. John Penn.

[Bradſtreet and Amherſt MSS., p. 155.]

PRESQUE ISLE, 14 AUG. 1764.

To Governor Penn.

SIR:

AS it may be agreeable to you and the People under your Government to know as ſoon as poſſible of the Peace concluded with all the Nations of Indians, who have done you ſo much Damage, I encloſe you a Copy of what has paſſed on the Occaſion.

I am, &c.

JNO. BRADSTREET.

P. S. Perhaps under preſent Circumſtances of the Troops acting from your Quarter and the advanc'd Seaſon, it may be agreeable to the ſouthern Governments to have early Information of this Affair in which you will pleaſe ſo act as may be moſt agreeable to you.

Letter from Colonel Bradſtreet to Colonel Bouquett.

[Bradſtreet and Amherſt MSS., p. 159.]

PRESQUE ISLE, 14th Aug. 1764.

SIR:

AGREEABLE to Gen. Gages Orders to me to grant Peace and His Majeſtys Protection to all Savages that may lay down their Arms & beg for Peace, I encloſe you what has paſſ'd between me and the Deputys of all the Nations of Indians who inhabit the Lands of Sanduſky, the Scioto Plains, Muſkinham, the Ohio, near this Place, &c. and doubt not if you are

are in readyneſs to march you will firſt receive Gen. Gages Directions how you are to act after his receiving my Letters and Articles of Peace.

I am, &c.

JNO. BRADSTREET.

Col. Bouquett.

PRESQUE ISLE. 14th Aug. 1764.

SIR:

I SEND you encloſ'd Copy of a Peace I have made with all the Nations of Savages upon the Banks of the Ohio, Scioto Plains, &., &c., &c., and Letters for Gen. Gage, &c. which I muſt deſire you to forward with the utmoſt Diſpatch.

I am, &c.

JNO. BRADSTREET.

Letter from Colonel Bradſtreet to Sir Wm. Johnſon.

[Bradſtreet and Amherſt MSS.]

DETROIT, 28th Aug. 1764.

DEAR SIR:

I HAVE only Time to ſay by Major Gladwin we have ſhown the Savages in this Quarter we could have cut them up in Part at leaſt had they not aſk'd Peace, that the Outawas, Petewatamas, &c. Chepewas are to be all in ſix or ſeven Days to end the general Peace & comply with every thing I demand, amongſt which Bondeac is to be given up to be ſent down to the Seacoaſt & maintain'd at his Majeſtys Expence the Remainder of his Days. Major Gladwin will tell your Ex. the ſad State of this Place reſpecting the Quarters

for

for the Troops. I shall do all I can towards building Barracks, it being absolutely necessary. The Troops you ordered for to Garrison Michilimicanack with two Companys of fifty Men each which I have raised out of the Inhabitants here, go of to morrow and one of the Vessells shall be got into Lake Huron, tho' no more than six feet Water is as yet found over the Barr in Lake St. Clair, and no Pains shall be wanting to know how to fix the Navigation from Neagara Falls to Michigan Lake, &c.

Inclosed you have a Copy of the Peace made with the Shawanes, &c. and I shall be at Sandusky at the Time appointed for the Chiefs & Prisoners to be there & to march against them to Scioto if they do not fulfill their Engagements.

From very good Information I found necessary to give the Inhabitants & Savages of the Elliones & the Nations on this Side of it to the Miames to know that unless they carry themselves well to His Majestys Troops who were to take Possession of that Country, they might expect to hear from us and ye Savages of the Six Nations, those of Canada, the Shawanes, &c. that we have made Peace with, together with the Nations surrounding this Place soon, for which Purpose I have sent Capt. Morris of 17th Regiment and Savages with the usual Belts. Should Capt Morris succeed he is to push on to all the Nations of Savages on the Banks of the Missisippi to the Sea, as your Ex. will see by his Instructions a Copy of which is herein enclosed, as also the Oath the Inhabitants are to take.

Letter

Letter from Colonel Bradstreet to Lieut. Sinclair.

DETROIT, 12th Sept. 1764.

SIR:

YOU are hereby requir'd and directed the Beginning of May next to receive on board the Schooner Gladwin a Load of Provisions for the Garrison of Michilimicanack & with it proceed to that Place, and as soon as you have delivered it you are to sail for the Bottom of the Bay where we had a Fort, & from thence round the Lake Michigan, steering up the River St. Josephs as far as you can, making throughout the whole Voyage such Remarks & Observations as the Importance of the Service you are ordered on requires for the Safety of the future Navigation of those Lakes, observing the same on Lake Huron, the whole of which you will report in Writing to Lt. Col. Campbell or Officer commanding here on your Return and receive from him Directions for your further Conduct.

As you will doubtless see many Savages before you return you will inform them, that the Reason of your sailing round those Lakes is to find out if it is practicable for Vessels agreeable to my Promise to them at Neagara.

I am, &c.

J. B.

Lt. Sinclair.

Letter from Col. Bradſtreet to Lt. Col. Campbell.

[Bradſtreet and Amherſt MSS., p. 155.]

SANDUSKY, 10th Oct. 1764.

To Lt. Col. Campbell.

SIR:

YOUR Letter by Chain, without Date, I have received and I have great Pleaſure to find you have in ſo ſhort a Time gained ſo much Influence over the Indians as you mention. I doubt not but you will improve it as His Majeſtys Service much requires it at this Time to correct the Shawanes & Delawares; but I muſt obſerve for the good of the Service, that it is abſolutely neceſſary that every Perſon that may have Influence with the Indians ſhould be employ'd to gain their Affection and to engage them not only to keep the Peace with us but act for us againſt the Kings Enemies. The Savages love the Inhabitants of Detroit in general and the latter may by gentle Treatment be brought to exert themſelves in our Favor with the former with little or no Expence to Government; but after all, Affability & Attention in the Officer commanding at Detroit is abſolutely neceſſary, to the Savages in general, particularly thoſe going out to War, without which all will go wrong. You will pleaſe to uſe your utmoſt Endeavours to make up & ſend out againſt the Shawanes & Delawares all the Parties of Indians in Friendſhip with us you can poſſibly collect & continue it until further Orders, unleſs you ſhall receive Letters from Col. Bouquett telling you to deſiſt, he having made Peace with thoſe two Nations of Savages, the Shawanes & Delawares, & you are to fit out all ſuch Parties as you ſend out againſt thoſe

two

two Nations in the Manner the French did thofe Indians they fent to War, and pay for every Scalp or Prifoner brought in by them, you fend out four Blankets, four fhirts, four Pair of Stockings and one Pound of Paint. The Goods wanted for this Service you are to purchafe as Occafion requires and add it to your other public Accounts. You will alfo employ fuch of the Inhabitants of Detroit in each Party as you think can be trufted. Mr. Royome, that was with Capt. Morris, offers his Service. I fhall fend you what I can from Niagara this Fall, & fet off for that Place this Day. Much depends upon the Manner you receive thofe Indians now going againft the Delawares on their Return; if they do any thing pay them for each Scalp or Prifoner as above mentioned, & if not fucceffful be kind & give them what will fend them Home fatiffied, with fome Rum to the Chief of the Party. At the Requeft of the Ottawas, Chepewas, etc. I have appointed *Chain* an Interpreter to thofe Nations, he is much beloved by them & will be of great ufe in getting Parties to go out & go with them when neceffary. You will allow him one Mans Provifion to be given to his Mother when he is on Service & pay him the fame Pay and in the fame way as you do the other Interpreters. You have enclofed Copy of my Letter to the Officer commanding the Places at Fort Chefter with the Inftructions to Godfroy & Maifonville whom I order thither &·when they return the latter may proceed to me with the Anfwer if he thinks proper, otherwife you will forward the Officers Letter and the Anfwer from the Indian Nations they fpeake with.

 You have the Copy of the Peace, &c. with the Hurons on   of this Place to be added to the one made at Detroit, and it being highly neceffary to acquaint all the Nations of Indians we poffibly can that

our

our continuing the War with the Shawanes, &c. is owing to their sending out Parties, killing and taking our People Prisoners after having sued for Peace and neglecting to come to Sandusky with their Prisoners & Chiefs to ratify that Peace agreeable to their . . . . . .

You will therefore use every Means in your Power for that Purpose, and I send an Order to Mr. Morsac having great Influence, he being well acquainted with the upper Nations, to proceed to the Falls of St. Marys for that Purpose, also as you will see by the Copy of his Instructions herein enclosed, all Passes that I thought proper to give when I left Detroit for carrying on the Ind^n Trade you will allow to be carry'd into Execution, giving Instructions to the People to acquaint all the Indians when they go of the perfiduous Behaviour of the Shawanes & Delawares, and to use their utmost Endeavours to prevent any bad Impressions being on them by the . . . .

FINIS.

INDEX.

AARON, 70, 72, 76, 79, 87, 94, 95, 176, 177, 178, 184, 192, 204.
Abbot, Lieut., 59, 73.
Abenaques, 65, 116.
Abercrombie, Maj., 175.
Ague, 193.
Alarm, 161.
Albany, xvi, xxiii, 68, 139, 153, 164, 165, 168, 169, 170, 172, 173, 183, 186, 187, 188, 190, 191, 195, 200, 202, 209, 219, 223, 230, 243, 251, 252, 253, 265, 268, 269, 273.
Algonquin, xvii.
Allegiance, Oath of, 109.
Amboy, 242, 251, 252.
Ambuscade, 16, 17, 55, 60, 63, 80.
Amherst, Sir Jeffrey, 1, 8, 12, 32, 109, 139, 161, 164, 165, 167, 170, 171, 172, 173, 175, 181, 182, 185, 186, 187, 188, 194, 195, 197, 198, 201, 219, 245, 273, 276, 279.
André, the Huron, 52, 53, 54, 112, 114.
Andrew, 51, 82, 89, 113, 115, 204.
Andrews, Collin, 75.
Arbre Croche, 29, 276.
Assembly, General, 196, 197, 198, 213, 215, 253.
Augusta, 207.
Auquago (see Oquago).
Aurora, 178.

BABIE, M., 10, 21, 33, 34, 37, 39, 40.
Babi, M., 45, 62, 65.
    the Huron, 51, 52, 67, 72, 85, 86.
Baggattway, 29.
Ball playing, 29, 31, 134.
Banyar, Goldsbrow, 201.
Barracks, 4, 109.
Barrois, M., 64, 65, 71.
Bayard Hall, 272.
Bayard, Nicholas, 272.
Beaulieu, 83.
Beaver, 89, 103, 190, 225.
Beaver, Vessel named the, 4.
Bedding, 167, 185, 186.
Beef, a full Supply of, 166.
Belletre, M., 6.
Belts, xii, xv, xviii, 18, 25, 27, 28, 31, 32, 33, 42, 47, 56, 73, 77, 83, 86, 87, 88, 90, 91, 92, 94, 95, 97, 99, 100, 101, 106, 108, 115, 117, 173, 174, 177, 184, 189, 203, 221, 248, 249.
Big Jaco, 95.
Billets, 70.
    issued by Pontiac, 34, 35.
Billeting of Troops, 194.
Biographical Notices of
    M. P. Belletre, 6
    Col. Bradstreet, 109.
    Major Donald Campbell, 5.
    Capt. James Dalyal, 54.
    Saml Dunlop, 218.
                    Biographical

Index.

Biographical Notices of
  Major Henry Gladwyn, 1.
  Capt. Hopkins, 7.
  Capt. McKean, 250.
  Ensign Christopher Paully, 15.
  Pierre Reaume, 69.
  Robert Wells, 250.
Birch bark Bills of Credit, 35.
Birthday of his Majesty, 92.
Bishoprick, 236.
Blockhouses, 4, 36, 38, 131, 134, 196, 201, 202.
Bloody Run, 56.
Board of Trade, 50.
Bogardus, 185.
Bois Blanc Isle, 108, 109.
Bondeac, 283.
Borgard, 102.
Boston Schooner, 99, 104, 107, 108, 109, 110, 111.
Bostwick, Henry, 225.
Bounties, 223.
Bouquet, Col., 20, 212, 280, 282, 286.
Braddock's Expedition, 1.
Bradstreet, Col. John, 2, 8, 109, 110, 111, 113, 119, 139, 141, 157, 161, 165, 167, 170, 172, 173, 185, 186, 187, 188, 194, 195, 209, 210, 214, 245, 262, 273, 274, 276, 279, 281, 282, 283, 285, 286.
Brands found, 87.
Bread, Price of, 145.
Breastwork, 9, 16, 66.
Brehm, Lieut., 67, 73, 74.
Bridges, 185.
Brisar, M. 79.
Broome Co., 255.
Brown, Lieut., 56, 60, 76.
  Capt., 173.
Browning, Lt. Col., 171.
  Major, 203.
  Col., 274.

Bull, Capt., 256, 261, 262, 271, 272.
Burlington, 253, 269.
Burton, Gen., 186, 239.
Bushy Run, 20.
Butter, Price of, 145.
Buxton, 83.

CAHOKIA, xx, xxi.
Cahugees, 177.
Callender, Mr., 131.
Calumet Dance, 1.
Campbell, Col., xviii, 111, 115, 276.
  Lt. Col., 166, 173, 185, 285, 286.
  Major Donald, 1, 5, 6, 10, 13, 15, 16, 19, 40.
  Capt., 35, 40, 41, 47, 86, 126, 127, 129, 134.
  Lt., 269.
  John, 271.
Campeau, Michael, 83.
Campo, Baptiste, 79.
  M., 39, 42, 50, 56, 76, 108.
Canada, viii, ix, x, xii, xvii, 17, 94, 139, 143, 145, 151, 153, 156, 168, 169, 216, 236, 237, 239, 240, 246, 253, 273, 281, 284.
Canadians, 28, 124, 131, 142, 148.
Canajoharie, 218.
Canawaroghere, 257, 262, 269, 271.
Cannard River, 69.
Cannibalism, 3, 5, 41, 89.
Canoes taken, 7, 12.
Cape Breton, ix.
Capitulation of Canada, vii, x.
Caps, Style worn, 212, 213.
Carver, Jonathan, 11.
Cataracqui, 174.
Catawbas, 206.
Catfish Creek, 75.
Catskill Cr., 182.

Cattle

Index.   291

Cattle, 3, 13, 34, 57, 87.
Caughnawagas, 175, 178.
Cayuga, 213, 215, 227.
Cavaliers made, 14, 15, 41.
Cavalier, Mr., 23.
Cecote, Mr., 65, 77, 84, 85.
Certificate of Behavior, 87.
Chain, 287.
Chairs taken by Pontiac, 34.
Chapman, Mr., 45, 46, 82.
    a Trader, 12.
Charleston, 205, 230.
Charlotte, Sloop, 106, 110, 112, 115, 116, 117.
Chartres, Fort, 13.
Chemin du Ronde, 4.
Chenussco, 180, 189, 190, 211, 214, 217, 222, 227, 269, 272.
Cheppaton, Mr., 111.
Cherokees, 65, 82, 193, 205, 251.
Cherry Valley, 178, 182, 213, 219, 242, 250, 251, 261, 266.
Chevalier, 114.
Chickasaws, 206.
Chimney Island, 58.
Chinn, Edward, 225.
    Jno., 225.
Chippewas (variously spelled), 21, 29, 31, 32, 40, 43, 48, 50, 51, 62, 65, 76, 77, 83, 86, 87, 91, 92, 97, 99, 103, 106, 107, 108, 110, 111, 115, 117, 128, 157, 213, 215, 224, 276, 283, 287.
Choctaws, 206.
Christie, Ensign, 37, 44, 133.
Chughnot, 227.
Church within Fort at Detroit, 4.
Claus, Daniel, 29, 31, 173, 175, 239, 240.
Clermont, 48, 101, 115.
Clincincourt, 102, 103.
Clothing, 169, 170, 172, 175.
Cochrane, Gavin, 192, 193.
Cohorn Shells, 61.

Colden, Lt. Gov., 165, 180, 181, 182, 196, 198, 214, 221, 226, 233, 252, 265.
Commissaries, 146, 152, 153.
Confederacy, Indian, 143.
Congress, 175, 205, 206, 207.
Connecticut, xvi, 73, 243.
Connistoga, 231, 241.
Conokgorasse, 247, 248.
Coon, Figure of, 35.
Cornwell, Mr., 63.
Corpses buried, 23.
Costume of Troops, 200.
Council, 2, 5, 10, 16, 21, 23, 26, 29, 31, 38, 51, 52, 76, 83, 84, 90, 94, 96, 110, 126, 127, 129, 133, 145, 177, 193, 204.
Coureurs de Bois, 143.
Courts, 147, 150.
Coville, Mr., 109.
Cowaha, 248.
Crawford, Mr., 11, 38, 46.
Creeks, 205, 231.
Creoles, xxi.
Crofton, Mr., 110.
Croghan, Geo., xx, 75, 116, 176.
Crosthwaite, Ensign, 169.
Crown Point, 168, 169, 170.
Cuellierreys, Mr., 86.
Cuesiere, M., 9, 20, 21, 53, 77, 102.
Cut-the-Pumpkin, 248, 249.
Cuyler, Lieut., 17, 19, 35, 37, 132,
    Mr., 19, 22, 56.

DACOTAH Indians, 50.
Daly, Capt., 274.
Dalyel, Capt. James, 54, 55, 56, 60, 65, 72, 123, 165.
Dances, 105.
Daniel, a Mohawk, 81, 176, 183, 192, 208.
Darlington, Wm., 272.
Davers, Sir Robert, 2, 3, 17, 128.
                                Death

Index.

Death Song, 14.
Debts, Payment of, 147, 224, 225.
De Couagne, T., 18, 61, 75, 81, 183, 184, 202, 203, 208, 209, 225.
Defeat of Capt. Dalyel's Party, 55.
DeGraff, Daniel, 201.
Delawares, 14, 20, 52, 61, 88, 96, 97, 101, 106, 107, 110, 111, 113, 114, 115, 116, 118, 152, 153, 154, 157, 182, 183, 199, 204, 211, 212, 215, 240, 258, 262, 264, 265, 266, 272, 278, 279, 286, 287, 288.
Dellius, Godfredius, 253.
Deneyon, Mr., 77, 94, 102.
Deriverre, Baptiste, 71.
De Roen, M., 79.
DesCheine, M., 79.
Deserters, 101, 270.
Detroit, x, xvii, xviii, xx, 3, 6, 7, 8, 15, 17, 21, 31, 32, 36, 56, 60, 70, 75, 80, 81, 84, 94, 95, 96, 98, 123, 125, 129, 133, 135, 141, 143, 144, 145, 146, 147, 148, 149, 150, 151, 153, 155, 156, 164, 167, 170, 171, 174, 176, 177, 182, 183, 187, 189, 193, 198, 199, 203, 204, 209, 212, 213, 221, 224, 236, 278, 279, 285, 287, 288.
Detroit River, 56, 62, 128.
Devils Hole, 80.
Diary, Notice of Authorship, xviii.
Dioaga, 227, 260.
Dobbs, Gov., 207.
Doctor's Son, 86.
Douw, Volkert P., 190.
Duncan, Alex'r, 170, 172.
Duncan, John, 269.
  Maj., 165, 166, 170, 274, 276.
Dunlop, Rev. Samuel, 218, 219, 220.
Duquendse, M., 77, 80.
Duties, xiii, 147, 152.

EAST India Co., 149.
Eckers, Capt. Tho., 238.
Eckersons, Capt., 263.
Edgar, Wm., 189.
Ehle, Dirk, 182.
Elder, Rev. John, 241, 242.
Elliott, Lt. Col., 169, 173, 187, 265.
Emissaries, 148, 216.
Episcopal foundation, 236.
Erse, Letter written in, 81.
Esopus, 179, 180, 181, 182.
Etherington, Capt., 29, 30, 31, 32, 33, 50, 58, 66, 133, 134.
Eyre, Col.; 179, 180, 228, 234.

FAC Similes.
  Jeffrey Amherst, 164.
  John Bradstreet, 157.
  Daniel Claus, 175.
  Gavin Cochrane, 193.
  T. De Couagne, 184.
  Volkert P. Douw, 190.
  Alexander Duncan, 172.
  Sam'l Dunlop, 220.
  Guy Johnson, 192.
  Wm. Johnson, 213.
  Gerret A. Lansing, 202.
  Robert McKeen, 250.
  Thomas McKee, 245.
  Robert Rogers, 135, 177.
  John Stuart, 208.
  David Vanderheyden, 183.
Faies, Jean, 79.
Farli, M., 30, 32.
Ferguson, Mr., 65.
Fire Rafts, 44, 46, 48, 49, 51.
Fisher, James, 3.
  Serjeant, 71.
Five Nations, 173, 177, 204, 212, 226, 234, 237, 266.

Flag

Index. 293

Flag, 26, 38, 42, 45.
Fletcher, Gov., 253.
Florida, 206.
Folles Avoines, 50, 51, 88, 100, 108
Fort at Albany, 186.
   Augusta, 227.
   Charters, 156.
   at Detroit, 4, 5, 6, 7, 8, 9, 10, 11, 14, 15, 16, 17, 19, 20, 21, 34, 35, 36, 38, 43, 44, 49.
   Edward, 168, 169, 253, 254.
   Erie, 112, 280.
   George, 168, 169, 198.
   Levi, 58.
   Miami, 132.
   Ontario, 163, 166, 168.
   Pitt, 20, 33, 51, 53, 54, 66, 79, 87, 96, 115, 116, 117, 143, 144, 156, 279, 281.
   Schloffer, 80, 203.
   Stanwix, 144, 145, 163, 166, 168, 169, 170, 173, 185, 193, 228, 271.
   William, 58.
   Wm. Augustus, 58, 149, 163, 165, 166, 172.
Fortville, M., 65, 71.
Foxes, 50.
Frank, Mr., 190.
Franks, Conradt, 178.
French, vii, viii, x, xiv, xvi, xvii, xxi, 26, 83, 86, 88, 94, 97, 99, 102, 107, 114, 116, 117, 118, 129, 130, 133, 141, 143, 145, 146, 148, 149, 151, 152, 154, 155, 156, 174, 175, 189, 205, 215, 216, 221, 233, 234, 235, 236, 287.
Frontenac, 149.
Frost, 37.
Fur Trade, vii, 4, 7, 11, 17, 19, 29, 30, 32, 33, 38, 56, 59, 65, 145, 217.

GAGE, General Thomas, 32, 155, 157, 171, 172, 174, 184, 209, 210, 219, 224, 226, 254, 258, 270, 281, 282, 283.
Gamelin, Mr. 22, 38, 85.
Garrison at Detroit, Strength of, 4.
Gauntlet, running of the, 5.
Genesco, (see Chenuffco), 154, 155, 277.
Geneva, 211.
German Flatts, 185, 189, 190, 230.
Germantown, 241.
Gladwyn, Major Henry, 1, 2, 4, 5, 8, 79, 82, 97, 109, 126, 129, 130, 131, 164, 176, 186, 187, 188, 195, 204, 270, 279, 280, 283.
Gladwyn, Vessel named the, 4, 11, 35, 103, 106, 107, 108, 109, 110, 112, 113, 285.
Glen, Jn, 178.
Goddard, James Stanly, 225.
Godfoy, 53, 287.
Goods, Bill of, 178.
Goodwin, Lt., 187.
Gorrel, Lieut., 50.
Gouin, M., 5.
Gowaha, 249.
Grand Marais, 62.
Grand River, 23, 56, 86, 87, 171.
Grant, Capt., 55, 57, 60, 77, 106, 109, 275.
Grants of Land, 229.
Gray, Capt., 56, 76.
Great Falls on Otter Creek, 253.
Great Spoon, 91.
Green Bay, 30, 50, 69.
Grenon, M., 79.
Grofs Isle, 56.
Grofs Point, 49, 91.
Groote Imbogt, 182.

Hair

HAIR, Style of cutting, 212.
Hanfen, John R., 238, 263, 264.
Hardenbergh, Col., 180.
Hare, Wm., 247, 249, 255, 257, 260, 261.
Hatchet, 15, 18, 27, 78.
Havana, 167.
Hay, Lieut., 40.
Heckewelder, Account by, 7.
Hecotte, M., 39.
Henry, Alexander, 30, 32.
Herkimer, 190.
Hogan, Maj., 273.
Hog Ifland, 3, 74.
Hog feized by the Indians for a Feaft, 247.
Holmes & Memfen, 225.
Holmes, Lieut., 6, 20, 22, 26, 132.
Hombach, 189.
Hopkins, Cap., 7, 19, 29, 34, 37, 39, 41, 46, 59, 63, 68.
Hornbach, 79.
Horfes ftolen, 42.
Horfey, Mr., 68, 71, 73.
Hofpital, 187.
Houfes burned, 6, 8, 9, 10, 23, 65.
Howard, James, 225.
Hudfons Bay Co., 143.
Hudfon River, 182.
Huron River, 11, 16, 17, 40, 44, 79.
Huron Village, 7, 13, 33, 36, 45, 51, 53, 54.
Hurons, 7, 12, 13, 15, 16, 26, 37, 38, 43, 44, 45, 48, 51, 52, 53, 56, 59, 66, 67, 68, 70, 72, 76, 83, 86, 89, 90, 96, 97, 100, 101, 105, 108, 109, 110, 111, 112, 113, 115, 116, 118, 157, 178, 212.
Huron's Point, 93, 118.

ILLINOIS, xii, xx, xxi, xxiii, 10, 13, 22, 24, 28, 48, 49, 51, 52, 53, 57, 67, 71, 77, 78, 79, 80, 86, 91, 94, 101, 102, 104, 105, 110, 115, 116, 117, 118, 129, 131, 132, 142, 148, 155, 156, 189, 216, 217, 284.
Impreffing Carriages, 194.
Ireland, 218, 219.
Iroquois, 225.
Irondequoit, 277.
Ifle au Boisblond, 80.
  au Cochon, 31, 63, 77, 109.
  au Diende, 34, 36.
  la Motte, 253.
  Royal, 58.

JACOB, 86, 176, 192, 208, 248.
Jadeau, M., 78, 80, 82, 83, 89, 91, 101, 108, 115.
Jamet, Lieut., 30, 133.
Jenkins, Lt. Edward, 24, 133.
Jerfey, 273.
Jefuits, xii, 29, 31, 32, 48, 91, 133, 263.
Johnfon, Capt. Guy, 191, 192.
Johnfon Hall, 179, 180, 183, 184, 192, 210, 214, 221, 226, 229, 231, 234, 239, 252, 258, 262, 265, 268.
Johnfon, Sir John, 254.
  Lt., 193, 229, 254.
  Sir William, ix, xiii, xix, xx, 18, 31, 50, 60, 70, 72, 75, 81, 82, 91, 95, 96, 97, 101, 116, 123, 124, 135, 161, 166, 170, 173, 176, 177, 179, 180, 181, 182, 183, 184, 185, 189, 190, 191, 192, 193, 201, 202, 204, 205, 208, 210, 213, 214, 220, 221, 225, 226, 227, 228, 229, 230,

Johnfon

Index.   295

Johnfon, Sir William, 231, 234,
    238, 239, 241, 242, 243, 247,
    249, 250, 251, 252, 254, 255,
    258, 260, 261, 262, 263, 264,
    265, 268, 270, 271, 272, 274,
    276, 277, 278, 280, 282.
Johnfon (Veffel), 166.
Johnfton, John, 247, 249, 255,
    257, 260, 261.
Jonois, Father, 29.
Jofeph, 263.
Journal of Robert Rogers, 125.

KAGOUGHSHOUTONG,
    96, 182.
Kanadafaga, 211, 214.
Kafkafkia, xxi, 13.
Kaunawau Kohare, 247.
Keys found, 66.
Kiggel, Enfign, 63.
Killed and Wounded of Lieut.
    Dalyel's Company, 56.
King, Thomas, 265.
Klock, Geo., 218.

LA Bay, 32, 50, 88, 99, 141,
    143, 144, 150.
La Beuf, 134, 135.
La Butte, M., 5, 15, 26, 40, 65,
    86, 103, 106, 107.
La Croffe, 29.
L'Efperance, 91.
La Farge, 174.
Lafayette, 24.
Lafontaine, 82.
Lagaffe, 91.
Lake Erie, 11, 23, 36, 70, 75,
    109, 113, 150, 156, 185,
    193, 199, 203, 236, 280.
    George, xvi, 254.
    Huron, 3. 99, 128, 149, 150,
        151, 284, 285.
    Michigan, 50, 143, 144, 151,
        184, 185.

Lake Ontario, 99, 149, 203, 275.
    St. Clair, 111, 284.
    Superior, 102, 143, 144, 150,
        151.
Lake, Mr., 281.
Lancafter, 241, 242, 243.
Langlade, M., 30, 32, 33.
Lanfingh, Gerret A., 201, 202.
    Robert, 182.
La Platon, 180.
Lafcelle, Mr., 23.
Lead, 30, 39, 44, 67.
Leake, Mr., 164.
Le Grand, Mr., 82.
Lehigh, 241.
Le Ronde, Mr., 66.
Leffley, Lieut. Jas., 30, 31, 133, 134.
Levy, Mr., 45, 46.
    Gorfen, 225.
Lies punifhed, 27.
Lindefay, John, 218.
Little Aaron, 219.
    Chief, 106, 107, 111.
    Niagara, 203.
    Sandufky, 108.
Lizott, M., 79.
Londonderry, 218.
Long Cane River, 231.
Long Point, 178.
Lorain, Com., 58.
Lords of Trade, 207, 210, 237.
Loring, Capt., 166, 195.
    Commodore, 106, 109.
Louifiana, xii, 206.
Louifburgh, ix.
Luke, Lieut., 56.
Lydius, Mr., 253.
    Rev. John, 253.

McCORMICK, Mr., 7, 176.
    McDonald, Lieut., 76.
McDougall, Lieut., xviii, 5, 6, 19,
    35, 38, 60, 86, 88, 108, 116,
    129, 134.
                                    McKee

Index

McKee, Thomas, 241, 245.
McKeen, Robert, 249, 251.
Mackoy, 83.
Marchioquiſſe, 106, 114.
Magazine, 87, 153.
Maiſonville, 44, 112, 115, 116, 117, 287.
Manitoo, 71, 104.
Manuſcript, Notice of the, xix, 139, 161.
Marble Quarries, 253.
Marſacks, M., 64, 84, 91, 92, 108, 288.
Marſh, Witham, 272.
Martinico, 67, 167.
Maſcoutons, 117.
Matthews, 80.
Maumee, xx, 20.
Mediators, 153.
Meldrum, M., 65.
Meloche, M., 5, 35.
Memorial of Traders, 224.
Merchandiſe, 6, 7, 12, 23, 30, 31, 45, 58, 59, 73.
Meſſage of Gov. Colden, to General Aſſembly, 196.
Miami (variouſly ſpelled), 20, 21, 22, 26, 42, 45, 46, 65, 66, 76, 101, 102, 103, 104, 106, 107, 108, 110, 111, 115, 116, 117, 143, 144, 178, 224, 284.
Michilimackinac, 17, 28, 29, 30, 31, 32, 35, 48, 50, 51, 58, 70, 86, 88, 99, 100, 106, 108, 110, 113, 116, 128, 133, 141, 142, 143, 144, 145, 148, 150, 236, 276, 284, 285.
Middleburgh, 263.
Mikouder, 248.
Militia, 119, 182.
Millehomme, M., 79.
Mindoghquay, 26, 83, 99, 106.
Minechefne, 111.
Mingoes, 11.

Mintiwaby, 87, 106.
Miſſionaries, French, 7.
Miſſiſagues (variouſly ſpelled), 21, 66, 76, 88, 173, 174, 208, 209, 276.
Miſſiſſippi, viii, 13, 73, 78, 97, 102, 110, 142, 143, 145, 146, 148, 149, 155, 156, 216, 217, 284.
Mohawks, 67, 68, 69, 70, 72, 76, 84, 94, 95, 97, 113, 116, 176, 177, 180, 182, 193, 194, 200, 204, 208, 212, 213, 219, 221, 249, 263, 264, 265.
Monckton, Gen., 198, 228.
Moncrief, Major, 81, 170, 187, 246.
Montreal, vii, x, 13, 23, 32, 33, 58, 59, 65, 66, 71, 99, 100, 153, 173, 186.
Montreſor, Capt., 75.
Monture, Henry, 247, 249, 255, 257, 260, 261.
Moravians, 241, 242.
Morris, Capt., 110, 111, 173, 186, 187.
Murray, Gov. James, 246.
Muſkingum, 281.
Mynders, Rynier, 201.

NAIN, 241.
Naintaw, 84.
Napier, Mr., 185.
Navarre, M., 39, 40, 51.
Negroes, 64, 101, 130, 155, 183.
New Hampſhire, 218.
New Jerſey, 188, 199, 212, 243.
New Orleans, 53, 67.
Newtimas, Joe, 272.
New Years Call, 85.
New York, 141, 142, 144, 146, 153, 166, 168, 169, 172, 181, 183, 185, 186, 187, 188, 193, 194, 196, 198, 199, 212, 243, 253, 254, 268, 270, 274.
Neyon

Index. 297

Neyon, M., 13, 57, 67.
Niagara, xiv, xv, 6, 10, 11, 17, 19, 23, 26, 35, 36, 47, 48, 53, 59, 60, 61, 67, 70, 75, 80, 81, 82, 84, 86, 88, 91, 93, 99, 100, 101, 102, 103, 104, 105, 107, 108, 110, 113, 115, 116, 117, 129, 131, 132, 143, 144, 149, 150, 151, 156, 164, 165, 166, 170, 171, 172, 173, 174, 177, 178, 180, 182, 183, 198, 199, 202, 208, 213, 225, 227, 228, 234, 245, 270, 274, 275, 276, 281, 284, 285, 287.
Nichols, 248.
Nixon, Thomas, 201.
North Carolina, 207.
Northwest Fur Co., 58.

ODINGHQUANOORON, 67.
Oenentois, 115.
Ogdensburgh, 58, 275.
Ohio, iv, 33, 52, 142, 143, 156, 180, 212, 254, 279, 281, 283.
Ojibwas, xvii, 2, 21, 50,
O'Moke, George, 264.
Oneida Lake, 275.
Oneidas, 193, 237, 248, 257, 260, 262, 265, 269, 271.
Onoghquagey, 262, 263, 264, 265.
Onondagoes, 96, 118, 228, 248, 265.
Ontario, 81, 228, 234, 240.
Oquago, (variously spelled), 219, 249, 255, 256, 260, 169.
Oraconenton, 58.
Orange County, 193.
Oswegatchie, 149, 275.
Oswego, xiii, xx, 144, 165, 166, 170, 183, 188, 194, 200, 209, 210, 276.
Ottawa, ix, xi, xiii, xiv, xvii, 1, 2, 3, 5, 11, 12, 15, 16, 22, 24, 26, 27, 28, 30, 31, 32, 41, 43, 44,

Ottawa, 46, 47, 48, 49, 50, 51, 52, 53, 58, 61, 65, 70, 71, 72, 79, 83, 87, 100, 101, 102, 103, 104, 107, 108, 109, 110, 116, 117, 125, 157, 189, 212, 215, 224, 280, 283, 287.
Otter Creek, 253.
Otter, Figure of, 35.
Ouapacamigatte, 208.
Oughnour, Daniel, 75.
Ouquickare, 261.
Outattanon, 24, 44, 65, 67, 114, 116, 117, 133.
Outers, Forrest, 225.
Owego, 212.

PALISADES, 4.
Panees, 45, 174, 175.
Parent Creek, 5, 35, 57.
Parkman, Francis, Jr., xx.
Parley, 128, 130.
Parole, xviii.
Passes, 82, 171.
Passport, xv, 208.
Patteraros, 49, 61, 63.
Paully, Ensign Christopher, 3, 15, 41, 110.
Paxton Riots, 241, 242, 243, 252.
Peace, xix, 10, 12, 13, 16, 21, 26, 27, 28, 39, 40, 41, 42, 43, 46, 47, 53, 67, 76, 79, 82, 84, 92, 93, 95, 97, 98, 100, 102, 103, 104, 105, 110, 112, 115, 118, 146, 148, 178, 189, 196, 211, 221, 223, 224, 225, 233, 236, 244, 246, 247, 269, 270, 278, 279, 280, 281, 284, 286, 287, 288.
Peltry, 44.
Penn, Gov. John, 231, 251, 252, 253, 282.
Pennsylvania, xvi, 131, 152, 212, 227, 268, 272.
Pepiquaghquey, 227.

Perry

298   Index.

Perry, Ensign, 63.
Peter, 91,
Petet, Mr., 67.
Philadelphia, 227, 239, 241, 242, 243, 244.
Pians, 100, 117.
Pickering, Sir Edward, 115.
Picquet, Francis, 275.
Pipe of Peace, 3, 77, 83, 91, 92, 106, 127, 150.
Pittiaugers, 44.
Pittsburgh, 18.
Plains of Scioto, 281.
Point au Pain, 81.
Point au Pelée, 17, 178.
Pontiac, xvii, xviii, xix, xx, xxi, xxiii, 1, 2, 3, 5, 6, 8, 9, 10, 12, 13, 14, 15, 16, 21, 22, 23, 24, 26, 28, 31, 32, 34, 35, 37, 38, 39, 40, 41, 42, 43, 45, 51, 53, 54, 56, 60, 61, 66, 70, 71, 77, 78, 79, 80, 94, 104, 106, 107, 116, 117, 126, 127, 130, 131, 161, 212, 279, 280, 283.
Pork, Price of, 145.
Post, Capt. 272.
Post Vincent, 107.
Pottawatamies, xvii, 2, 6, 20, 21, 22, 23, 24, 25, 26, 27, 33, 34, 38, 41, 42, 43, 44, 46, 47, 48, 52, 56, 59, 63, 65, 69, 70, 71, 72, 84, 85, 87, 91, 94, 99, 106, 107, 108, 110, 114, 117, 128, 157, 224, 280, 283.
Pouchot, M., 58.
Powder, 7, 30, 39, 67, 83, 97, 102, 107, 147, 172, 189, 202, 204, 222, 274.
Prentice, Mr., 79, 89, 131, 189.
Presque Isle, 36, 37, 70, 75, 85, 91, 134, 156, 279, 281, 282, 283.
Prizes, 114, 144, 151.
Priest, French, 4, 39.

Prisoners, 3, 5, 7, 9, 11, 12, 15, 17, 19, 20, 21, 24, 25, 27, 31, 37, 38, 40, 42, 43, 44, 46 52, 54, 56, 59, 76, 77, 83, 84, 85, 87, 88, 89, 91, 92, 93, 97, 98, 99, 100, 101, 103, 104, 106, 107, 112, 114, 115, 116, 117, 118, 126, 129, 131, 133, 134, 190, 230, 255, 257, 262, 264, 265, 270, 278, 281, 287, 288.
Proclamations, 210, 211, 215.
Profits of Fur trade, 144.
Prophecy, pretended, 52.
Provender, 172.
Provisions, 5, 6, 8, 10, 17, 18, 37, 58, 68, 69, 70, 79, 80, 145, 151, 163, 271.
Provosts, 174.
Prudhomme, Mr., 83.
Pruyn, Samuel, 183.
Puante, 88, 100 102.

QUAGHQUOANDAX, 182.
Quebec, 82, 141, 142, 146, 153, 216, 253.
Queen's Rangers, 132.
Queenston, 81.
Quilleriez, M., 35.
Quotas, 188, 199, 200.

RACCOON Skins, 253.
Rainbeau, 91.
Randolph County, Ill., 13.
Reaume, Mr., 39, 69, 99, 112.
Reinforcements sent, 8, 36, 37, 54.
Renards, 50, 100 102.
Rescue of Prisoner, 7, 18.
Rifle Barrel Guns, 152.
Riggell, Ensign, 73.
Rioters, 232.
River Au Roche, 119.
River Rouge, 62, 113, 115.
Robertson, Captain, 128.
                                Robinson

Index. 299

Robinson, Capt., 2, 3, 9, 17, 73.
Rogers, Major Robert, 3, 6, 35, 60, 63, 64, 82, 84, 123, 135, 176, 177, 178, 208.
Rossin, 209.
Royal Americans, 132.
Royal Charlotte, Sloop, 104.
Royome, Mr., 287.
Ruiard, France, 88.
Rum, xiv, 7, 17, 49, 94, 102, 128, 150, 175, 187.
Rutherford, Mr., 9, 17, 20, 21, 56.

SABOLE, M., 71.
Saggina, 23, 26, 27, 28, 29, 33, 38, 89, 92, 102, 106, 225.
St. Albans, 253.
 Ange, xx, xxii.
 Clair, Arthur, 111.
 Clair, M., 111.
 Clair, Lake, 73.
 Clair, Capt., 113.
 Josephs, 11, 20, 24, 25, 42, 67, 69, 70, 79, 80, 88, 94, 102, 106, 114, 117, 133, 143, 144, 148, 150, 189, 285.
 Lawrence, 58, 217.
 Louis, xx, xxi, xxii, 83.
 Martin, Mr., 9, 10, 12, 14, 16, 21, 22, 37, 38, 64, 71, 86, 97, 105.
 Marys, 32, 141, 142, 144, 150, 288.
 Vincent, 117.
Salteux, 102, 114, 116.
Sandusky, 12, 15, 16, 54, 60, 66, 70, 72, 79, 82, 89, 95, 96, 99, 100, 101, 104, 108, 110, 112, 113, 116, 131, 178, 189, 204, 279, 280, 281, 284, 286, 288.
Saqui, (variously spelled), 84, 87, 91, 100, 102, 114, 157.
Scalp, 5, 18, 20, 39, 40, 287.

Schenectady, xv, 177, 179, 180, 182, 191, 201, 202, 250, 254, 269, 273.
Schlosser, Ensign, 20, 21, 22, 23, 25, 133.
Schoharie, 213, 219, 238, 249, 250, 263, 266.
School, 219.
Schuyler, Capt. Stephen, 183.
Scuyler, Lieut., 17, 18.
Scioto, 143, 144, 279, 283, 284.
Seckaho, 106, 107, 115, 117.
Senecas, xiii, xix, xv, xvii, 18, 61, 75, 80, 173, 177, 180, 182, 199, 204, 209, 211, 212, 213, 214, 215, 223, 225, 226, 229, 233, 248, 258, 259, 265, 269, 278.
Settlement on Lakes, 157.
Shaguomigan, 106.
Shamokin, 179, 180, 182.
Shataquau, 279.
Shaw, Sergeant, 16.
Shawanese, 14, 20, 33, 51, 88, 96, 97, 106, 107, 110, 111, 112, 113, 114, 115, 117, 118, 152, 153, 154, 157, 199, 204, 211, 212, 215, 240, 258, 272, 278, 279, 284, 286, 288.
Shells, 39, 41, 49, 64.
Sibbold, 86.
Siege of Detroit, began, 3, 4, 8.
Sieus, 100.
Silver Heels, 81, 194.
Simpson, Capt., 119.
Sinclair, Lt., 285.
Singsink, 227.
Sioux, 32.
Six Nations, 21, 144, 145, 154, 155, 214, 215, 232, 284.
Sledges, 188.
Smallman, Mr., 12.
Small Pox, 100, 243.
Smith, Matthew, 241.

Sortie

Sortie, 7, 16, 23, 33, 34, 37, 38, 39, 40, 54, 57, 88, 123.
Sowers, Capt., 172.
Spaniards, 142, 143, 145, 146.
Speeches, 90, 91, 94, 95.
Spy, 116, 183.
Squafhcutter, 261.
Sterling, Mr., 7, 17, 40, 47, 53, 81.
Statement by Gen. Bradftreet, 141.
Stationery, Order for, 247.
Statiftics of Fur trade, 144.
Stedman, Mr., 80, 184.
Stewart, Lt., 115.
Storming of the Fort threatened, 6.
Stockade, 44, 118, 201.
Stockbridge, 248.
Stone Arabia, 249.
Strouds, 147, 178.
Stuart, John, 205, 208, 230, 231, 268.
Suit at Law, 165.
Surprife, 2, 132.
Surrender of Fort demanded, 6, 8, 9, 35, 39.
Sufquehanna, 179, 180, 182, 212, 227, 241, 254, 255, 262.
Swegachie, 174, 275.
Swit, Mr., 170.

TAWAYS, 125, 128, 177, 178, 204.
Tawaniowe, 174.
Taylor, Jacob, 59.
Teata, 95, 96, 97.
Teedyufcung, 262.
Ten Eyck, Mr. 214.
Tennefie, 190.
Tents, 201.
Teurogoa, 248.
Theata, 45, 52, 67, 85, 86, 90, 94, 95.
Thefault, 99.
Tice, Mr., 254.
Ticonderoga, 168, 169.
Tioga, 227, 260.

Tobacco, 150.
Tobacco Pouch made from the Skin of Capt. Robinfon's Arm, 3.
Tohicon, 227.
Toronto, 76, 87, 171, 173.
Toways, 178.
Tracy, Mr., 29, 30, 31.
Traders, 76, 141.
Traders, Memorial of, 224.
Tranfportation, Coft of, 144.
Treachery of Indians, 2, 5, 11, 15, 20, 22, 24, 25, 26, 29, 30, 51, 68, 69, 96, 227.
Treaty, 7, 8, 17, 19, 33, 67, 101.
Trenton, 242.
Trinkets, 147.
Truce, xviii.
Turkey Ifland, 34.
Turnbull, Mrs., killed, 4.
Tucaroras, 96, 207, 231, 237, 265.
Twightwees, 268.

ULSTER County, 193.

VANDERHIDEN, David, 84, 86, 182, 183.
Vanderheyden, Lt. Col., 238.
Van Eps, Widow, 201.
Van Slyke, Col., 192.
Venango, 51, 135, 152.
Venifon, 225.
Vermillion, 82.
Vermont, 253, 254.
Veffels fired upon, 4, 6, 7, 8, 10, 11, 14, 16, 17, 19, 20, 21, 33, 34, 35, 36, 37, 38, 44.
Veffel loft on Lake Erie, 11, 75.
Victory, Schooner, 99, 105, 109, 111, 113, 115, 118.
Vincennes, 107.
Virginia, xx, 113.
Voifegamigate, 203.

Wabafh

Index.

WABASH, 24, 107, 143, 144, 148.
Wabagommigot (variously spelled), 76, 87, 97, 98, 99, 184, 313.
Wade, Ferrall, 239.
Wade, Wells &, 171.
Wages, 214.
Walsh, Mr., 22, 26, 133.
Wampum, xii, xv, 27, 28, 45, 82, 90, 91, 93, 115, 174, 184, 203, 204.
War Dance, 99.
War Song, 53, 94, 129.
Washashe, 25, 26.
Washee, 24.
Washtinon, 86.
Wassong, 62, 88, 103.
Watch, Gold, 45.
Watkins, Mr., 7, 15, 62, 63.
Wawaukaugee, 248.
Wecquetank, 241.
Weiser, Conrad, 263.
Weiserſdorp, 263.

Wells, Capt. Robert, 250.
Wells, Mr., 261.
Wells & Wade, 171.
Weſtbrook, Capt., 212.
Whitewood, 104, 109.
Wilkins, Major, 8, 164, 165, 171, 184, 193, 203, 208.
Willero, Mr., 80.
Williamſon, xxi.
Windmill burned, 67.
Windſor, 255.
Winnepreſs, Capt., 163, 164.
Winſton, Mr., 79, 189.
Wyndotes (variouſly ſpelled), 2, 53, 70, 95, 128, 129, 131, 177, 204.
Wyaluſing, (variouſly ſpelled), 212, 227, 241, 269.
Wyoming, 241, 243.
Wyyautaukeen, 248.

YORKERS, 273, 275, 276.

www.ingramcontent.com/pod-product-compliance
Lightning Source LLC
Chambersburg PA
CBHW021205230426
43667CB00006B/571